T0318455

Lesbian and Bisexual Women's Mental Health

Lesbian and Bisexual Women's Mental Health has been co-published simultaneously as *Journal of Psychology & Human Sexuality*, Volume 15, Numbers 2/3 and 4 2003.

The *Journal of Psychology & Human Sexuality* Monographic "Separates"

Below is a list of "separates," which in serials librarianship means a special issue simultaneously published as a special journal issue or double-issue *and* as a "separate" hardbound monograph. (This is a format which we also call a "DocuSerial.")

"Separates" are published because specialized libraries or professionals may wish to purchase a specific thematic issue by itself in a format which can be separately cataloged and shelved, as opposed to purchasing the journal on an on-going basis. Faculty members may also more easily consider a "separate" for classroom adoption.

"Separates" are carefully classified separately with the major book jobbers so that the journal tie-in can be noted on new book order slips to avoid duplicate purchasing.

You may wish to visit Haworth's website at . . .

http://www.HaworthPress.com

. . . to search our online catalog for complete tables of contents of these separates and related publications.

You may also call 1-800-HAWORTH (outside US/Canada: 607-722-5857), or Fax 1-800-895-0582 (outside US/Canada: 607-771-0012), or e-mail at:

docdelivery@haworthpress.com

Lesbian and Bisexual Women's Mental Health, edited by Robin M. Mathy, MSW, LGSW, MSc, MSt, MA, and Shelly K. Kerr, PhD (Vol. 15, No. 2/3/4, 2003). *Explores the interrelationship between lesbian and bisexual women's mental health and the diverse social contexts in which they live.*

Masturbation as a Means of Achieving Sexual Health, edited by Walter O. Bockting, PhD, and Eli Coleman, PhD (Vol. 14, No. 2/3, 2002). *"Finally, here is an excellent book filled with research illustrating how positive attitudes toward masturbation in history, across cultures, and throughout the life span can help in the achievement of sexual health. This book is an invaluable resource and I highly recommend it for all who are teaching health or sexuality education or are involved in sex counseling and therapy." (William R. Strayton, PhD, ThD, Professor and Coordinator, Human Sexuality Program, Widener University)*

Sex Offender Treatment: Accomplishments, Challenges, and Future Directions, edited by Michael H. Miner, PhD, and Eli Coleman, PhD (Vol. 13, No. 3/4, 2001). *An easy-to-read collection that reviews the major issues and findings on the past decade of research on and treatment of sex offenders. The busy professional will find this book a quick and helpful update for their practice. The reviews presented are succinct, but capture the main issues to be addressed by anyone working with sex offenders." (R. Langevin, PhD, CPsych, Director, Juniper Psychological Services and Associate Professor of Psychiatry, University of Toronto)*

Childhood Sexuality: Normal Sexual Behavior and Development, edited by Theo G. M. Sandfort, PhD, and Jany Rademakers, PhD (Vol. 12, No. 1/2, 2000). *"Important . . . Gives voice to children about their own 'normal' sexual curiosities and desires, and about their behavior and development." (Gunter Schmidt, PhD, Professor, Department of Sex Research, University of Hamburg, Germany)*

Sexual Offender Treatment: Biopsychosocial Perspectives, edited by Eli Coleman, PhD, and Michael Miner, PhD (Vol. 10, No. 3, 2000). *"This guide delivers a diverse look at the complex and intriguing topic of normal child sexuality and the progress that is being made in this area of research."*

New International Directions in HIV Prevention for Gay and Bisexual Men, edited by Michael T. Wright, LICSW, B. R. Simon Rosser, PhD, MPH, and Onno de Zwart, MA (Vol. 10, No. 3/4, 1998). *"Performs a great service to HIV prevention research and health promotion. . . . It takes the words of gay and bisexual men seriously by locating men's sexual practice in their love relationships and casual sex encounters and examines their responses to HIV." (Susan Kippax, Associate Professor and Director, National Center in HIV Social Research, School of Behavioral Sciences, Macquarie University, New South Wales, Australia)*

Sexuality Education in Postsecondary and Professional Training Settings, edited by James W. Maddock (Vol. 9, No. 3/4, 1997). *"A diverse group of contributers all experienced sexuality educators–offer summary information, critical commentary, thoughtful analysis, and projections of future trends in sexuality education in postsecondary settings. . . . The chapters present valuable resources, ranging from historical references to contemporary Websites."* (Adolescence)

Sexual Coercion in Dating Relationships, edited by E. Sandra Byers and Lucia F. O'Sullivan (Vol. 8, No. 1/2, 1996). *"Tackles a big issue with the best tools presently available to social and health scientists. . . . Perhaps the most remarkable thing about these excellent chapters is the thread of optimism that remains despite the depressing topic. Each author . . . chips away at oppression and acknowledges the strength of women who have experienced sexual coercion while struggling to eliminate sexist assumptions that deny women sexual autonomy and pleasure."* (Naomi B. McCormick, PhD, Professor, Department of Psychology, State University of New York at Plattsburgh)

HIV/AIDS and Sexuality, edited by Michael W. Ross (Vol. 7, No. 1/2, 1995). *"An entire volume on the topic of HIV and sexuality, bringing together a number of essays and studies, which cover a wide range of relevant issues. It really is a relief to finally read some research and thoughts about sexual functioning and satisfaction in HIV-positive persons."* (Association of Lesbian and Gay Psychologists)

Gender Dysphoria: Interdisciplinary Approaches in Clinical Management, edited by Walter O. Bockting and Eli Coleman (Vol. 5, No. 4, 1993). *"A useful modern summary of the state-of--the-art endocrine and psychiatric approach to this important problem."* (Stephen B. Levine, MD, Clinical Professor of Psychiatry, School of Medicine, Case Western Reserve University; Co-Director, Center for Marital and Sexual Health)

Sexual Transmission of HIV Infection: Risk Reduction, Trauma, and Adaptation, edited by Lena Nilsson Schönnesson, PhD (Vol. 5, No. 1/2, 1992). *"This is an essential title for understanding how AIDS and HIV are perceived and treated in modern America."* (The Bookwatch)

John Money: A Tribute, edited by Eli Coleman (Vol. 4, No. 2, 1991). *"Original, provocative, and breaks new ground."* (Science Books & Films)

Lesbian and Bisexual Women's Mental Health

Robin M. Mathy, MSW, LGSW, MSc, MSt, MA
Shelly K. Kerr, PhD
Editors

Lesbian and Bisexual Women's Mental Health has been co-published simultaneously as *Journal of Psychology & Human Sexuality*, Volume 15, Numbers 2/3 and 4 2003.

Routledge
Taylor & Francis Group

LONDON AND NEW YORK

Lesbian and Bisexual Women's Mental Health has been co-published simultaneously as *Journal of Psychology & Human Sexuality*, Volume 15, Numbers 2/3 and 4 2003.

First published 2003 by The Haworth Press, Inc.

Published 2013 by Routledge
2 Park Square, Milton Park, Abingdon, Oxon OX14 4RN
711 Third Avenue, New York, NY 10017, USA

Routledge is an imprint of the Taylor & Francis Group, an infoma business

Cover design by Lora Wiggins

Library of Congress Cataloging-in-Publication Data

Lesbian and bisexual women's mental health / Robin M. Mathy, Shelly K. Kerr, editors.
    p. cm.
    "Lesbian and Bisexual Women's Mental Health has been co-published simultaneously as Journal of Psychology & Human Sexuality, Volume 15, Numbers 2/3 and 4 2003."
    Includes bibliographical references and index.
    ISBN 978-0-789-02682-8 (pbk)

    1. Lesbians–Mental health. 2. Bisexual women–Mental health. I. Mathy, Robin M. II. Kerr, Shelly K. III. Title: Journal of Psychology & Human Sexuality.
RC451.4.G39L46 2004
616.89'14'086643–dc22

                                                                            2004018286

Indexing, Abstracting & Website/Internet Coverage

Journal of Psychology & Human Sexuality

This section provides you with a list of major indexing & abstracting services. That is to say, each service began covering this periodical during the year noted in the right column. Most Websites which are listed below have indicated that they will either post, disseminate, compile, archive, cite or alert their own Website users with research-based content from this work. (This list is as current as the copyright date of this publication.)

Abstracting, Website/Indexing Coverage . . . . Year When Coverage Began

- *Business Source Corporate: coverage of nearly 3,350 quality magazines and journals; designed to meet the diverse information needs of corporations; EBSCO Publishing <http://www.epnet.com/corporate/bsourcecorp.asp>* 2001

- *Cambridge Scientific Abstracts is a leading publisher of scientific information in print journals, online databases, CD-ROM and via the Internet <http://www.csa.com>* 1992

- *Educational Administration Abstracts (EAA)* 1995

- *e-psyche, LLC <http://www.e-psyche.net>* 2001

- *Family & Society Studies Worldwide <http://www.nisc.com>* 1996

- *Family Index Database <http://www.familyscholar.com>* 2003

- *Family Violence & Sexual Assault Bulletin* 1991

- *GenderWatch <http://www.slinfo.com>* 1999

- *Health & Psychosocial Instruments (HaPI) Database (available through online and as a CD-ROM from Ovid Technologies)* . . . . *

- *Higher Education Abstracts, providing the latest in research and theory in more than 140 major topics* 1991

(continued)

*Exact start date to come.

Special Bibliographic Notes related to special journal issues
(separates) and indexing/abstracting:

- indexing/abstracting services in this list will also cover material in any "separate" that is co-published simultaneously with Haworth's special thematic journal issue or DocuSerial. Indexing/abstracting usually covers material at the article/chapter level.
- monographic co-editions are intended for either non-subscribers or libraries which intend to purchase a second copy for their circulating collections.
- monographic co-editions are reported to all jobbers/wholesalers/approval plans. The source journal is listed as the "series" to assist the prevention of duplicate purchasing in the same manner utilized for books-in-series.
- to facilitate user/access services all indexing/abstracting services are encouraged to utilize the co-indexing entry note indicated at the bottom of the first page of each article/chapter/contribution.
- this is intended to assist a library user of any reference tool (whether print, electronic, online, or CD-ROM) to locate the monographic version if the library has purchased this version but not a subscription to the source journal.
- individual articles/chapters in any Haworth publication are also available through the Haworth Document Delivery Service (HDDS).

ABOUT THE EDITORS

Robin M. Mathy, MSW, LGSW, MSc, MSt, MA, is a Licensed Graduate Social Worker who has authored or coauthored more than 50 peer-reviewed articles and book chapters. She is the coauthor of *Male Homosexuality in Four Societies: Brazil, Guatemala, the Phillipines, and the United States* (Greenwood/Praeger, 1986), which the *New York Times Review of Books* identified as one of the best books in print in Anthropology. Robin's work focuses on cultural competence and research methods in clinical research and practice, particularly as factors that interact with suicide symptoms, stress-related disorders, and service utilization. She has graduate degrees in Sociology (Indiana University–Bloomington), Social Work and Family Education (University of Minnesota–Twin Cities), International Relations (University of Cambridge) and Evidence-Based Health Care (University of Oxford). She has worked as an executive director of a social service agency as well as a research consultant. She is currently Director of Research and Assistant Professor of Arts & Sciences at Presentation College in Aberdeen, South Dakota, and is a Licensed Graduate Social Worker in Minnesota.

Shelly K. Kerr, PhD, is Assistant Director, Training Director, and a licensed psychologist at the University of Oregon Counseling and Testing Center. She earned her master's degree in College Student Personnel from Western Illinois University and her doctorate in Counseling Psychology from Washington State University. Her dissertation research is entitled *Bias in Diagnosis and Assessment of Lesbian Clients by Counselor Trainees.* Dr. Kerr's professional areas of interest include training and supervision, lesbian, gay, bisexual and transgender issues, multicultural issues, hate and bias related crimes and incidents, and white privilege. She has presented professional trainings in the areas of working with LGBT clients and white privilege.

Lesbian and Bisexual Women's Mental Health

CONTENTS

Foreword:
Lesbian and Bisexual Women's
Mental Health

Beverly Greene, PhD, ABPP

The mental health literature supports the view that sexual orientation is an important, often understudied variable in women's mental health problems. Just as women were often a footnote in the mental health literature in general, lesbians have been a footnote in the mental health literature on women. For the most part, women's mental health problems are discussed as if women were a homogeneous group and as if sexism were the same for all of them. This occurs in spite of what we know about the ways that poverty, education, age, ethnicity, and sexual orientation not only transform and inform the experience of being a woman, but also complicate the challenge of sexist barriers in our society.

We know that lesbians face a level of social marginalization and disadvantage that, put simply, makes life more difficult for them. From the moment they are aware of their sexual minority status, they are equally aware of the challenges that their status will bring to their lives. Lesbians must negotiate the sexism that all women face. If they are members of ethnic minority groups they must negotiate racism. If they have a physical or perceptual disability, they must negotiate ableism. Of course, if they are old, they must negotiate ageism as well. All of those locations of social disadvantage are intensified for lesbians, who face

Beverly Greene is Professor of Psychology, St. John's University, Jamaica, NY.

[Haworth co-indexing entry note]: "Foreword: Lesbian and Bisexual Women's Mental Health." Greene, Beverly. Co-published simultaneously in *Journal of Psychology & Human Sexuality* (The Haworth Press, Inc.) Vol. 15, No. 2/3, 2003, pp. xvii-xviii; and: *Lesbian and Bisexual Women's Mental Health* (ed: Robin M. Mathy, and Shelly K. Kerr) The Haworth Press, Inc., 2003, pp. xiii-xiv. Single or multiple copies of this article are available for a fee from The Haworth Document Delivery Service [1-800-HAWORTH, 9:00 a.m. - 5:00 p.m. (EST). E-mail address: docdelivery@haworthpress.com].

the additional and ubiquitous challenges that are a function of their sexual minority status, heterosexism. Hence, lesbians may be seen as being required to routinely manage double, triple, or even quadrupled jeopardies. These jeopardies challenge the mental health and wellbeing of lesbians in a way that makes their understudied condition an irony. Many of the routine life transitions and challenges that all women face are intensified for lesbians, who are always required to negotiate a normal range of life stressors in a ubiquitous climate of hostility because of their sexual orientation. It is little wonder that many lesbians develop mental health problems; what perhaps is unusual is that perhaps most do not! Certainly those mental health problems found among women are intensified for lesbians. Lesbians may, in fact, be said to be at greater risk for developing less than optimal mental health outcomes because there are so many barriers that they must negotiate to have families and relationships that everyone else takes for granted and that everyone else is allowed to celebrate.

Perhaps the paucity of empirical research on lesbians can be attributed in part to the very heterosexism that challenges their wellbeing. Women are presumed to be heterosexual unless they say otherwise and because they are less visible, lesbians can be easily overlooked. This kind of behavior represents just one form of their social marginalization. There are, however, realistic methodological obstacles to conducting such research that must be acknowledged, which speaks to the challenges faced by the contributors to this collection. A traditional obstacle is that of representative sampling. Conducting research in a way that goes beyond the most immediate samples is important. For many researchers who recognize the need for more of this research there is the ongoing problem of finding subjects who in some way may be seen as representative of lesbians as a group, challenging traditional stereotypes of what lesbians can be or who they are. Hence, this volume breaks new ground not only in its exploration of mental health problems that are under-explored among lesbians, but its acknowledgement of the heterogeneity of this group as well.

The chapter contributors break new ground in helping us to better understand not only the complexities of development among this group but also of the diversity reflected in geographic, religious, ethnic and other differences between them and the contribution of those diversities to their dilemmas. This is an important contribution to our knowledge base and fills a void in the literature. By improving on what we know about lesbians with mental health problems we have hope of developing preventive paradigms as well as treatment approaches that take the uniqueness of this population into account. Hopefully this will be among the first of many efforts to follow.

Introduction:
The Human Ecology of Lesbian
and Bisexual Women's Mental Health

Shelly K. Kerr, PhD
Robin M. Mathy, MSW, LGSW, MSc, MSt, MA

SUMMARY. This introduction to *Lesbian and Bisexual Women's Mental Health* reviews the need for research specific to lesbian and bisexual women's mental health. We also emphasize the need to provide research sensitive to the multidimensional nature of lesbian and bisexual women's lives. We provide a human ecological perspective consistent with lifespan developmental psychology and compatible with Clinical Social Work and Counseling Psychology as well as other interdisciplinary disciplines. With a strong emphasis on empirical research, this volume introduces readers to research that explores and reexamines the interactions between lesbian and bisexual women's mental health and the diverse social contexts in which they (we) live. *[Article copies available for a fee from The Haworth Document Delivery Service: 1-800-HAWORTH. E-mail address: <docdelivery@haworthpress.com> Website: <http://www.HaworthPress.com> © 2003 by The Haworth Press, Inc. All rights reserved.]*

KEYWORDS. Human ecology, lesbian, bisexual, mental health

Shelly K. Kerr is affiliated with the Counseling and Testing Center, University of Oregon. Robin M. Mathy is Director of Research and Assistant Professor of Arts & Sciences at Presentation College in Aberdeen, South Dakota, and is a Licensed Graduate Social Worker in Minnesota.

Address correspondence to Shelly K. Kerr, Counseling and Testing Center, University of Oregon, 1590 East 13th Avenue, Eugene, OR (E-mail: skerr@uoregon.edu).

[Haworth co-indexing entry note]: "Introduction: Human Ecology of Lesbian and Bisexual Women's Mental Health." Kerr, Shelly K., and Robin M. Mathy. Co-published simultaneously in *Journal of Psychology & Human Sexuality* (The Haworth Press, Inc.) Vol. 15, No. 2/3, 2003, pp. 1-9; and: *Lesbian and Bisexual Women's Mental Health* (ed: Robin M. Mathy, and Shelly K. Kerr) The Haworth Press, Inc., 2003, pp. 1-9. Single or multiple copies of this article are available for a fee from The Haworth Document Delivery Service [1-800-HAWORTH, 9:00 a.m. - 5:00 p.m. (EST). E-mail address: docdelivery@haworthpress.com].

http://www.haworthpress.com/web/JPHS
© 2003 by The Haworth Press, Inc. All rights reserved.
Digital Object Identifier: 10.1300/J056v15n02_01

The American Psychiatric Association removed homosexuality from its list of mental disorders in 1973. Since then, there have been many calls for the mental health profession to provide affirmative services to the gay and lesbian community (Garnets, Hancock, Cochran, Goodchilds, & Peplau, 1991; Gonsiorek, 1982). Gonsiorek (1982) noted that the key elements of affirmative psychotherapy must (a) be relevant to the actual life experiences of gays and lesbians, (b) incorporate relevant ideas from mainstream psychology, and (c) begin to accumulate empirical support. More recently, a final report from a joint meeting between the American Psychological Association and the Association of Lesbian, Gay, and Bisexual Psychologies of Europe (ALGBP) presented a consensus statement that recommended "affirmative care for lesbian, gay, and bisexual persons" (2003, p. 4). The purpose of this meeting was to "improve mental health care and prevent mental illness with lesbian, gay, and bisexual populations" (p. IV). The recommendations presented in the final report from this meeting included removing prejudice and discrimination in psychological practice, creating new and changing existing mental health care delivery systems, and preventing mental health and adjustment problems among lesbian, gay, and bisexual individuals.

Many scientists and practitioners have contributed relevant, meaningful, and affirmative literature on sexual orientation and mental health. However, empirical literature specific to lesbian and bisexual women has lagged behind their sexual minority male peers. In addition to books produced primarily for and about gay men, much of the literature specific to mental health and sexual orientation includes papers that address gay men and lesbians as a homogeneous group. We conceived this volume as a project that would empirically examine issues relevant to lesbian and bisexual women's mental health from a social ecological perspective.

There is substantial need for greater attention to lesbian and bisexual women's mental health. The Institute of Medicine (IOM) (National Academy Press, 1999) identified lesbians as a subgroup of women whose health issues have been neglected for the past two decades. The IOM used the term health to reflect "physical, mental, and social well-being and not merely the absence of disease or infirmity" (p. 17). The IOM also endorsed a socioecological view of health that focuses on the interaction between lesbians and their environments. The IOM report findings and recommendations, as well as an ecological model of human development and mental health, provided our foundation for developing *Lesbian and Bisexual Women's Mental Health*.

The IOM's report suggested that the study of lesbian health is important in order to "gain knowledge that is useful for improving the health status and health care of lesbians, to confirm beliefs and counter misperceptions that exist about the health risks to lesbians, and to identify health areas in which lesbians are at risk or tend to be at greater risk than heterosexual women or women in general" (pp. 20-21). The papers in this volume address these issues. For example, relevant to improving the quality of mental health care provided to lesbians, Kerr, Walker, McNeill, and Warner's paper (Counselor Trainees' Assessment and Diagnosis of Lesbian Clients with Dysthymic Disorder) reviews literature citing biased and inadequate mental health assessment, diagnosis, and treatment of lesbians. Their study suggests that the mental health assessment and diagnostic decisions that counselor trainees make about lesbians may be influenced by their perceptions that sexual orientation plays a role in mental health functioning. In terms of addressing myths and misperceptions regarding the mental health of sexual minorities, Mathy and Schillace's paper (Psychosexual Development, Rural-Urban Gradients, and Community Victimization in Three Cross-Sectional Studies of Lesbian and Bisexual Women) contradicts perceptions that lesbian and bisexual women raised in rural areas are at higher risk for negative developmental outcomes than those raised in metropolitan centers. Other papers compare heterosexual and sexual minority women's risks for developing mental health problems. For example, Wagenbach's "Lesbian Body Image and Eating Issues" examined body image and eating behavior in order to compare lesbian and heterosexual women's attitudes toward their bodies as well as their dieting behaviors. In "Depressive Distress and Prevalence of Common Problems among Homosexually Active African American Women in the United States," Mays, Cochran, and Roeder compared depressive distress among sexual minority and heterosexual African-American women. In "Mental Health and Sexual Minority Females in Taiwan," Kuang, Nojima, Carol, and Mathy compared Taiwanese lesbian and bisexual females to heterosexual females to investigate differences in levels of stress by gender role and sexual orientation.

The IOM's report emphasized that it is important for mental health care providers and lesbians to have access to research that reveals mental health problems faced by lesbians as well as to research that addresses protective factors. Going beyond a literature review that compares lesbian and heterosexual women's experiences of depression and anxiety, Kerr and Emerson's article (A Review of Depression and Anxiety) also discusses protective factors that mediate or moderate clinical depression. In "Lesbians in Psychotherapy: Relationship of Shame and Attachment Style," Wells found that secure attachment might be considered a protective factor that buffers against internalized shame of sexual minority identity. In addition, the papers by Mathy and her colleagues suggest that rural residence and religiosity may be protective factors for lesbian and bisexual women.

As endorsed by the IOM, a socioecological perspective on lesbian health includes an examination of lesbian mental health in the context of women, the mental health care system, and society. Such a perspective also includes studying the mental health of lesbians across the lifespan. Thus, developmental issues are not limited to children and adolescents. For example, in "The Impact of Religiosity on Lesbian and Bisexual Women's Psychosexual Development" Mathy et al. examined the impact of parental religiosity on psychosexual development of adult lesbian and bisexual women. Wagenbach found that age was a factor in lesbians' investment in physical fitness and the evaluation of their appearance. Wells conducted a study of attachment and shame that involved a sample of lesbians, aged 35 to 55, in the highest stage of identity integration. Thus, this volume addresses lesbian and bisexual women's mental health issues across the entire socioecological spectrum.

Bronfenbrenner's (1977;1979) ecological model of human development provides an appropriate framework for approaching the study of lesbian and bisexual women's mental health and a model that corresponds with the IOM's socioecological perspective. Bronfenbrenner described human development as taking place within four different systems that affect development directly and indirectly. The microsystem involves the interactions between the individual and his or her immediate setting, such as family, school, and church. Not only do the specific individuals within these systems affect development, but there also are patterns that develop within microsystems that influence individuals' development. Bronfenbrenner described the reciprocal nature of relationships within systems. Not only do patterns within a system affect an individual's experience, an individual's patterns also may have an impact on the larger system. For example, Kerr and Emerson's review of depression and anxiety in lesbians identifies aspects of microsystems such as family and work as well as social and intimate relationships that can increase or buffer symptoms of depression and anxiety. Mathy et al. examined the role of lesbian and bisexual women's religiosity on the self-disclosure of their sexual orientation.

Individuals participate in more than one microsystem, creating links between those systems. Bronfenbrenner conceptualized these links as the mesosystem. Indirect linkages can form between systems as well, wielding multidirectional influences on individuals. For example, a child's parent (family microsystem) might participate in a conference with the child's teacher (school microsystem). These indirect links are also part of the mesosystem. Mathy et al.'s findings about the effect of maternal religiosity on self-disclosure of sexual orientation and its relation to acceptance and rejection following self-disclosure can be viewed as the interaction of one microsystem (church) on another (parent) that affects lesbian and bisexual women's psychosexual development.

The exosystem is comprised of contexts with which one does not have direct contact, but that nonetheless exerts an indirect influence on an individual. Bronfenbrenner included neighborhoods, mass media, government agencies, and informal social networks in this system. Bronfenner's broadest system is the macrosystem, which like the exosystem, exerts its influence indirectly. Cultural, economic, social, educational, legal, and political systems comprise the macrosystem. Mathy, Carol, and Schillace's study of rural lesbians addresses both exosystem and macrosystem issues involving rural culture, the influence of rural neighborhoods, and the social networks that develop in rural environments. Mays et. al's examination of depressive distress among African-American women and Kuang et. al's study of lesbian and bisexual women in Taiwan consider cultural variables in relation to the mental health issues faced by lesbian and bisexual women. In addition to considering the ethnicity of their sample, Mays et al. also describe economic and other problems faced by women in their sample, including financial and housing problems.

The papers in *Lesbian and Bisexual Women's Mental Health* examine mental health issues within a social ecological context, examining the ways in which systemic factors play a role in psychological and emotional wellbeing. We could have addressed other issues. However, we sought to fulfill the IOM's call for empirical research. Earlier works that have focused on lesbian and bisexual women's mental health have been rich in clinical experience and insight. In agreement with the IOM's assessment, we believe that more studies of an empirical nature are necessary. Such studies will enable scientist-practitioners as well as sexual minorities and their allies to enhance lesbian and bisexual women's mental health.

Gathering empirical research concerning lesbian and bisexual women can be a daunting task. Historically, feminists, historians, and scholars of English have led the study of lesbian and bisexual women's issues. Their postmodern inquiries have correctly underscored the limits of positivist research. All positivist research is correlational, and no study can explain all of the variance in lesbian and bisexual women's mental health outcomes. Further, positivist research concerning sexual minorities often has excluded females or neglected the differences between gay men and lesbians. The external validity of such research for lesbian and bisexual women is highly questionable. Conversely, positivist researchers have questioned the reliability of research about sexual minorities because few samples are representative of the general population. Yet representative samples of sexual minorities are extremely difficult and expensive to obtain. Indeed, until the stigma and oppression of same-sex fantasies, attraction, and behaviors abate, it may be impossible to obtain a truly representative sample of sexual minorities. To be sure, the use of convenience samples and a focus on positivist vis-à-vis hermeneutic studies limits the generalizability and external validity of the findings presented in this volume. Nonetheless, each of the papers included in this volume enhances our understanding of lesbian and bisexual women across multiple social ecologies.

We need further research concerning lesbian and bisexual women, particularly at the interstices of physical and mental health. For far too long, sex researchers have studied physical and mental health separately. For example, some researchers (Cochran, Keenan, Schober, & Mays, 2000; Cochran & Mays, 2000; Gilman, Cochran, Mays, Hughes, Ostrow, & Kessler, 2001; Mays & Cochran, 2001) have examined the mental health burden of oppression on sexual minorities by examining sexual orientation differences in stress-related disorders, such as suicide attempts, depression, anxiety, and substance abuse. Researchers also have examined physical health issues among sexual minority women (Cochran, Mays, & Bowen et al., 2001; Yancey, Cochran, Corliss, & Mays, 2003). However, self-injurious behaviors, substance abuse, and psychosocial stress also affect physical health. Yet physicians who treat lesbian and bisexual women may simultaneously minimize their reproductive health system (Ryan & Bradford, 1993) and overlook the adverse physical effects of enduring oppression and stigma. Further, there is considerable variation in oppression and stigma of sexual minorities cross-culturally. Cross-cultural studies of sexual minority women's physical and mental health may help elucidate the ways in which cultural norms and formal legal codes might mediate or moderate the relationship between social structures and psychosexual development. Heretofore, a disproportionate number of health-related studies have focused on lesbian and bisexual women in North America. Cross-cultural studies must control for variance in the status of women. Although women in the Global North (i.e., the Australia, European, and North American continents) remain oppressed, they have made far greater gains than their peers in the Global South (i.e., Africa, Asia, and South America). We know very little about the physical or mental health of sexual minority women in the Global South.

Lesbian and Bisexual Women's Mental Health attempts to lay an empirical foundation for further *empirical* research. For example, we do not expect that all readers will agree with Mathy and her colleagues' findings regarding the protective influence of religion or rural areas in lesbian and bisexual women's development. However, we hope it will stimulate further research and discussion about the differences between gay men and lesbians in socioecological contexts. Despite their sexual minority status, gay men and lesbian women rarely occupy the same socioecological space. Lesbian and bisexual women are subject to both sexism and heterosexism, whereas gay and bisexual men primarily endure heterosexism.

Lesbian and Bisexual Women's Mental Health could not examine every issue that readers might have hoped we would include. Nonetheless, we remain committed to advancing understanding in this area, and to encouraging other scientist-practitioners to develop gender and sexual orientation specific theories and to reexamine questionable hypotheses. This work may help put to rest the notion that lesbian and bisexual women are a pale shadow of their gay male peers. Although most sophisticated scientist-practitioners are aware that there are differences between sexual minority men and women, the dearth of research specific to lesbian and bisexual women has undermined the ability to articulate these differences. For example, Mathy and her colleagues are careful to articulate that the developmental outcomes of lesbian and bisexual women raised in rural areas or in religious families may differ from those of gay and bisexual men.

In sum, this book represents the beginning of a long journey on a path to greater understanding of lesbian and bisexual women's health. We hope readers will genuinely enjoy as well as appreciate the individual and collective efforts of this book's authors. Many of the authors are relatively new to publishing, and they subjected themselves to the ardors of learning to write for peer-reviewed publication while striving to make a meaningful contribution to the literature. We also hope this work will empower other young scholars to begin their own bold adventures into lesbian and bisexual women's health. To be sure, studying lesbian and bisexual women's health issues is the path less traveled, but the adventure promises to bring greater discoveries, deeper understanding, and a potentially rewarding journey for those who take it. It also promises to provide evidence-based information that scientist-practitioners need to improve the quality of care provided to lesbian and bisexual women. We aim to continue this journey, and we hope readers will feel free to join us and suggest other paths on the road to lesbian and bisexual women's empowerment and self-actualization.

REFERENCES

American Psychological Association & Association of Lesbian, Gay, and Bisexual Psychologies of Europe. (2003). Sexual orientation and mental health: Toward global perspectives on practice and policy. (Final Report). An international meeting on lesbian, gay, and bisexual concerns in psychology.

Bronfenbrenner, U. (1977). Toward an experimental ecology of human development. *American Psychologist, 32*(7), 513-531.

Bronfenbrenner, U. (1979). *The ecology of human development: Experiments by nature and design.* Cambridge, MA: Harvard University Press.

Cochran, S. D., Keenan, C., Schober, C., & Mays, V. M. (2000). Estimates of alcohol use and clinical treatment needs among homosexually active men and women in the U.S. population. *Journal of Consulting & Clinical Psychology, 68*(6), 1062-1071.

Cochran, S. D., & Mays, V. M. (2000). Lifetime prevalence of suicide symptoms and affective disorders among men reporting same-sex sexual partners: Results from NHANES III. *American Journal of Public Health, 90*(4), 573-578.

Cochran, S. D., Mays, V. M. Bowen, D., Gage, S., Bybee, D., Roberts, S. J., Goldstein, R. S., Robinson, A., Rankow, E. J., & White, J. (2001). Cancer-related risk indicators and preventive screening behaviors among lesbians and bisexual women. *American Journal of Public Health, 9*(4), 591-597.

Cochran, S. D., Sullivan, J. G., & Mays, V. M. (2003). Prevalence of mental disorders, psychological distress, and mental services use among lesbian, gay, and bisexual adults in the United States. *Journal of Consulting & Clinical Psychology, 71*(1), 53-61.

Garnets, L., Hancock, K.A., Cochran, S. D., Goodchilds, J., & Peplau, L. A. (1991). Issues in psychotherapy with lesbians and gay men: A survey of psychologists. *American Psychologist, 46*(9), 964-972.

Gilman, S. E., Cochran, S. D., Mays, V. M., Hughes, M., Ostrow, D., & Kessler, R. C. (2001). Risk of psychiatric disorders among individuals reporting same-sex sexual partners in the National Comorbidity Survey. *American Journal of Public Health, 91*(6), 933-939.

Gonsiorek, J. C. (1982). Introduction: Present and future directions in gay/lesbian mental health. *Journal of Homosexuality, 7,* 5-7.

Mays, V. M., & Cochran, S. D. (2001). Mental health correlates of perceived discrimination among lesbian, gay, and bisexual adults in the United States. *American Journal of Public Health, 91*(11), 1869-1876.

McMillan, B. W. (1990). An ecological perspective on individual human development. *Early Childhood Development and Care*, *55*, 33-42.

Ryan, C., & Bradford, J. (1993). The National Lesbian Health Care Survey: An overview. In L. D. Garnets & D. C. Kimmel (Eds.), *Psychological perspectives on lesbian and gay male experiences* (pp. 541-556). New York: Columbia University Press.

Solarz, A. (Ed) (1999). *Lesbian health: Current assessment and directions for the future*. Washington, DC: National Academy Press.

Yancey, A. K., Cochran, S. D., Corliss, H. L., & Mays, V. M. (2003). Correlates of overweight and obesity among lesbian and bisexual women. *Preventive Medicine*, *36*(6), 676-683.

Counselor Trainees' Assessment and Diagnosis of Lesbian Clients with Dysthymic Disorder

Shelly K. Kerr, PhD
W. Rand Walker, PhD
Dennis A. Warner, PhD
Brian W. McNeill, PhD

SUMMARY. Graduate-level counselor trainees completed an Assessment and Diagnostic Inventory consisting of clinical vignettes and a series of questions pertaining to conceptualization of client problem, diagnosis, and assessment of overall level of psychopathology. We hypothesized that participants would assign different diagnoses to clients with lesbian versus heterosexual sexual orientation. Participants responded to vignettes in which clients were identified as either a lesbian or a heterosexual female, with all other content identical. Participants

Shelly K. Kerr, W. Rand Walker, Dennis A. Warner, and Brian W. McNeill are affiliated with the Department of Educational Leadership and Counseling Psychology, Washington State University.

Shelly K. Kerr is now Assistant Director and Training Director at the University Counseling and Testing Center, University of Oregon. W. Rand Walker is now Affiliate Associate Professor, Center for Disabilities and Human Development, College of Education, University of Idaho.

Address correspondence to Shelly K. Kerr, University Counseling and Testing Center, 1590 East 13th Avenue, University of Oregon, Eugene, OR (e-mail: skerr@uoregon.edu).

[Haworth co-indexing entry note]: "Counselor Trainees' Assessment and Diagnosis of Lesbian Clients with Dysthymic Disorder." Kerr et al. Co-published simultaneously in *Journal of Psychology & Human Sexuality* (The Haworth Press, Inc.) Vol. 15, No. 2/3, 2003, pp. 11-26; and: *Lesbian and Bisexual Women's Mental Health* (ed: Robin M. Mathy, and Shelly K. Kerr) The Haworth Press, Inc., 2003, pp. 11-26. Single or multiple copies of this article are available for a fee from The Haworth Document Delivery Service [1-800-HAWORTH, 9:00 a.m. - 5:00 p.m. (EST). E-mail address: docdelivery@haworthpress.com].

were significantly more likely to perceive lesbian clients' problems to be related to sexual orientation for the vignette corresponding to dysthymic disorder. However, they were not more likely to assign personality disorder diagnoses, nor did they attribute a greater degree of psychopathology to lesbian clients with dysthymic disorder. *[Article copies available for a fee from The Haworth Document Delivery Service: 1-800-HAWORTH. E-mail address: <docdelivery@haworthpress.com> Website: <http://www.HaworthPress.com> © 2003 by The Haworth Press, Inc. All rights reserved.]*

KEYWORDS. Counselor education, clinical training, assessment and diagnosis, lesbian, depression

Case formulation and diagnosis are essential components in the process of planning and implementing counseling treatment. Assessment and diagnosis are prone toward inaccuracies, due in part to biases and distortions on the part of clinicians (Dumont & Lecomte, 1987; Spengler & Strohmer, 1994; Strohmer, Shivy, & Chiodo, 1990). There are a number of sources of error based on counselor characteristics. These include (a) preconceived notions or expectancies (Arkes, 1981), (b) the tendency to focus on information that confirms an original hypothesis, while disregarding disconfirmatory information (Arkes, 1981; Faust, 1986; Strohmer, Shivy, & Chiodo, 1990), (c) the tendency to use the first set of information adequately explaining the situation at hand and to weigh such information more heavily in making diagnoses (Dumont & Lecomte, 1987), and (d) anchoring bias (Friedlander & Phillips, 1984; Pain & Sharpley, 1989).

Judgment errors may also occur when clinicians rely on inferential strategies such as "knowledge structures" and "judgment heuristics." Knowledge structures involve already established sets of beliefs, theories, and schemas that are helpful in classifying and interpreting information quickly and easily. Judgment heuristics are cognitive strategies that enable individuals to reduce complex inferential tasks to more simple judgmental operations (Nisbett & Ross, 1980). Although these strategies can be efficient and useful in the diagnostic process, over-reliance on diagnostic shortcuts can result in biased and inaccurate decision-making.

Studies addressing the influence of client variables on diagnostic decision-making have demonstrated that unwarranted shifts of emphasis can occur based on a single characteristic (e.g., gender or ethnicity) (Gray-Little, 1995). Biased clinical judgment may be influenced by client race (Rahimi, Rosenthal, & Chan, 2003; Garb, 1997; Pavkov, Lewis, & Lyons, 1989), gender or gender roles (Wisch & Mahalik, 1999; Garb, 1997), cultural background (Lopez & Hernandez, 1986), and social class (Lopez, 1989). Given the substantial body of literature highlighting problems in clinical assessment due to both clinician and client variables, this study examined bias in the context of one client variable: sexual orientation.

In spite of efforts to depathologize homosexuality by the American Psychiatric Association (Eldridge & Barnett, 1991) and admonitions by the American Psychological Association to eliminate bias from the treatment of gay and lesbian clients (Conger, 1975), some mental health professionals have continued to view homosexuality as an undesirable deviance. Rudolph's (1988) review of literature noted that as many as one-third of counseling professionals expressed negative attitudes toward gays and lesbians. Even more recently, Jordan and Deluty (1995) found that some therapists continue to believe that a gay or lesbian sexual orientation is indicative of a personality disorder or psychosexual disorder.

Wisch and Mahalik's (1999) study of male therapists revealed that male clients' sexual orientation and emotional expression influenced the therapists' ratings of prognosis, as well as the degree of liking, empathy for, comfort with, and willingness to see clients. Biaggio et al.'s (2000) study of members of the American Psychological Association's Psychotherapy division yielded mixed results about the influence of sexual orientation on the clinical judgment of therapists who read case vignettes and answered questions about psychological functioning. Lesbians and heterosexual men received higher ratings for alcohol dependence and schizophrenia than did gay men and heterosexual women. Gay men and lesbians were also perceived to be in greater need for pharmacological intervention. However, gay and lesbian clients were also evaluated as functioning better in their significant relationships and being more motivated for therapy.

The American Psychological Association's Task Force on Bias in Psychotherapy with Lesbians and Gay Men (1990) cited instances of therapist bias in areas of assessment, diagnosis, and intervention. Some therapists described a gay or lesbian sexual orientation as a form of psychopathology or developmental arrest, or attributed clients' problems to sexual orientation without evidence that it was actually at the root of clients' difficulties. Some therapists automatically assumed a client was heterosexual or discounted clients' own identification of themselves as gay or lesbian. There were also examples of therapists discouraging clients from adopting a gay or lesbian identity, actively attempting to change clients' sexual orientations without being requested by clients to do so, or terminating therapy with clients upon learning that they were gay or lesbian (Garnets, Hancock, Cochran, Goodchilds, & Peplau, 1991; Task Force on Bias in Psychotherapy with Lesbians and Gay Men, 1990).

Graduate students are subject to similar biases. These biases appear to continue throughout their training. Gay men and lesbians were perceived as less psychologically healthy than heterosexual clients and as being more dissatisfied with themselves (Garfinkle & Morin, 1978). Glenn and Russell (1986) found that counselor trainees identified "relationship life-style" as an issue to be addressed significantly more often for lesbian clients than for heterosexual or unidentifiable clients. More recently, Barrett and McWhirter (2002) found that counseling and clinical psychology graduate students with higher levels of homophobia (based on the Index of Homophobia) were significantly more likely to assign negative adjectives to lesbian clients, but not to gay male clients. Trainees who had higher levels of homophobia did assign significantly fewer positive adjectives to both lesbian and gay male clients than to heterosexual clients. These researchers also noted that the mean level of homophobia among their sample was relatively low (mean score of 41.04 on a scale ranging from 1-100) and that graduate students who reported having a gay male or lesbian friend had significantly lower levels of homophobia.

Given that clinicians are susceptible to a number of judgment errors, and that client variables such as ethnicity, gender, cultural background, and sexual orientation have been found to influence the judgment of clinicians, this study investigated the extent to which the sexual orientation of clients influences the clinical judgment of counselor trainees. The authors hypothesized that counselor trainees would (a) conceptualize lesbian client problems in terms of the client's sexual orientation, (b) assign personality disorder diagnoses to lesbian clients, and (c) attribute higher levels of psychopathology (greater level of disturbance, poorer prognosis for therapy, longer duration of therapy) to lesbian clients than to heterosexual female clients.

METHOD

Participants

Counselor trainees ($n = 157$) completing master's and doctoral level degrees in Counseling Psychology and Clinical Psychology participated in this study. Participants were solicited from training sites across the United States, including doctoral programs and internship sites. Two hundred inventories were distributed and 157 were returned, yielding a 79% return rate. Demographic characteristics of the sample are found in Table 1.

TABLE 1. Demographic Characteristics of Participants (n = 157)

Demographic Variable	Frequency	Percent
Gender		
Male	039	25.00
Female	117	75.00
Age		
21-29	82	55.78
30-39	35	23.81
40-49	27	18.37
50+	03	02.04
Theoretical Orientation		
Client Centered	17	11.56
Cognitive	04	02.72
Cognitive Behavioral	31	21.09
Eclectic	52	35.37
Existential	21	14.29
Gestalt	00	00.00
Psychoanalytic/Psychodynamic	04	02.72
Other	18	12.24
Degree Program		
Clinical Psychology	37	24.18
Counseling Psychology	80	52.28
Psy D	15	09.80
Other	21	13.72
Year In Program		
1st year masters	57	37.25
2nd year masters	31	20.26
3rd year masters	01	00.65
1st year doctoral	11	07.19
2nd year doctoral	19	12.42
3rd year doctoral	08	05.23
4th year doctoral	03	01.96
Intern	19	12.42
Other	04	02.61
Clinical Experience (4 months = 1 semester)		
No experience	37	23.57
1-3 semesters	73	46.50
4-6 semesters	18	11.46
7-9 semesters	15	09.55
10-12 semesters	06	03.82
13-15 semesters	02	01.27
19-21 semesters	01	00.64
22-24 semesters	01	00.64

Instrument

Assessment and Diagnostic Inventory. The Assessment and Diagnostic Inventory was developed to investigate assessment and diagnostic decisions made by counselor trainees about hypothetical female clients. The inventory was adapted from similar instruments developed by Paul Spengler, PhD, who has done extensive research in the area of clinical judgment (personal communication, October 4, 1995). The inventory consists of three clinical vignettes representing three diagnostic categories (dysthymic disorder, generalized anxiety disorder, obsessive-compulsive disorder), followed by questions pertaining to assessment of the client's problem, DSM-IV diagnosis, and overall level of psychopathology. The final page of the Assessment and Diagnostic Inventory solicits information about the participants themselves (e.g., gender, theoretical orientation, educational background, counseling experience, knowledge about diagnosis, importance placed on diagnosis, level of comfort with diagnostic ability).

This paper presents information related to the dysthymic disorder vignette that was developed based on DSM-IV criteria. The sexual orientation of the client was presented as either lesbian or heterosexual female. The vignette read as follows:

> Client #1: Susan is a 26-year old [*heterosexual female*] [*lesbian*] who reports feeling "depressed" since adolescence. She indicates that she feels lethargic, has little interest in and derives little pleasure from anything, has trouble concentrating, and often feels inadequate and pessimistic. She reports rarely feeling "good" about herself or anything else and those "good periods" do not last more than a day or two. Throughout adolescence, Susan reports having few close friends and always feeling as if she did not fit in. She reports that she did not date much in high school and did not attend school dances or proms. She earned Bs throughout school and attended college the year immediately following graduation. She found herself having increasing academic difficulties throughout college as she no longer had her parents to push her to complete assignments and study for tests. Susan reports that she had difficulty making friends, which she attributes to her low self-esteem.

To achieve face validation, faculty and interns at Washington State University's Counseling Services read the vignette and provided a primary diagnosis. This procedure was done to determine whether the vignette accurately described symptoms leading to the intended diagnosis of dysthymic disorder. Eight individuals assigned a diagnosis of dysthymic disorder to the dysthymic disorder vignette and one individual assigned a diagnosis of depression.

Question #1 reads "Based on the information presented about this client, indicate your assessment of how likely the client is experiencing problems in the following areas." This statement is followed by a list of 12 potential client problems and a scale ranging from 1 (not likely client is experiencing that problem) to 7 (very likely that client is experiencing that problem). This question includes several items designed as distractors, ranging from academic concerns to suicide or death. The variable of interest is the item "sexual orientation."

Question #2 reads, "Based on the information presented about (the client), indicate the likelihood that the following diagnoses apply to this client." The question is followed by a list of 27 possible diagnoses and a scale ranging from 1 (very likely that the diagnosis is appropriate for that client) to 7 (not likely that the diagnosis is appropriate for that client).

Question #3 reads "Each statement is followed by descriptors on a continuum. Circle the number on the Likert scale which best describes your opinion about the statement for (the client). Participants are asked to circle the number on the scale which best describes their opinion in six areas: (a) level of clients' disturbance (7 = unable to function; 1 = no disturbance), (b) the degree to which clients have control for their problems (7 = cannot control problems; 1 = in control of problems), (c) prognosis for successful therapy (7 = very poor; 1 = very good), (d) duration of therapy (7 = long term; 1 = short term), (e) onset of client's problems (7 = chronic; 1 = acute), and (f) the degree to which subjects would like to work with the clients (7 = very little; 1 = very much).

Procedure

Participants were randomly divided into three groups: one "lesbian client" group and two "heterosexual client" groups. The "lesbian client" group read vignettes in which hypothetical clients were identified as lesbian, and the two "heterosexual client" groups read vignettes in which clients were identified as a heterosexual female. Mean scores on the dependent variables of the "lesbian client" group were compared to the mean scores on the dependent variables of the two "heterosexual client" groups, rather than just one "heterosexual client" group. The "heterosexual client" groups were compared to each other. If client sexual orientation was the only piece of information presented differently to the groups, one would expect that the mean scores for one "heterosexual client" group would not differ significantly from those of the other "heterosexual client" group, because they responded to identical information. If those scores did differ significantly, one could conclude that factors other than sexual orientation were at work in the diagnostic and assessment decision-making process. If the mean scores for the "lesbian client" group differed significantly from one, or both, "heterosexual client" groups, but the mean scores of the two "heterosexual client" groups did not differ significantly from one another, one could conclude with greater certainty that client sexual orientation affected the decisions made by these subjects.

Participants received a packet with a cover letter and the Assessment and Diagnostic Inventory. All instruments were coded to protect subjects' anonymity. Materials were distributed and collected with the assistance of training directors, and faculty who were identified in the publication "Graduate Faculty Interested in Gay and Lesbian Issues" (APA, 1993).

Subject group (one "lesbian client group," and two "heterosexual client groups"), based on the sexual orientation of the hypothetical client, was the primary independent variable that was expected to influence the assessment and diagnostic decisions made by the subjects. We had planned to investigate the extent to which gender played a role in assessment and diagnosis. However, the low number of male subjects in this study resulted in cell sizes that were too small to detect significant differences.

Dependent variables included conceptualization of client problem (sexual orientation), personality disorder diagnoses (borderline personality disorder, histrionic personality disorder, narcissistic personality disorder, avoidant personality disorder, dependent personality disorder, and obsessive compulsive personality disorder), and three measures of overall assessment of psychopathology for each hypothetical client [the client's level of disturbance (7 = unable to function; 1 = no disturbance), prognosis for therapy (7 = very poor; 1 = very good), and duration of therapy (7 = long term/30 + sessions; 1 = short term/less than 10 sessions)].

RESULTS

We hypothesized that the "lesbian client" group would have a significantly higher mean score on the dependent variable "Client Problem-Sexual Orientation" than would the "heterosexual client" groups.

We also hypothesized that there would be no significant mean differences between the two "heterosexual client" groups on this dependent variable. Subject scores on the dependent variable "Conceptualization of Client Problem-Sexual Orientation" were analyzed using a one-way fixed-model analysis of variance. Group (lesbian or heterosexual) was the independent variable. A significant effect for group was found for the dependent variable "Conceptualization of Client Problem-Sexual Orientation" for dysthymic disorder vignette, $F = 13.006$ (2, 153), $p < .000$. ANOVA results are located in Table 2.

Post-hoc comparisons of cell means of the independent variable groups (lesbian or heterosexual) using Tukey's HSD (alpha = .05) revealed that the "lesbian client" group had a significantly higher mean score ($M = 4.41$) on the dependent variable "Conceptualization of Client Problem-Sexual Orientation" than the first "heterosexual client" group ($M = 2.96$) and the second "heterosexual client" group ($M = 3.16$). No significant mean differences were found between the two "heterosexual client" groups for this diagnostic vignette. Means and standard deviations for each group are presented in Table 3.

Secondly, we hypothesized that the "lesbian client" group would have significantly higher mean scores on the personality disorder diagnoses than would either of the "heterosexual client" groups. Subject scores on a linear combination of the dependent variables comprising the personality disorder cluster (borderline, histrionic, narcissistic, avoidant, dependant, and obsessive-compulsive personality disorders) were analyzed using a multivariate analysis of variance. Group (lesbian or heterosexual) was the independent variable. The multivariate analysis of variance revealed no significant differences between groups for the linear combination of these dependent variables for the dysthymic disorder vignette [Wilks' Lambda F (12,292) = 1.366, $p = 0.181$]. Because the overall F-values were found to be non-significant, no additional univariate analyses were conducted.

TABLE 2. ANOVA Source Table for Conceptualization of Client Problem–Sexual Orientation

Source	SS	DF	MS	F	P
Group	65.194	2	32.597	13.066	0.000
Error	381.704	153	2.495		

TABLE 3. Means and Standard Deviations for Group on Conceptualization of Client Problem–Sexual Orientation

	Mean	Standard Deviation
Heterosexual Group (n = 51)	2.96	1.31
Lesbian Group (n = 54)	4.41	2.01
Heterosexual Group (n = 51)	3.16	1.29

Finally, we hypothesized that the "lesbian client" group would have significantly higher mean scores on the dependent variables "Level of Disturbance," "Prognosis for Therapy," and "Duration of Therapy" than would either "heterosexual client" group. We also hypothesized that there would be no significant mean differences between the two "heterosexual client" groups. Subject scores on a linear combination of these dependent variables were analyzed using a multivariate analysis of variance. Group (lesbian or heterosexual) was the independent variable. The multivariate analysis of variance revealed no significant differences among groups for the linear combination of dependent variables for the dysthymic disorder vignette (Wilks' Lambda F (6, 304) = 1.338, p = 0.240). Subsequently, no additional univariate analyses were performed for these diagnostic vignettes.

DISCUSSION

The analysis of the data strongly supported the hypothesis that participants who read a dysthymic disorder vignette in which the client was identified as lesbian would be significantly more likely to attribute her problems to sexual orientation than would participants who read an identical vignette identifying the client as a heterosexual female. This study used two "heterosexual client" groups as a means of strengthening the conclusions drawn from the data. If some random factor were operating, one might have expected the "lesbian client" group to differ from only one of the groups reading about heterosexual clients, or for one of the "heterosexual client" groups to differ from the other in addition to one of these groups differing from the "lesbian client" group. However, participants in the "lesbian client" group were significantly more likely to attribute clients' problems to sexual orientation than were participants in both of the "heterosexual client" groups. Additionally, the "heterosexual client" groups did not differ significantly from each other. This finding allows one to be more confident that the identification of the client as lesbian was the primary factor that resulted in differences between groups.

Overall, it appears that client sexual orientation did influence these research participants' conceptualization of client problems. Support for this hypothesis is consistent with earlier studies that reflected a tendency for undergraduate subjects (Davison & Friedman, 1981), counselor trainees (Glenn & Russell, 1986), and psychologists (Morin, 1977; Task Force on Psychotherapy with Lesbians and Gay Men, 1990) to perceive and to overemphasize sexual orientation as relevant to the etiology of clients' problems. One explanation for this finding might be the ease with which participants could recall similar instances with lesbian clients. It would not be surprising for a number of this study's participants to have had limited experience or contact with lesbian clients. Participants may have worked with (or known a trainee colleague who worked with) one lesbian client for whom sexual orientation was a primary problem. Participants may have drawn conclusions about the study's hypothetical clients based on their recall of that one client who seemed to have problems with her sexual orientation. A second explanation for this finding is that participants were considering sexual orientation as a possible problem, not the conclusive problem. This explanation seems plausible in light of the fact that the lesbian subject group ranked three or four other presenting problems higher than sexual orientation.

The hypothesis that counselor trainees would be more likely to assign a personality disorder diagnosis to lesbian clients was not supported by this research. In fact, a review of mean scores for each of the personality disorders according to group suggests that participants were unlikely to assign a personality disorder diagnosis at all. The vignettes were written to closely meet the DSM-IV criteria and it is likely that trainees operating with some working knowledge of the DSM-IV did not assign personality disorder diagnoses because information in the vignettes did not meet criteria for any of those diagnoses. In other words, given unambiguous diagnostic information, counselor trainees were not more likely to label lesbian clients as personality disordered compared to heterosexual females.

The data analysis did not support the hypothesis that a lesbian sexual orientation would result in clients being regarded as having a higher level of disturbance, a poorer prognosis for therapy, or requiring a longer duration of therapy. This lack of support may be due to an actual absence of bias; trainees may not have considered the issue of sexual orientation when determining the severity of clients' disturbance, the prognosis for therapy, and the estimated length of therapy. However, it is quite possible that diagnosis, not client sexual orientation, was the mediating factor in the assessment of overall psychopathology.

This study contradicted previous literature regarding assessment of severity of psychopathology. Earlier studies revealed that undergraduates viewed gays and lesbians as being more maladjusted than heterosexuals (Page & Yee, 1985), and practicing psychologists perceived heterosexual clients to be more psychologically healthy than gay clients (Garfinkle & Morin, 1978). The Task Force on Psychotherapy with Lesbians and Gay Men (1990) cited numerous instances in which clinicians expressed the belief that gay men and lesbians were more psychologically maladjusted than heterosexuals. However, most studies examining perceptions of psychological adjustment involved assessment of gay men rather than lesbians. Perceptions of gay men tended to be based on gender-role stereotypes and the extent to which gay men were believed to be "stereotypically feminine." A paucity of research exists that examines perceptions of the psychological adjustment of lesbians. Additionally, no studies were located that examined specific indicators of psychological adjustment such as ratings of the level of disturbance, prognosis for therapy, and duration of therapy. Finally, Shemberg and Doherty's (1999) recent study found that clinicians tend to take a conservative approach to assessing psychopathology. They suggested that clinicians perceive psychopathology to be rare and they require a substantial amount of evidence to assign labels of psychopathology to clients. It appears that this conclusion may hold true for clinicians-in-training as well.

While this study does suggest that counselor trainees made assumptions that sexual orientation could be problematic for clients, it does not tap into how those assumptions are used in actual practice with clients. Lesbians may actually struggle with issues related to sexual orientation and it is appropriate to explore this important aspect of their identity. A question that cannot conclusively be answered by this particular study is, "Were these participants entertaining a hypothesis about sexual orientation or had they drawn a firm conclusion?" In all likelihood, some participants in this study were probably certain that sexual orientation was a problem. This is a biased and inaccurate assumption that could interfere with the effectiveness of therapy. Unaware that there may be other issues that are more relevant, clinicians who focus exclusively on sexual orientation as the client's primary therapeutic issue may fail to accurately conceptualize and diagnose clients' actual concerns. This poses problems in that there are empirically validated treatments for a number of psychological disorders (Division 12, American Psychological Association, 1995). Implementation of these treatments depends upon accurate formulation and conceptualization of clients' problems. Clinicians who focus unnecessarily on addressing clients' sexual orientation may derail treatment rather than guide it. Clients may lose the opportunity to receive appropriate and effective treatment because clinicians are treating the wrong problem.

Limitations of This Study

This study goes further than most research related to lesbian issues in that it addresses the assessment and diagnostic decisions that trainees make about lesbian clients, rather than simply inquiring about their attitudes about a lesbian sexual orientation. While some researchers caution that the analogue nature of the research might limit its generalizability to actual practice, others suggest that this methodology can quickly establish whether raters know criteria and interpret case records in the same way (Grove et al., 1981), that counselors use similar hypotheses testing strategies with actual clients as with written case material (Strohmer & Newman, 1983), and that experts make the same judgments in hypothetical situations that they do in vivo (Dawes, 1986). In spite of differing perspectives on this issue, one must consider the possibility that participants' responses in this study may not be consistent with the formulation and assessment process with actual clients.

A second possible problem area in this study pertains to demand characteristics. It is possible that participants deduced the hypotheses of the study and modified their responses accordingly. For example, some participants may have avoided identifying sexual orientation as the client's problem in order to appear unbiased. Others may have thought that the desired response was to consider sexual orientation as a problem for lesbian clients and believed that failure to do so might cause them to appear unknowledgeable about sexual orientation issues.

A third limitation is that this research did not elicit information about possible emotional and motivational factors that may have influenced how trainees attended to client sexual orientation. For example, in order to disguise the hypotheses of the study, the Diagnostic and Assessment Inventory did not ask questions to assess participants' knowledge about gay and lesbian issues or their attitudes about a gay or lesbian sexual orientation.

Finally, the instrument itself must be considered as a possible limitation. Because no valid instruments appropriate to test the hypotheses of this study were found, the *Assessment and Diagnostic Inventory* was developed. Further work needs to be done to establish validity and reliability of this instrument.

Future Research

This study lays the foundation for additional research pertaining to assessment and diagnosis of lesbians. Several studies could be conducted using this methodology with variations in demographics of hypothetical clients or research participants. For example, the literature suggests that gay men may be rated less favorably than lesbians. The current study did not reveal serious diagnostic problems or excessive assessment of psychopathology that could be attributed to clients' lesbian sexual orientation. However, using vignettes with four types of hypothetical clients (gay men, heterosexual men, lesbians, and heterosexual women) may reveal differences based on gender and sexual orientation.

Participant demographics could be modified to determine whether experienced clinicians assess and diagnose lesbian clients differently than heterosexual clients, or whether there are differences between trainees' and practicing clinicians' assessments of lesbian clients. The influence of participant gender was not adequately addressed in this study because of the low number of male subjects. It would be useful to target responses from male trainees in order to achieve a large enough sample of men to address the role of gender in assessment and diagnosis of lesbian clients.

Additional research could be conducted to reduce the influence of demand characteristics. For example, the diagnostic vignettes used in the current study were fairly transparent and were designed to match a specific diagnostic category. A study utilizing more ambiguous diagnostic vignettes that are not as easy to diagnose may be more sensitive to bias and distortion. Follow-up questionnaires could be utilized to ascertain the extent to which participants were aware that sexual orientation was the variable of interest. Different methodologies, such as the use of audiotaped or videotaped (rather than written) vignettes, would allow participants to hear or observe a client and therapist's interaction. This methodology would enable participants to base decisions about clients on more information than can be provided in a brief written description.

REFERENCES

Arkes, Hal R. (1981). Impediments to accurate clinical judgment and possible ways to minimize their impact. *Journal of Consulting and Clinical Psychology, 49,* 323-330.

Barrett, Kathleen A. & McWhirter, Benedict T. (2002). Counselor trainees' perceptions of clients based on client sexual orientation. *Counselor Education and Supervision, 41,* 219-233.

Biaggio, Maryka, Roades, Laurie A., Staffelbach, Darlene, Cardinali, John, & Duffy, Rosemary. (2000). Clinical evaluations: Impact of sexual orientation, gender, and gender role. *Journal of Applied Social Psychology, 30,* 1657-1669.

Committee on Lesbian and Gay Concerns. (1993). *Graduate Faculty in Psychology Interested in Lesbian and Gay Issues.* Washington, D.C.: American Psychological Association.

Conger, John. (1975). Proceedings of the American Psychological Association, for the year 1974: Minutes of the annual meeting of Council of Representatives. *American Psychologist, 30,* 620-651.

Davison, Gerald C. & Friedman, Steven. (1981). Sexual orientation stereotypy in the distortion of clinical judgment. *Journal of Homosexuality, 6,* 37-44.

Dawes, Robyn M. (1986). Representative thinking in clinical judgment. *Clinical Psychology Review, 6,* 425-441.

Division 12, American Psychological Association (1995). Training and dissemination of empirically-validated psychological treatments: Report and recommendations. *Clinical Psychologist, 48,* 3-23.

Dumont, Florent & Lecomte, Conrad. (1987). Inferential processes in clinical work: Inquiry into logical errors that affect diagnostic judgments. *Professional Psychology: Research and Practice, 18,* 433-438.

Eldridge, Natalie S. & Barnett, David C. (1991). Counseling gay and lesbian students. *In beyond tolerance: Gays, lesbians, and bisexuals on campus.* Evans, N. J. & Wall, V. A., Eds.

Faust, David. (1986). Research on human judgment and its application to clinical practice. *Professional Psychology: Research and Practice, 17,* 420-430.

Friedlander, Myrna L. & Phillips, Susan D. (1984). Preventing anchoring errors in clinical judgment. *Journal of Consulting and Clinical Psychology, 52,* 366-371.

Garb, Howard N. (1997). Race bias, social class bias, and gender bias in clinical judgment. *Clinical Psychology: Science and Practice, 4,* 99-120.

Garfinkle, Ellen M. & Morin, Stephen F. (1978). Psychologists' attitudes toward homosexual psychotherapy clients. *Journal of Social Issues, 34,* 101-112.

Garnets, Linda, Hancock, Kristin A., Cochran, Susan D., Goodchilds, Jacqueline, & Peplau, Letitia A. (1991). Issues in psychotherapy with lesbians and gay men: A survey of psychologists. *American Psychologist, 46,* 964-972.

Glenn, Audrey A. & Russell, Richard K. (1986). Heterosexual bias among counselor trainees. *Counselor Education and Supervision, 26,* 222-229.

Gray-Little, Bernadette. (1995). The assessment of psychopathology in racial and ethnic minorities. In J. Butcher (Ed), *Clinical personality assessment: Practical approaches* (pp. 140-157).

Grove, William M. & Keller, Martin B. (1981). Reliability studies of psychiatric diagnosis. *Archives of General Psychiatry, 38*, 408-413.

Jordan, Karen M. & Deluty, Robert H. (1995). Clinical interventions by psychologists with lesbians and gay men. *Journal of Clinical Psychology, 51*, 448-456.

Lopez, Steven R. (1989). Patient variable biases in clinical judgment: Conceptual overview and methodological considerations. *Psychological Bulletin, 106*, 184-203.

Lopez, Steven & Hernandez, Priscilla. (1986). How culture is considered in evaluations of psychopathology. *The Journal of Nervous and Mental Disease, 176*, 598-606.

Morin, Stephen F. (1977). Heterosexual bias in psychological research on lesbianism and male homosexuality. *American Psychologist, 32*, 629-637.

Nisbett, Richard & Ross, Lee. (1980). *Human inference: Strategies and shortcomings of social judgment*. Englewood Cliffs, NJ: Prentice-Hall, Inc.

Page, Steward & Yee, Mary. (1986). Conception of male and female homosexual stereotypes among university undergraduates. *Journal of Homosexuality, 12*, 109-117.

Pain, Michelle D. & Sharpley, Christopher F. (1989). Varying the order in which positive and negative information is presented: Effects on counselors' judgments of clients' mental health. *Journal of Counseling Psychology, 36*, 3-7.

Pain, Michelle D. & Sharpley, Christopher F. (1988). Case type, anchoring errors and counselor education. *Counselor Education and Supervision, 28*, 53-58.

Pavkov, Thomas W., Lewis, Dan A., Lyons, John S. (1989). Psychiatric diagnoses and racial bias: An empirical investigation. *Professional Psychology: Research & Practice, 20*, 364-368.

Rahimi, Maryam, Rosenthal, David A., & Chan, Fong. (2003). Effects of client race on clinical judgment of African-American undergraduate students in rehabilitation. *Rehabilitation Counseling Bulletin, 46(3)*, 157-163.

Rudolph, James. (1988). Counselors' attitudes toward homosexuality: A selective review of the literature. *Journal of Counseling and Development, 67*, 165-168.

Shemberg, Kenneth M. & Doherty, Michael E. (1999). Is diagnostic judgment influenced by bias to see pathology? *Journal of Clinical Psychology, 55*, 513-518.

Spengler, Paul M. & Strohmer, Douglas C. (1994). Clinical judgmental biases: The moderating roles of counselor cognitive complexity and counselor client preferences. *Journal of Counseling Psychology, 41*, 8-17.

Strohmer, Douglas C. & Newman, Lisa J. (1983). Counselor hypothesis-testing strategies. *Journal of Counseling Psychology, 30*, 557-565.

Strohmer, Douglas C., Shivy, Victoria A., & Chiodo, Anthony L. (1990). Information processing strategies in counselor hypothesis testing: The role of selective memory and expectancy. *Journal of Counseling Psychology, 37*, 465-472.

Task Force on Psychotherapy with Lesbians and Gay Men. (1990). *Bias in psychotherapy with lesbians and gay men (Final Report)*. Washington, DC: American Psychological Association.

Wisch, Andrew F. & Mahalik, James R. (1999). Male therapists' clinical bias: Influence of client gender roles and therapist gender role conflict. *Journal of Counseling Psychology, 46*, 51-60.

Depressive Distress and Prevalence of Common Problems Among Homosexually Active African American Women in the United States

Vickie M. Mays, PhD, MSPH
Susan D. Cochran, PhD, MS
Michele R. Roeder, BA

SUMMARY. We report findings from a national survey of 603 homosexually experienced African American women who self-identified as lesbian, gay, or bisexual. Levels of psychological distress greatly exceeded population norms for African American women. The most frequent problems participants reported were romantic relationship and financial difficulties. Problems with using drugs or alcohol to self-medicate psychological distress were the most chronic stressors. Although

Vickie M. Mays is affiliated with the Department of Psychology, University of California, Los Angeles. Susan D. Cochran is affiliated with the Epidemiology School of Public Health, University of California, Los Angeles. Michele R. Roeder is affiliated with the Department of Psychology, University of California, Los Angeles.

Address correspondence to Vickie M. Mays, University of California, Los Angeles, 1285 Franz Hall, Box 951563, Los Angeles, CA (E-mail: mays@ucla.edu).

This work was supported by grants from the National Institute of Mental Health, the National Institute on Allergy and Infectious Diseases, and the National Institute of Drug Abuse (MH42584, MH44345, AI38216, DA15539).

[Haworth co-indexing entry note]: "Depressive Distress and Prevalence of Common Problems Among Homosexually Active African American Women in the United States." Mays, Vickie M., Susan D. Cochran, and Michele R. Roeder. Co-published simultaneously in *Journal of Psychology & Human Sexuality* (The Haworth Press, Inc.) Vol. 15, No. 2/3, 2003, pp. 27-46; and: *Lesbian and Bisexual Women's Mental Health* (ed: Robin M. Mathy, and Shelly K. Kerr) The Haworth Press, Inc., 2003, pp. 27-46. Single or multiple copies of this article are available for a fee from The Haworth Document Delivery Service [1-800-HAWORTH, 9:00 a.m. - 5:00 p.m. (EST). E-mail address: docdelivery@haworthpress.com].

31% of women indicated they received emotional support from a counselor or other professional in the prior month, the least likely to receive support were those reporting chronic financial, housing, anger, or substance use problems. These findings underscore the vulnerability of African American women, who navigate the triple stigma of having a minority ethnicity, sexual orientation, and gender. *[Article copies available for a fee from The Haworth Document Delivery Service: 1-800-HAWORTH. E-mail address: <docdelivery@haworthpress.com> Website: <http://www.HaworthPress.com> © 2003 by The Haworth Press, Inc. All rights reserved.]*

KEYWORDS. Lesbians, African-American, depressive distress, life stressors

Recent studies suggest that homosexually active women experience greater lifetime prevalence rates of common mental health disorders, such as alcohol dependence, depression, and drug abuse, attempted suicide, and psychiatric help-seeking than those reported by exclusively heterosexually active women (Matthews, Hughes, Johnson, Razzano, & Cassidy, 2002; Cochran, Keenan, Schober, & Mays, 2000; Cochran & Mays, 2000; Bux, 1996; Cochran, Bybee, Gage, & Mays, 1996; Gillow & Davis, 1987; Saghir, Robins, Walbran, & Gentry, 1970). Mental health concerns among lesbians who are racial/ethnic minorities have been greatly understudied despite research findings indicating that these women may experience a number of stressors commonly associated with higher burden of mental disorders, even more so than White lesbians (Greene, 1994, 2000,2000; Matthews & Hughes, 2001; Mays, Cochran & Rhue, 1994; Cochran & Mays, 1994). For example, a previous study observed that homosexually active African American women may be especially vulnerable to depressive disorders (Cochran & Mays, 1994). This group was found to evidence symptoms more likely to fall into a clinically diagnosable category of depression than gay men who had been diagnosed with AIDS or HIV-related illnesses.

Identifying the specific problems that may be associated with depressive distress among homosexually active African American women might improve both treatment and prevention programs targeting depressive distress (Cochran & Mays, 1994; Matthews & Hughes, 2001). One early study by Bell and Weinberg (1978) found that African American lesbians, relative to white lesbians, more often perceived themselves to be (a) lonely, (b) in poorer health, (c) evidencing a greater number of somatic symptoms, (d) manifesting more tension, and (e) they reported less job satisfaction. Recently, Matthews and Hughes (2001) examined some of the specific problems faced by homosexually active African American women in a study that measured African American women's rates of mental health service use. They found that the most common reasons for seeking help among lesbian and heterosexual African American women were similar (i.e., feeling sad or depressed). Most studies, however, have more generally examined problems affecting either lesbians or African American women. Overall, these studies have found that the prevalence and consequences of alcohol abuse is higher among African American than among White women (Mays, Beckman, Oranchak, & Harper, 1994; Clark & Midanik, 1982; Herd, 1985; Caetano, 1984), that lesbian couples earn less than heterosexual couples (Badgett, 1998), and that lesbians in general often feel isolated (Mays et al., 1994; Greene, 1996) and have difficulty finding positive role models of lesbian relationships (Matthews & Hughes, 2001).

The present study examines the self-reported prevalence of common stressors, depressive distress, and help-seeking among a national sample of 603 homosexually active African American women. Our interest is in understanding the types of stressors that highly stressed and help-seeking African American lesbians and bisexual women report. This information might prove useful in tailoring at both individual and social levels interventions that may reduce the elevated levels of depressive distress thought to be commonly experienced by these women.

METHOD

Procedures

A national sample of 603 homosexually active African American women was recruited from across the United States to complete anonymous questionnaires (Cochran & Mays, 1994; Mays & Cochran, 1988a; Mays & Jackson, 1991; Peplau, Cochran & Mays, 1997). In order to ensure a heterogeneous sample, a variety of recruitment methods were employed. Questionnaires were mailed to the members of national Black gay and lesbian political, social, and health care organizations, such at the National Coalition of Black Lesbians and Gays. Each nondescript manila envelope contained a questionnaire as well as a stamped, preaddressed envelope with which to return the questionnaire. A post-card was also included, which could be returned separately if the respondent wished to request additional questionnaires for friends or flyers to be distributed or posted in the meeting places of various gay organizations and social groups. In addition, flyers were mailed to lesbian organizations and business establishments describing the study. We also used announcements in the lesbian press to publicize the survey.

Participants responded voluntarily to the self-administered, anonymous questionnaires. A cover letter informed subjects about the purpose of the study and the protection of their privacy. We conducted several focus groups and pretests of preliminary instruments in locations throughout the United States, including both rural and urban areas, to assist us in the modification of our previous instruments. Our goals in the focus groups and pretests were to: (a) determine areas of specific concerns in the lives of African American lesbians; (b) develop language that would be reflective of the culture of African American lesbians regardless of regional, education, and class differences (see Mays et al., 1992, for discussion); (c) determine the best ordering of items, tolerable length of questionnaire, and format of the instrument; and (d) learn more about methodological parameters for reaching "hidden" African American lesbians who, despite being homosexually active, did not identify as such and were not likely to be reached through organized lesbian networks.

Study Participants

Questionnaires were completed by 603 African-American women who reported having had homosexual sex and whose sexual orientation was not heterosexual. Eighty-five percent considered themselves lesbian or gay (see Table 1). Women ranged in age from 18 to 60 years with a median age of 32 years. On average, women had completed approximately 15 years of schooling (X = 15.4, S.D. = 2.6). The great majority of participants reported being employed more than 20 hours per week. The median annual income was $17,500. Two thirds of participants reported being in a current lesbian relationship.

Questionnaire

The self-administered questionnaire extensively asked women about their life experiences. Sections relevant to the present study included:

Frequency of common problems. Using the National Survey of Black Americans (Jackson, 1991; Jackson & Gerald, 1999) as a guide in de-

TABLE 1. Demographic Characteristics of the African American Lesbians and Bisexual Women

Demographic Characteristic	N	Percent
Age		
18-24 years	90	15.0%
25-34 years	283	47.2%
35-44 years	171	28.5%
45+ years	56	9.3%
Education		
High school or less	70	11.8%
Some college	247	41.5%
Bachelor's	127	21.3%
Graduate school	151	25.4%
Employment status		
Employed more than 20 hours/week	489	81.5%
Employed less than 20 hours/week	51	8.5%
Not employed	60	10.0%
Annual income		
< $ 5,000	52	8.8%
$ 5,000-$10,999	102	17.7%
$11,000-$19,999	202	34.1%
$20,000-$39,999	200	33.8%
> $40,000	33	5.6%
Sexual orientation		
Lesbian/gay	504	85.1%
Bisexual	66	11.1%
Other (but not heterosexual)	22	3.7%
Relationship status		
Single	205	34.0%
In current lesbian relationship	398	66.0%
Geographic location		
Northwest/West Coast/Southwest	293	49.2%
Northeast/East Coast	131	21.9%
Midwest	85	14.4%
Southeast/South	87	14.4%

Note. N = 603, except for missing data.

veloping the questionnaire, we asked respondents to indicate the frequency with which they experienced problems in each of nine areas of their lives. Three were related to economic factors including job, financial, and housing problems. Two were relationship-based including problems with one's love life or family. Four were personal including health problems, using drugs or alcohol as a means of coping, suicidal thoughts, and anger (thoughts of doing harm to someone else). Frequency was measured using 5-point items anchored by "never," "rarely," "sometimes," "often," and "most of the time." Problems responded to as occurring "often" or "most of the time" were considered to be frequent problems of the past year. After completing this measure, women were asked to indicate which of the problems was their most distressing. Eighty-three percent of women ($n = 503$) surveyed listed one of the nine problems, 9% ($n = 54$) listed two, 3% ($n = 15$) listed 3, and 5% ($n = 31$) did not answer the question. Next, women were asked how long they had been troubled by their most distressing problem.

Psychological help. The questionnaire did not ask women specifically whether or not they were currently in psychotherapy. However, women were asked about several possible sources of emotional support in the month prior to completing the questionnaire, including the receipt of emotional support from a "counselor, social worker or other professional." Using this variable as a proxy for current therapy utilization, we considered those women who indicated receiving emotional support from this target to have a therapist. Similarly, we assumed that women who did not indicate support from this target were not utilizing psychotherapy services. Necessarily, this proxy represents a somewhat imprecise assessment of therapy utilization because some women may be referring to service providers other than therapists. Women were also asked how frequently in the past year they had had thoughts about seeking professional help for their problems. The 5-item measure was anchored with "never," "rarely," "sometimes," "often," and "most of the time." Women who reported thinking about seeking help "often" or "most of the time" were considered as having frequent thoughts of seeking help.

Depressive distress. Respondents completed the Center for Epidemiologic Studies-Depression Scale (Radloff, 1977). This 20-item inventory of common symptoms indicative of depression was developed for use with non-psychiatric samples. Scores range from 0 to 60, with scores > 15 used to indicate probable depression.

Demographic characteristics. The questionnaire also assessed age, educational achievement, employment, annual income, current relationship status, and self-rated sexual orientation.

Data Analysis

Data were analyzed by chi-square analyses and logistic regression. We examined correlates of reported problems using stepwise logistic regression procedures (Hosmer & Lemeshow, 1989). Variables we considered for entry in these equations included respondents' age, education, relationship status, sexual orientation, employment status, income, and presence of depressive distress. To conduct the analyses, we categorized respondents into one of four age categories (under age 25, between age 25 and 34, between age 35 and 44, and age 45 and older). Similarly, we recorded educational achievement as high school or less, some college, bachelor's degree, and evidence of graduate education. Sexual orientation was coded into two categories, gay or lesbian versus bisexual or other. Employment status was divided into three categories: employed 20 hours per week or more, employed 20 hours per week or less, and not employed. The latter category included 36 unemployed women, 10 who were disabled or retired, 11 who survived by "side hustle," and 3 who were being supported by their partner. Income was divided into five categories (less than $5,000 per year, $5,000 to $10,999, $11,000 to $19,999, $20,000 to $39,999, and $40,000 or more per year). Using the standard CES-D cutoff score of 16 and above, we categorized women as either not depressed or depressed. Variables were entered on a forward stepwise manner with evaluation of model improvement via an improvement of fit chi-square test. Fit of the final equations was evaluated by Hosmer-Lemeshow goodness-of-fit tests, with all equations reported achieving model fit. We report prevalence odds ratios and their 95% confidence intervals. Intervals that do not include 1.00 indicate a statistically significant association between the correlate and the dependent variable at the .05 level. Odds ratios greater than 1.00 indicate a positive association; those less than 1.00 indicate a negative association. Logistic regression was also used to examine associations between presence of a counselor and different problems, after adjusting for levels of depressive distress. Again, we report adjusted prevalence odds ratios and their 95% confidence intervals. Intervals that do not encompass 1.00 indicate a statistically significant association.

RESULTS

Depression, Chronicity of Distressing Problems, and Desires for Help

As anticipated, the African American women participating in this survey indicated high levels of depressive distress. In prior population-based studies, approximately 26% of African American women scored above 15 on the CES-D (Vernon, Roberts, & Lee, 1982;

Comstock & Helsing, 1976; Cochran & Mays, 1994). However, in the current sample 38% of the women scored above the cut-point for probable depression (> 15) (see Table 2).

Approximately half of the sample reported that their most distressing problem in the past year was one of a chronic nature, lasting more than six months. Depressed women were significantly more likely than non-depressed women to report that their most distressing problem in the past year had lasted more than six months (59% vs. 46%, X^2 (1) = 7.40, $p < .01$).

Thirty-one percent of women reported receiving emotional support from a counselor or other professional in the past month. Also, 22% of women indicated frequent thoughts of seeking professional help in the past year. As might be expected, women who reported frequent thoughts of seeking help in the past year were significantly more likely than women who had not to report recent emotional support from a therapist (60% vs. 22%, X^2 (1) = 68.31, $p < .001$). Also, women who reported frequent thoughts of seeking help were more likely to be depressed than those who did not (62% vs. 32%, X^2 (1) = 37.76, $p < .001$).

TABLE 2. Depressive Distress, Chronicity of Most Upsetting Problem, and Presence of a Therapy Relationship Among African-American Lesbians and Bisexual Women

Characteristic	N	Percent
Duration of most upsetting problem in past year		
Less than one month	79	16.7%
One to 6 months	154	32.6%
Seven to 12 months	103	21.8%
One year or more	136	28.8%
CES-D Depression Score		
Nondepressed (score < 16)	372	61.5%
Probable depression (score 16 or above)	233	38.5%
Reports emotional support from a therapist		
No	417	69.3%
Yes	186	30.8%
Thoughts of getting help in past year		
Never/infrequent	464	78.4%
Often or most of the time	128	21.6%

Note. N = 603, except for missing data.

Frequency of Problems

As can be seen in Table 3, the two most prevalent problems that women reported were problems with their love life and financial problems. More than a third of the sample reported frequent problems within these areas. These two problems also represented the most distressing problems in the past year. Less commonly, women were bothered by job and family problems.

Though 18% of women reported using drugs or alcohol frequently to make themselves feel better, only 7.2% of women reported that drug or alcohol use was their most distressing problem. However, for nearly two-thirds of those who did so, this problem was chronic, defined as lasting more than 6 months. Also, a small percentage of women reported frequent problems with anger and suicidal thoughts. Approximately 5% reported frequent thoughts of doing harm to someone else, with 4% of women reporting that this was their most distressing problem. Problems with anger appeared to trouble women for shorter peri-

TABLE 3. Self-Reported Problems Experienced by African-American Lesbian and Bisexual Women in the Past Year

Problem area	Reports problem occurs often[1]		Reports problem as most upsetting[2]		Most upsetting problem has lasted more than 6 months
	Percent	(95% CI)	Percent	(95% CI)	Percent
Problems with love life	39.5%	(35.6%-43.5%)	32.6%	(28.9%-36.6%)	48.0%
Financial problems	35.4%	(31.6%-39.3%)	30.0%	(26.3%-33.9%)	51.1%
Job problems	22.2%	(19.0%-25.6%)	10.4%	(8.0%-13.0%)	58.3%
Problems with family members	17.8%	(14.9%-21.0%)	12.8%	(10.2%-15.7%)	56.9%
Used drugs or alcohol to make self feel better	18.1%	(15.2%-21.3%)	7.2%	(5.3%-9.5%)	63.3%
Health problems	13.4%	(10.9%-16.3%)	7.2%	(5.3%-9.5%)	46.9%
Housing problems	10.5%	(8.2%-13.2%)	4.0%	(2.6%-5.9%)	61.9%
Thoughts of doing harm to someone else	5.5%	(3.9%-7.5%)	4.0%	(2.6%-5.9%)	27.8%
Thoughts of suicide	4.3%	(2.9%-6.2%)	4.6%	(3.1%-6.5%)	42.9%

Note. N = 603, except for missing data. S.D. = standard deviations.
[1]Percent reporting problem occurring "often" or "most of the time."
[2]Sums to greater than 100% because individuals sometimes listed more than one problem.

ods of time than other difficulties. Only 28% reported that thoughts of doing harm to someone else had lasted over 6 months. More than 4% of women reported frequent suicidal thoughts, and 4.6% indicated that suicidal thoughts were their most distressing problem.

Correlates of Frequent Problems

Overall, depressive distress was positively associated with reports of frequent problems regardless of their nature (see Table 4). Reporting frequent problems with one's love life was also associated with being single. In contrast, reporting problems with family members was positively associated with lower income, being in a current relationship, and higher levels of depressive distress.

As might be expected, predictors of reporting financial problems included lower income, being employed part-time, and greater levels of depressive distress. Frequent job difficulties were associated with being employed part-time or not at all, lower income, and greater depressive distress. Also, frequent housing related problems were associated with lower income and depressive distress. Frequent health problems in the last year were associated with both depressive distress and being in a current relationship. Frequent use of drugs or alcohol as a coping response was related to being unemployed and reporting greater levels of depressive distress. Frequent thoughts of doing harm to someone else were related both to depressive distress and younger age. Finally, frequent suicidal thoughts were positively related to depressive distress.

Presence of Therapist Among Those Reporting Frequent Problems

As can be seen in Table 5, women who reported problems with their love life, job, health, and suicidal thoughts were more likely to indicate that they had emotional support from a counselor or professional in the past month, even after controlling for differences in depressive distress. In addition, findings suggest that reporting problems with one's family members might be associated with the presence of a counselor or therapist. However, the degree of uncertainty in estimating the prevalence odds ratio is such that this conclusion may be premature.

DISCUSSION

Results of the present study provide some insight into common problems affecting homosexually active African American women and the

TABLE 4. Demographic Correlates of Frequent Problems of African American Lesbian and Bisexual Women: Results of Stepwise Logistic Regression Analyses[1]

Problem area correlates	Odds Ratio	95% CI	Improvement of Fit X^2 Probability
Problems with love life			
Depression, greater	2.22	(1.56-3.17)	.001
Relationship status, coupled	.45	(.32-.66)	.001
Financial problems			
Income, higher	.58	(.48-.70)	.001
Depression, greater	1.65	(1.14-2.40)	.005
Employment status[2]			.03
Employed parttime	2.35	(1.20-4.64)	
Not employed	1.37	(.76-2.50)	
Job Problems			
Employment status[2]			.001
Employed parttime	2.14	(1.06-4.32)	
Not employed	4.37	(2.34-8.14)	
Depression, greater	2.59	(1.69-3.97)	.001
Income, higher	.78	(.63-.97)	.02
Problems with family members			
Depression, greater	2.08	(1.33-3.25)	.001
Relationship status, coupled	1.81	(1.09-3.00)	.02
Income, higher	.80	(.65-.99)	.04
Using drugs or alcohol			
Depression, greater	1.90	(1.23-2.95)	.002
Employment status[2]			.04
Employed parttime	.69	(.28-1.70)	
Not employed	2.14	(1.15-3.98)	
Health problems			
Depression, greater	3.02	(1.81-5.02)	.001
Relationship status, coupled	1.92	(1.07-3.44)	.02
Housing problems			
Income, higher	.60	(.47-.78)	.001
Depression, greater	1.88	(1.09-3.24)	.02
Thoughts of doing harm			
Age, older	.46	(.28-.77)	.001
Depression, greater	2.56	(1.20-5.46)	.006
Employment status[2]			.08
Employed parttime	1.79	(.56-5.69)	
Not employed	2.94	(1.18-7.28)	
Suicidal thoughts			
Depression, greater	3.94	(4.36-81.5)	.001

[1]Variables considered for entry included age, education, relationship status, sexual orientation, employment status, income, and depression.
[2]Referent is employed > 20 hours per week.

TABLE 5. Prevalence of Frequent Problems[1] and Reports of Emotional Support from a Counselor or Other Professional: Results of Logistic Regression Analyses Predicting Counselor Presence

Problem areas	Number reporting problem	Counselor present	Adjusted[2] Odds Ratio	95% CI	Improvement of Fit[2]
Problems with love life	235	39.1%	1.70	(1.18-2.44)	.004
Financial problems	215	34.7%	1.25	(.86-1.79)	ns
Job problems	132	43.2%	1.94	(.95-2.32)	.002
Problems with family members	107	40.2%	1.49	(.95-2.32)	.004
Used drugs or alcohol to make self feel better	109	35.0%	1.23	(.78-1.92)	ns
Health problems	81	45.7%	1.93	(1.19-3.16)	.009
Housing problems	63	30.1%	1.32	(.76-2.30)	ns
Thoughts of doing harm to someone else	33	42.4%	1.59	(.77-3.27)	ns
Thoughts of suicide	26	57.7%	2.65	(1.15-6.11)	.02

Note. N = 603. CI = Confidence Interval. Probability indicated for Improvement of Fit Chi-Square. ns = not significant.
[1]Problems occurring in the past year "often" or "most of the time."
[2]Odds ratio adjusted for depressive distress.

relationship of these problems to depressive distress. Approximately half of the sample reported that their most distressing problem in the past year was chronic, lasting more than six months, with the two most prevalent and upsetting problems involving difficulties with love relationships and finance (Peplau, Cochran & Mays, 1997; Cochran & Mays, 1994). Problems with job, family, and alcohol or drugs were less commonly reported, as were problems with health, housing, anger, and suicidal intent. One encouraging finding is that difficulties with drugs and alcohol seem to be less serious than reported previously among the general lesbian population (Cochran, 2001; Cochran, Keenan, Schober, & Mays, 2000; Diamant, Wold, Spritzer, & Gelberg, 2000; Roberts & Sorenson, 1999; Lewis, Saghir, & Robins, 1982). However, this result was based on self-reports, and as such may not be a wholly accurate reflection of the severity of alcoholism within the sample. Use of drugs and alcohol appeared to trouble women for longer periods of time than other problems; however, only slightly more than 7 percent of those who reported using drugs and alcohol to feel better indicated that this problem was their most upsetting.

Homosexually active African American women, as a whole, experience elevated levels of depressive distress when compared to African American women in general (Cochran & Mays, 1994). In prior population-based studies (Vernon et al., 1982; Comstock & Helsing, 1976), approximately 26% of African-American women scored above 15 on the CES-D, but in the current study, 38% of the women scored above the cut-point for probable depression. The triple stigmatization of being a racial/ethnic minority, being a female, and being lesbian or bisexual may be important risk factors that help to explain the high level of depressive distress observed in our sample (Langer & Michael, 1963; Cochran & Mays, 1994; Mays et al., 1994). This concept is what Greene (1994) calls the "Triple Jeopardy" in which the individual stressors associated with race, gender, and sexual orientation discrimination compound and result in detrimental effects on mental health. African American lesbians must not only deal with the stress of managing the dominant culture's racism, homophobia, and sexism but must also deal with racism within the gay communities (Matthews et al., 2002; Greene, 1994; Mays et al., 1994). Effective targeting of mental health interventions may be enhanced by understanding the sources of higher distress levels (Greene, 1996). At the same time, while discrimination and other social factors may be important contributors to these women's distress levels (Cochran, 2001), presenting complaints in therapy are often focused around the mundane details of common life difficulties.

In the current study, women who had frequent problems in the past year with their job, health, love life, and suicidal thoughts were most likely to report the presence of a counselor or therapist. Those who were depressed were also more likely to think about seeking help than those who were not depressed. In contrast, women reporting problems that may be more difficult to address in therapy, such as difficulties with finances, housing, feelings of anger, and use of drugs or alcohol were among those least likely to report support from a counselor in the past month. Further, only 38% of respondents who scored above the cut-point for probable depression frequently thought of getting help in the past year. This suggests that there is unmet need for professional mental health services among African American lesbians and bisexual women.

There are several possible reasons for this. First, African Americans in general are more likely to use informal sources of care as opposed to formal help-seeking of psychotherapy (Matthews & Hughes, 2001; Cooper-Patrick, Gallo, Powe, Steinwachs, Eaton, & Ford, 1999; Snowden, 1999; Neighbors, 1988; Neighbors & Jackson, 1984). Ethnic communities and extended families often serve as the primary reference groups providing support for their members at times of distress (Mays, Howard-Caldwell, & Jackson, 1996; Green, 1998; Boyd-Franklin, 1989). In a study that examined the usage of African American ministers as a source of help for serious emotional problems among African Americans, Neighbors and colleagues (1998) found that regardless of the type or severity of the emotional problem, those who sought help from clergy first were less likely to seek help from other professionals.

Second, a number of studies suggest that African Americans in general are significantly less likely than other groups to seek and to receive adequate care (Smedley, Stith, & Nelson, 2002; Mays, Cochran, & Sullivan, 2000; Alegria, Canino, Rios, Vera, Calderon, Rusch & Ortega, 2002; Matthews & Hughes, 2001; Mays, Yancey, Cochran, Weber, & Fielding, 2002; Mays, Coleman, & Jackson, 1996; Snowden, 2003,1999; Sue, Fujino, Hu, Takeuchi, & Zane, 1991). Partly this is due to disparities in access to, utilization of, and satisfaction with mental health services (Snowden, 2003; Kohn & Hudson, 2002; Mays et al., 1996). For example, Sussman and colleagues (1987) found that some African Americans do not seek help for depression until it has reached a severe stage. Likewise, a study by Wang and colleagues (2002) that looked at the quality of treatment for serious mental illnesses in the United States found that being African American was a predictor of not even receiving "minimally adequate" treatment. In both national and smaller clinical studies, African Americans were less likely to receive appropriate mental health services for the treatment of anxiety or depression (Young, Klap, Sherbourne, & Wells, 2001; Wang, Berglund, & Kessler, 2000;). These findings are supported by research that suggest that there is a greater likelihood that African Americans will be misdiagnosed with schizophrenia rather than an affective disorder (Bell & Mehta, 1980; Mukherjee, Shukla, Woodle, Rosen, & Olarte, 1983; Neighbors, Trierweiler, Munday, Thompson, Jackson, Binion, & Gomez, 1999; Trierweiler, Neighbors, Munday, Thompson, Binion, & Gomez, 2000) and that when treated pharmacologically, African Americans will receive higher doses of antipsychotic medications (Lawson, 1986; Snowden, 2003; Strickland et al., 1995,1993,1991).

Third, it has been suggested that higher rates of unemployment (USDHHS, 2001; Darity, 2003) and lower likelihood of insurance coverage as compared to Whites (Burns, 2001; USDHHS, 2001; Brown, Ojeda, Wyn, & Levan, 2000) may result in reduced available treatment alternatives (Mays et al., 2000; Snowden, 2003; Amaro, Beckman, & Mays, 1987). Also, African Americans are over represented in emergency room care and tend to delay seeking regular mental health services (Snowden, 1999; USDHHS, 2001). For example, Brown and Tooley (1989) found that African Americans are less likely to seek treatment for problem drinking than any other ethnic or racial group.

Fourth, it may be that our measurement of help-seeking was too imprecise. The proxy we used to assess therapy utilization did not ask women specifically whether they were currently in psychotherapy; instead, we assumed that those who did not indicate receipt of emotional support from a "counselor, social worker or other professional" were not using psychotherapy services. Thus we may have underestimated help-seeking behaviors.

Two other limitations of the present study also need to be highlighted. First, because our sample is defined as a hidden population, random sampling was impractical. However, because national, diverse social networks within the African American homosexually active population were used to recruit subjects, the generalizability of our findings may not have been too greatly affected. Second, because participation involved self-administered questionnaires, the less educated segment of the African American homosexually active population may have been under-selected into our study.

Despite these study limitations, the present findings demonstrate quite clearly that levels of depressive distress are high among homosexually active African American women in the United States. Our findings underscore the vulnerability of an understudied population that navigates stressors associated with the triple stigmas of racial, sexual orientation and gender minority statuses. Highly distressing problems tend to be chronic, with finances and relationships being the greatest areas of concern among African American lesbians. At the same time, women with problems such as feelings of anger and drug and alcohol use appear less likely to be receiving needed services. Further research is needed to identify methods to address the unmet mental health needs of African American lesbian and bisexual women as part of the effort to reduce or eliminate health disparities in the African American population.

REFERENCES

Alegria, M., Canino, G., Rios, R., Vera, M., Calderon, J., Rusch, D., & Ortega, A.N. (2002). Inequalities in Use of Speciality Mental Health Services Among Latinos, African Americans, and Non-White Latinos. *Psychiatric Services, 53*(12), 1547-1555.

Amaro, H., Beckman, L.J. & Mays, V.M. (1987). A comparison of Black and white women entering alcoholism treatment. *Journal of the Studies of Alcohol, 48*(3), 220-228.

Aneshensel, C.S., & Fredicks, R.R. (1982). Stress, support, and depression: A longitudinal causal model. *Journal of Community Psychology, 10*, 363-376.

Badgett, M.V. Lee. (1998). Income inflation: The myths of affluence among gay, lesbian, and bisexual Americans. *The National Gay and Lesbian Task Force Policy Institute*, 5-6.

Bell, A.P., & Weinberg, M.S. (1978). The Institute For Sexual Research. *Homosexualities: A Study of Human Diversity*, Simon and Schuster.

Bell, C.C., & Mehta, H. (1980). The misdiagnosis of black patients with manic depressive illness. *Journal of the National Medical Association, 73*(2), 141-145.

Berndt, E.R., Finkelstein, S.N., Greenberg, P.E., Howland, R.H., Keith, A., Rush, A.J., Russell, J., & Keller, M.B. (1998). Workplace performance effects from chronic depression and its treatment. *Journal of Health Economics, 17*, 511-535.

Boyd-Franklin, N. (1989). Black families: A multisystems approach to family therapy. New York: Guilford Press.

Broadhead, W.E., Blazer, D.G., George, L.K., & Tse, C.K. (1990). Depression, disability days and days lost from work in a prospective epidemiologic survey. *Journal of the American Medical Association, 264*(19), 2524-2528.

Brown, E.R., Ojeda, V., Wyn, R., & Levan, R. (2000). Racial and Ethnic disparities in access to health insurance and health care. UCLA Center for Health Policy Research & The Kaiser Family Foundation.

Brown, F., & Tooley, J. (1989). Alcoholism in the black community. In G.W. Lawson & A.W. Lawson (Eds.), *Alcoholism and Substance Abuse in Special Populations* (pp. 115-130). Rockville, MD: Aspen Publishers.

Brown, G.W., & Harris, T.O. (1978). *Social origins of depression: A study of psychiatric disorder in women*. London: Tavistock.

Brown, T.N., Williams, D.R., Jackson, J.J., Neighbors, H.W., Torres, M., Sellers, S.L., & Brown, K.T. (2000). "Being Black and feeling blue": The mental health consequences of racial discrimination. *Race and Society, 2*(2), 117-131.

Bruce, M.L., & Kim, K.M. (1992). Differences in the effects of divorce on major depression in men and women. *American Journal of Psychiatry, 149*, 914-917.

Bruce, M.L., Takeuchi, D.T., & Leaf, P.J. (1991). Poverty and psychiatric status: Longitudinal evidence from the New Haven Epidemiologic Catchment Area Study. *Archives of General Psychiatry, 48*, 470-474.

Bruce, M.L., Wells, K.B., Miranda, J., Lewis, L., & Gonzalez, J.J. (2002). Overcoming barriers and creating opportunities to reduce burden of affective disorders: A new research agenda: Barriers to reducing burden of affective disorders. *Mental Health Services Research, 4*(4), 187-197.

Burns, R.J. (2001). Strengthening the mental health safety net: Issues and innovations. NGA Center for Best Practices.

Bux, D.A., Jr. (1996). The epidemiology of problem drinking in gay men and lesbians: A critical review. *Clinical Psychology Review, 16*(4), 277-298.

Caetano, R. (1984). Manifestations of alcohol-related problems in Latin America: A review. *PAHO Bulletin*, 18(3), 258-279.

Clark, W., & Midanik, L. (1982). *Alcohol use and alcohol problems among U.S. adults: Results of the 1979 national survey.* In National Institute on Alcohol Abuse and Alcoholism. Alcohol consumption and related problems. Alcohol and Health Monograph No. 1. DHHS Pub. No. (ADM) 82-1190. Washington, D.C.: Supt. of Docs., U.S. Government Printing Office: 3-52.

Cochran, S.D. (2001). Emerging issues in research on lesbians' and gay men's mental health: Does sexual orientation really matter? *American Psychologist, 56*(11), 929-947.

Cochran, S.D., Bybee, D., Gage, S. & Mays, V.M. (1996). Prevalence of HIV-related, self-reported sexual behaviors, sexually transmitted diseases, and problems with drugs and alcohol in three large surveys of lesbian and bisexual women: A look into a segment of the community. *Women's Health: Research on Gender, Behavior and Policy, 2*(1&2), 11-33.

Cochran, S.D., Keenan, C., Schober, C. & Mays, V.M. (2000). Estimates of alcohol use and clinical treatment needs among homosexually active men and women in the US population. *Journal of Consulting and Clinical Psychology, 68*(6), 1062-1071.

Cochran, S.D., & Mays, V.M. (2000). Relation between psychiatric syndromes and behaviorally defined sexual orientation in a sample of the U.S. population. *American Journal of Epidemiology, 151*, 5, 516-523.

Cochran, S.D., & Mays, V.M. (1994). Depressive distress among homosexually active African American men and women. *The American Journal of Psychiatry, 151*(4), 524-529.

Comstock, G.W., & Helsing, K.J. (1976). Symptoms of depression in two communities. *Psychological Medicine, 6*, 551-563.

Cooper-Patrick, L., Gallo, J.J., Powe, N.R., Steinwachs, D.M., Eaton, W.W., & Ford, D.E. (1999). Mental health service utilization by African Americans and Whites: The Baltimore Epidemiologic Catchment Area Follow-Up. *Medical Care, 37*(10), 1034-1045.

Darity, W. (2003). Employment discrimination, segregation, and health. *American Journal of Public Health, 93*(2), 226-231.

Diamant, A.L., Wold, C., Spritzer, K., & Gelberg, L. (2000). Health behaviors, health status, and access to and use of health care: A population-based study of lesbian, bisexual, and heterosexual women. *Archives of Family Medicine, 9*, 1043-1051.

Etner, S.L., Frank, R., & Kessler, R.C. (1997). The impact of psychiatric disorder on labor market outcomes. *Industrial and Labor Relations Review, 51*(1), 64-81.

Gillow, K.E., & Davis, L.L. (1987). Lesbian stress and coping methods. *Journal of Psychosocial Nursing, 25*(9), 28-32.

Greene, B. (2000). African-American lesbians and bisexual women. *Journal of Social Issues, 56*(2), 239-249.

Greene, B. (1998). Family, ethnic identity, and sexual orientation: African-American lesbians and gay men. In C.J. Patterson & A.R. D'Augelli (Eds.), *Lesbian, Gay, and Bisexual Identities in Families* (40-52). New York: Oxford University Press.

Greene, B. (1996). African-American women: Considering diverse identities and societal barriers in psychotherapy. *Annals of the New York Academy of Sciences, 789*, 191-209.

Greene, B. (1994). Lesbian women of color: Triple jeopardy. In L. Comaz-Diaz & B. Greene (Eds.), *Women of Color: Integrating Ethnic and Gender Identities in Psychotherapy* (pp.389-427). New York: Guilford Press.

Herd, D.A. (1985). Ambiguity in Black drinking norms. In L.A. Bennett and G.M. Ames (Eds.), *The American Experience with Alcohol: Contrasting Cultural Perspectives.* New York: Plenum Press.

Hosmer, D.W., & Lemeshow, S. (1989). *Applied Logistic Regression.* New York: John Wiley & Sons, Inc.

Jackson, J.S. (1991). *Life in Black America.* Newbury Park, CA: Sage Publications.

Jackson, J.S., & Gerald, G. (1999). *National Survey of Black Americans, 1979-1980.* Conducted by University of Michigan, Survey Research Center. Ann Arbor, MI: Inter-university Consortium for Political and Social Research.

Kessler, R.C., Avenevoli, S., & Ries, M.K. (2001). Mood disorders in children and adolescents: An epidemologic perspective. *Biological Psychiatry, 49*(12), 1002-1014.

Kohn, L.P., & Hudson, K.M. (2002). Gender, ethnicity and depression: Intersectionality and context in mental health research with African American women. *Perspectives, 8*(1), 174-184.

Langer, T.S., & Michael, S.T. (1963). *Life Stress and Mental Health.* Glencoe, Illinois: The Free Press.

Lawson, W.B. (1986). Clinical issues in the pharmacotherapy of African-Americans. *Psychopharmacology Bulletin, 32,* 275-281.

Lewis, C.E., Saghir, M.T., & Robins, E. (1982). Drinking patterns in homosexual and heterosexual women. *Journal of Clinical Psychiatry, 43,* 277-279.

Matthews, A.K., & Hughes, T.L. (2001). Mental health service use by African American women: Exploration of subpopulation differences. *Cultural Diversity and Ethnic Minority Psychology, 7*(1), 75-87.

Matthews, A.K., Hughes, T.L., Johnson, T., Razzano, L.A., & Cassidy, R. (2002). Prediction of depressive distress in a community sample of women: The role of sexual orientation. *American Journal of Public Health, 92*(7), 1131-1139.

Mays, V.M., Beckman, L.J., Oranchak, E. & Harper, B. (1994). Perceived social support for help-seeking behaviors of Black heterosexual and homosexually active women alcoholics. *Psychology of Addictive Behaviors, 8*(4), 235-242.

Mays, V.M., & Cochran, S.D. (2001). Mental health correlates of perceived discrimination among lesbian, gay and bisexual adults in the United States. *American Journal of Public Health,* 91(11), 1869-1876.

Mays, V.M., Cochran, S.D. & Rhue, S. (1994). The impact of perceived discrimination on the intimate relationships of Black lesbians. *Journal of Homosexuality, 25*(4), 1-14.

Mays, V.M., Cochran, S.D., & Sullivan, J.G. (2000). A profile of ethnic women's health care services in the United States. In C. Hogue, M.A. Hargraves & K. S. Collins (Eds.) *Minority Health in America: Findings and Policy Implications from the Commonwealth Fund Minority Health Survey.* Johns Hopkins University Press.

Mays, V.M., Coleman, L.M., & Jackson, J.S. (1996). Perceived race-based discrimination, employment status, and job stress in a national sample of Black women: Implications for health outcomes. *Journal of Occupational Health Psychology, 1*(3), 319-329.

Mays, V.M., Howard-Caldwell, C.S., & Jackson, J.S. (1996). Mental health symptoms and service use patterns of African American women. In H.W. Neighbors & J.S.

Jackson (Eds.), *Mental Health in Black America* (pp.161-176). Newbury Park: Sage Publications.

Mays, V.M., Yancey, A.K., Cochran, S.D., Weber, M. & Fielding, J.A. (2002). Heterogeneity of health disparities among African American, Hispanic, and Asian American women: Unrecognized influences of sexual orientation. *American Journal of Pubic Health, 92*(4), 632-639.

McGuire, T., Wells, K.B., Bruce, M.L., Miranda, J., Scheffler, R., Durham, M., Ford, D.E., & Lewis, L. (2002). Overcoming barriers and creating opportunities to reduce burden of affective disorders: A new research agenda: Burden of illness. *Mental Health Services Research, 4*(4), 179-185.

Miranda, J., Lawson, W., & Escobar, J. (2002). Overcoming barriers and creating opportunities to reduce burden of affective disorders: A new research agenda: Ethnic minorities. *Mental Health Services Research, 4*(4), 231-237.

Moos, R.H. (1990). Depressed outpatients' life contexts, amount of treatment, and treatment outcome. *Journal of Nervous and Mental Disease, 178*(2), 105-112.

Mukherjee, S., Shukla, S., Woodle, J., Rosen, A.M., & Olarte, S. (1983). Misdiagnosis of schizophrenia in bipolar patients: A multiethnic comparison. *American Journal of Psychiatry, 140*(12), 1571-1574.

Neighbors, H.W. (1988). The help-seeking behavior of black Americans. *Journal of the National Medical Association, 80*, 1009-1012.

Neighbors, H.W., & Jackson, J.S. (1984). The use of informal and formal help: Four patterns of illness behavior in the black community. *American Journal of Community Psychology, 12*, 629-644.

Neighbors, H.W., Musick, M.A., & Williams, D.R. (1998). The African American minister as a source of help for serious personal crises: Bridge or barrier to mental health care? *Health Education and Behavior, 25*, 759-777.

Neighbors, H.W., Trierweiler, S.J., Munday, C., Thompson, E.E., Jackson, J.S., Binion, V.J., & Gomez, J. (1999). Psychiatric diagnosis of African Americans: Diagnostic divergence in clinician-structured and semistructured interviewing conditions. *Journal of the National Medical Association, 91*(11), 601-612.

Peplau, L.A., Cochran, S.D, & Mays, V.M. (1997). A national survey of the intimate relationships of African American lesbians and gay men: A look at commitment, satisfaction, sexual behavior, and HIV disease. In B.Greene (Ed.) *Ethnic and Cultural Diversity Among Lesbians and Gay Men.* (pp. 11-38). Thousand Oaks, CA: Sage Publications.

Radloff, L.S. (1977). The CES-D Scale: A self-report depression scale for research in the general population. *Applied Psychological Measurement, 1*, 385-401.

Roberts S.J. & Sorensen, L. (1999). Health related behaviors and Cancer screening of lesbians: Results from the Boston Lesbian Health Project. *Women and Health, 28*(4), 1-12.

Saghir, M.T., Robins, E., Walbran, B., & Gentry, K.A. (1970). Homosexuality IV: Psychiatric disorders and disability in the female homosexual. *American Journal of Psychiatry, 127*, 147-54.

Sherbourne, C.D., Hays, R.D., & Wells, K.B. (1995). Personal and psychosocial risk factors for physical and mental health outcomes and course of depression among depressed patients. *Journal of Clinical and Consulting Psychology, 63*(3), 345-355.

Smedley, B.D., Stith, A.Y., & Nelson, A.R. (eds.). (2002). *Unequal treatment: Confronting Racial and Ethnic disparities in health care.* Washington, DC: National Academy Press.

Snowden, L.R. (2003). Bias in mental health assessment and intervention: Theory and evidence. *American Journal of Public Health, 93*(2), 239-242.

Snowden, L.R. (1999). African American service use for mental health problems. *Journal of Community Psychology, 27*(3), 303-313.

Strickland, T.L., Lawson, W., Lin, K.M., & Fu, P. (1993). Interethnic variation in response to lithium therapy among African-American and Asian-American populations. In K. Lin, R.E. Poland, et al. (Eds.), *Psychopharmacology and Psychobiology of Ethnicity,* (pp. 107-121). Washington, DC: American Psychiatric Press.

Strickland, T.L., Lin, K., Fu, P., et al. (1995). Comparison of lithium ratio between African-American and Caucasian bipolar patients. *Biological Psychiatry, 37*(5), 325-330.

Strickland, T.L., Ranganath, V., Lin, K., et al. (1991). Psychopharmacologic considerations in the treatment of Black American populations. *Psychopharmacology Bulletin, 27*(4), 441-448.

Sue, S., Fujino, D.C. Hu, L., Takeuchi, D.T., & Zane, N.W. (1991). Community mental health services for ethnic minority groups: A test of the cultural responsiveness hypothesis. *Journal of Consulting and Clinical Psychology, 42*, 794-801.

Sussman, L., Robins, L., & Earls, F. (1987). Treatment-seeking for depression by Black and White Americans. *Social Science and Medicine, 24*(3), 187-196.

Trierweiler, S.J., Neighbors, H.W., Munday, C., Thompson, E.E., Binion, V.J., & Gomez, J.P. (2000). Clinician attributions associated with the diagnosis of schizophrenia in African American and non-African American patients. *Journal of Consulting and Clinical Psychology, 68*(1), 171-175.

U.S. Department of Health and Human Services. (2001). *Mental Health: Culture, Race, and Ethnicity-A Supplement to Mental Health: A Report of the Surgeon General.* Rockville, MD: U.S. Department of Health and Human Services, Substance Abuse and Mental Health Services Administration, Center for Mental Health Services, National Institutes of Health, National Institutes of Mental Health.

Vernon, S.W., Roberts, R.E., & Lee, E.S. (1982). Response tendencies, ethnicity, and depression scores. *American Journal of Epidemiology, 116*, 482-495.

Wang, P.S., Berglund, P., & Kessler, R.C. (2000). Recent care of common mental disorders in the United States: Prevalence and conformance with evidence-based recommendations. *Journal of General Internal Medicine, 15*(5), 284-292.

Wang, P.S., Demler, O., & Kessler, R.C. (2002). Adequacy of treatment for serious mental illness in the United States. *American Journal of Public Health, 92*(1), 92-98.

Wells, K.B., Miranda, J., & Gonzalez, J.J. (2002). Overcoming barriers and creating opportunities to reduce burden of affective disorders: A new research agenda: Introduction. *Mental Health Services Research, 4*(4), 175-178.

Young, A.S., Klap, R., Sherbourne, C.D., & Wells, K.B. (2001). The quality of care for depressive and anxiety disorders in the United States. *Archives of General Psychiatry, 58*(1), 55-61.

The Impact of Community Size on Lesbian and Bisexual Women's Psychosexual Development: Child Maltreatment, Suicide Attempts, and Self-Disclosure

Robin M. Mathy, MSW, LGSW, MSc, MSt, MA
Helen M. Carol, MA
Marc Schillace

SUMMARY. We tested competing hypotheses about the impact of rural-urban gradients on sexual minorities with a public Internet chat room sample ($n = 82$) and a community-owned coffee house sample ($n = 92$). We found associations between rural-urban gradient and reports of pa-

Robin M. Mathy is Director of Research and Assistant Professor of Arts & Sciences at Presentation College in Aberdeen, South Dakota, and is a Licensed Graduate Social Worker in Minnesota. Helen M. Carol is affiliated with the Departments of Psychiatry and Pediatrics, University of Minnesota Medical School. Marc Schillace is affiliated with the Inter-College Program, University of Minnesota–Twin Cities.

Address correspondence to Robin M. Mathy (E-mail: math5577@umn.edu).

This work was supported, in part, by a grant from the American Foundation for Addiction Research, as well as a National Institute of Mental Health Supplemental Grant for an Individual with a Disability (5RO1MH063328) to Robin M. Mathy. The authors are grateful to Barrie E. Berquist and Sarah M. Coleman for their thorough reviews and suggestions of an earlier manuscript.

[Haworth co-indexing entry note]: "The Impact of Community Size on Lesbian and Bisexual Women's Psychosexual Development: Child Maltreatment, Suicide Attempts, and Self-Disclosure." Mathy, Robin M., Helen M. Carol, and Marc Schillace. Co-published simultaneously in *Journal of Psychology & Human Sexuality* (The Haworth Press, Inc.) Vol. 15, No. 2/3, 2003, pp. 47-71; and: *Lesbian and Bisexual Women's Mental Health* (ed: Robin M. Mathy, and Shelly K. Kerr) The Haworth Press, Inc., 2003, pp. 47-71. Single or multiple copies of this article are available for a fee from The Haworth Document Delivery Service [1-800-HAWORTH, 9:00 a.m. - 5:00 p.m. (EST). E-mail address: docdelivery@haworthpress.com].

47

ternal maltreatment as a child as well as self-disclosure of sexual orientation to a family member. In the coffee house sample, rural-urban gradient mediated the mean age at which participants self-disclosed their sexual orientation to another person, close friend, family member, and parent, though it was associated in the Internet sample only with disclosure of sexual orientation to a family member. Rural-urban gradient was not associated with suicidal intent or victimization. *[Article copies available for a fee from The Haworth Document Delivery Service: 1-800-HAWORTH. E-mail address: <docdelivery@haworthpress.com> Website: <http://www.HaworthPress.com> © 2003 by The Haworth Press, Inc. All rights reserved.]*

KEYWORDS. Religiosity, child abuse, suicide, lesbian, psychosexual development

This paper examines the relations between rural-urban gradients and child maltreatment, suicidal intent, self-disclosure, and others' reactions to self-disclosure of minority sexual orientation. First, we use Gallup Poll data to examine the relation between heterosexism and rural-urban gradients. Second, we present a hypothesis that predicts resilience in sexual minorities' psychosexual development despite increased risks associated with growing up in rural areas, where heterosexism is greater. Third, we test the resilience model against a Community Psychology risk paradigm by examining child maltreatment, suicidal intent, self-disclosure, rejection, and victimization among participants raised in urban (population > 50,000) and rural areas (population < 50,001). The outcomes of interest include retrospective reports of child maltreatment, suicidality, self-disclosure, rejection, and victimization. We conclude by discussing our findings in the context of negative attitudes toward rural residents as well as sexual minorities.

HETEROSEXISM AND COMMUNITY SIZE

Heterosexism may be defined as "an ideological system that denies, denigrates, and stigmatizes any nonheterosexual form of behavior, identity, relationship, or community" (Herek, 1993, pp. 89-90). Fernald (1995) argued that heterosexism is associated with growing up in rural areas and small towns. Gallup Poll surveys consistently reveal a statistically significant, inverse relation between community size and heterosexism. Thus, as population sizes decrease, heterosexist attitudes increase. These differences appear regardless of the specific content of questions concerning homosexuality. Relative to residents of urban areas (population > 50,000) and larger communities (population > 10,000), a significantly greater proportion of residents in rural areas (population < 50,000) and smaller communities (population < 10,000) disapprove of homosexual relations or behavior. To test whether the differences reported here are significant, we conducted two-tailed z-approximation tests of the difference of proportions, reported in standard deviations (z) and the associated probability (p) of erroneously rejecting the null hypothesis of equality.

In a 1991 national Gallup Poll, interviewers asked approximately 1,200 respondents, "Do you think homosexual relations between consenting adults should or should not be legal?" (Hugick & Leonard, 1991, p. 70). Of respondents with an opinion, 45.2% of those living in suburbs, medium-sized cities, and large cities answered, "Yes, should be legal." Conversely, only 32% of respondents living in small towns and rural areas answered this question affirmatively ($Z = 4.48$, $p < .00001$). A 1996 Gallup Poll asked approximately 1,000 participants the same question (Gallup, 1996). Of respondents who had an opinion, 49.9% of urban and suburban respondents answered, "Yes, should be legal." Conversely, only 41.8% of rural respondents answered this item affirmatively ($Z = 1.98$, $p < .048$). The Gallup Polls administered surveys containing questions identical to these in 1977 and 1982. They also revealed an inverse relation between heterosexism and community size (Table 1). Over the decades the Gallup Poll has administered this question, there has not been a statistically significant change in the proportions of urban and rural residents who disapprove of homosexual relations between consenting adults.

The relation between heterosexism and community size is not limited to questions regarding approval or disapproval of legal homosexual relationships between consenting adults. A 1996 Gallup Poll asked about 1,000 survey respondents, "Do you think marriages between homosexuals should or should not be recognized by the law as valid, with the same rights as traditional marriages?" (Moore, 1996). Of participants who had an opinion, 32.4% of urban and suburban residents answered, "Should." Conversely, among rural participants about half that proportion (17.8% of participants with an opinion) answered, "Should" ($Z = 4.92$, $p < .00001$). In 1997, the Gallup Poll conducted a survey that asked respondents, "Do you personally believe homosexual behavior is

TABLE 1. Heterosexism by Population Size

Population Size	June, 1977		June, 1982	
	Should	Should Not	Should	Should Not
1,000,000+	53%	32%	58%	29%
500,000-999,999	54	34	48	37
50,000-499,999	42	47	45	39
2,500-49,999	41	45	42	46
Under 2,500	34	51	35	45

morally wrong or is not morally wrong?" (Saad, 1997). Approximately 36.7% of urban and suburban residents replied, "Not wrong." About 27.3% of rural community members answered, "Not wrong" ($Z = 2.50$, $p < .012$). Thus, nationally representative surveys clearly and consistently indicate that sexual minorities in rural areas of the United States experience a social ecological milieu more hostile than gay, lesbian, and bisexual people who reside in urban areas.

SEXUAL MINORITY DEVELOPMENT IN RURAL AREAS

Community psychologists D'Augelli and Hart (1987) noted that research concerning gay men, women, and families has an urban bias. They recommended the development of "helping communities" in rural areas because sexual minorities who grow up in these areas are much more likely than peers raised in urban areas to be subjected to negative attitudes as well as limited exposure to gay persons and role models, lifestyles, and cultural symbols. They reasoned that the greater prevalence of nuclear and extended families in rural areas makes a sexual minority lifestyle appear highly unusual. They argued that self-disclosure of sexual minority status within the community is therefore limited and guarded.

D'Augelli and Hart (1987) accurately described rural communities as being comprised of more extended family networks. However, other aspects of rural communities also warrant consideration. Durkheim (1893/1984) argued that our collective conscience varies by the complexity in divisions of labor, with greater social heterogeneity but weaker social bonds and fewer moral constraints on individual thought and behavior in industrial societies than in agrarian cultures. Bellah et al. (1985) described significant differences between urban and rural residential enclaves. Lifestyles in the former are relatively unencumbered by ethnic and religious moral values that tend to constrain the behavior of individuals in smaller, relatively close, rural communities. Bellah et al. argued that America's shift from a predominantly rural, agrarian culture to a predominantly urban, industrial and post-industrial society has effectively promoted radical individualism at the expense of religious and other cultural constraints on individual behavior.

We hypothesized that the greater constraints on radical individualism in rural areas, particularly in combination with the increased importance of kinship and closer friendship networks in these settings, would mediate or moderate the relation between (relatively greater) heterosexism in rural vis-à-vis urban areas. Consequently, although heterosexism poses greater risks for rural than urban sexual minorities' psychosexual development, being raised in rural vis-à-vis urban communities may increase resilience sufficiently to overcome the relatively greater risks. We may define resilience as normal development despite adverse risks that we ordinarily would expect to compromise an individual's functioning (Masten, 2001). Because females are socialized to value relationships (Gilligan, 1982), lesbians and bisexual females raised in rural areas–where extended kin and friendship networks are more prevalent–might have better developmental outcomes than sexual minority females raised in urban settings.

This hypothesis challenges the relatively deficit-focused Community Psychology model postulated by D'Augelli and Hart (1987). The model has been difficult to test. Research concerning sexual minorities has been conducted primarily with male participants from urban areas (D'Augelli & Hershberger, 1993; Hammelman, 1993; Hershberger & D'Augelli, 1995; Hershberger, Pilkington, & D'Augelli, 1997; Hunter, 1990; Proctor & Groze, 1994; Remafedi, 1987; Remafedi, Farrow, & Deisher, 1991; Rich, Fowler, Young, & Blenkush, 1986; Rotheram-Borus, Hunter, & Rosario, 1994; Rotheram-Borus et al., 1995).

The Community Psychology model postulated by D'Augelli and Hart (1987) assumes that (negative) heterosexism (adversely) mediates or moderates the relation between family relationships and sexual minorities' development, leading to negative outcomes (top of Figure 1). Our resilience model hypothesizes that (positive) systems more proximal to the individual (e.g., kin relationships) (positively) mediate or moderate the relation between (relatively negative) community heterosexism and sexual minorities' development, leading to positive outcomes (bottom of Figure 1). Our model reflects somewhat greater emphasis on sociological and social work theory. Relative to Commu-

FIGURE 1. Community Psychology and Sociological Models of Relations Between Heterosexism, Family Relations, and Sexual Minority Developmental Outcomes

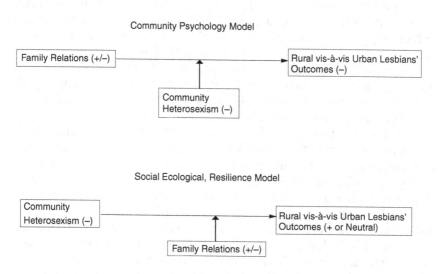

nity Psychology, Sociology and Social Work share interests in studying individuals in their social contexts. The latter differ somewhat in the relatively lower emphasis they give to individuals vis-à-vis their social contexts. Generally, Sociology and Social Work focus more heavily on the interaction of larger systems in human ecologies, whereas Community Psychology maintains its focus on individuals, as in its parent discipline, Psychology.

Were the Community Psychology model (D'Augelli & Hart, 1987) correct, we would expect a disproportionate number of sexual minorities who grew up in rural *vis-à-vis* urban areas to have negative experiences, such as child maltreatment, victimization related to their sexual orientation, and suicidality. Indeed, on the surface this assumption seems sensible precisely because there is a clear and consistent (inverse) relation between heterosexism and community size. However, this reasoning is open to ecological fallacies (Rubin & Babbie, 1997). Population-level data do not necessarily predict individual level probabilities. For example, globally, males complete suicide at a higher rate than females. However, females in specific countries in Asia complete suicide at higher rates than males. Therefore, we cannot predict suicide rates in an individual country merely by knowing sex ratios in suicide completions at the global level.

We based the development of our resilience model on sociological theory. In contrast to the Community Psychology paradigm, we would expect sexual minority females who grew up in rural areas to have risks of child maltreatment, suicidality, and victimization equal to those who grew up in urban areas. Kinship and community solidarity as well as decreased radical individualism may effectively buffer adverse risks endemic to living with increased heterosexism. Relative to rural communities, the solidarity of family and interpersonal relationships are weaker and more diffused in urban, industrialized areas. Sexual minority individuals raised in urban areas may have fewer interpersonal and community buffers against the risks of living in an (albeit less) heterosexist community. Thus, we would expect sexual minority individuals who grew up in smaller communities, where extended families and socially interconnected relationships are more prevalent, important, and less interchangeable, to have less child maltreatment, victimization, and suicidality than those who grew up in relatively large, urban areas. This paper tests the Community Psychology and Resilience models by comparing sexual minority females who grew up in urban vis-à-vis rural areas on a number of developmental outcomes. The outcomes of interest include child maltreatment, suicide attempts, self-disclosure, interpersonal rejection, and victimization. These are well-identified risk factors for sexual minorities (Hershberger, Pilkington, & D'Augelli, 1997; Corliss, Cochran, & Mays, 2003).

METHODS

We elected to replicate the results of an initial Internet study with an offline sample prior to publication. The validated methods of the Internet study appear elsewhere in the peer-reviewed literature (Mathy, Schillace, Coleman, & Berquist, 2002). Use of the Internet as a research tool remains controversial. Therefore, we replicated the Internet study with an offline sample obtained at a community-owned, easily accessible, Midwestern coffee house. The data for both studies have been archived with the Sexual Orientation and Families of Origin Project (Robin M. Mathy, Principal Investigator) archived at the Kinsey Institute for Research in Sex, Gender, and Reproduction at Indiana University–Bloomington. Our use of these data was approved by the Institutional Review Board at the University of Minnesota–Twin Cities.

Instrument for Sample 1 (Internet) and Sample 2 (Coffee House)

The survey contained 76 questions about demographics as well as history of child maltreatment by parents when they were a child or adolescent. Size of community was assessed by asking participants to complete the statement, "For most of my childhood and adolescence, I lived in a city or town of" with options including, "10 million or more," "5 to 9.99 million," "1 to 4.99 million," "100,001 to 999,999," "50,001 to 100,000," "10,001 to 50,000," and "10,000 or fewer." We classified rural as populations of 50,000 or fewer, consistent with the U.S. Census Bureau (2002). However, we also examined smaller communities (10,000 or fewer) relative to larger ones.

We explored participants' histories of child maltreatment. Categories of abuse included sexual, physical, verbal, psychological, spiritual, and neglect. Earlier ethnographic research had revealed that "emotional abuse" was synonymous with neglect (i.e., an act of omission and an absence of emotional warmth). Responses indicating non-sexual, non-physical abuse (neglect and verbal, psychological, and spiritual abuse) were also examined as "Other" abuse. Our previous ethnographic research found that this constituted acts of commission perceived as intentionally painful, including the use of words, gestures, stances, postures, and glances that did not result in physical contact.

The survey included questions about psychosexual developmental milestones, including self-awareness of same-sex attraction and intimacy as well as ages at which self-disclosure was made to others and the perceived reactions of those with whom they shared this information. We asked participants, "At what age did you first think you might be attracted to people of your own sex?" and, "At what age did you first become certain that you were attracted to people of your own sex?" and, "At what age, if ever, did you first become sexually intimate with a person of your own sex?" The answers to each of these 3 items was provided as, "At age" with a fill-in blank. We assessed self-disclosure of sexual orientation along a continuum, including (a) another person, (b) a close friend, (c) a family member, and (d) a parent. For each of these, respondents were asked, "At what age did you first tell [a-d in consecutive questions] of your sexual attraction to people of your own sex?" Answers were again recorded as, "At age" with a fill-in blank. We evaluated participants' perceptions of acceptance or rejection following self-disclosure to the individuals identified in self-disclosures a-d. We scored these on an unanchored Likert scale that ranged from "extremely rejected" to "extremely accepted." We scored the former as 1 and the latter as 7, with "neither accepted nor rejected" as 4. For each type of relationship (a-d), participants were asked to complete the statement, "When I first told [a-d in consecutive questions] that I am attracted to people of my own sex, I felt" followed by the Likert scale of extreme rejection through extreme acceptance.

We also asked participants questions about child maltreatment, suicidality, and victimization. Participants completed the statement, "For at least some of my childhood and adolescence, my mother (or primary female caregiver) was (indicate all that apply):" followed by a list including, "Sexually abusive," "Physically abusive," "Emotionally abusive," "Psychologically abusive," "Verbally abusive," "Spiritually abusive," and "None of the above." We used the same items used for fathers, substituting "father" for "mother" and "female" for "male." Suicidality was assessed by asking participants, "With which of the following statements would you most strongly agree?" followed by, "I never imagined suicide," "I have imagined suicide, but never seriously considered it," "I have imagined suicide, but never attempted it," "I have attempted suicide," and "I have attempted suicide more than once." Victimization was assessed by asking participants a series of six questions ("Have you ever been . . .") with 3 types of violence (verbally abused, physically assaulted, and threatened with physical violence) delineated by familiarity (i.e., "someone you know" vis-à-vis "a stranger"). The survey included questions about experiences of victimization, with questions delineated by physical assault, threats, and verbal abuse, and whether or not the perpetrator was known to the participant, and whether the assault was related to the participant's sexual orientation.

Data Analyses for Both Samples

We conducted data analyses using SPSS in a Windows operating environment, running on an IBM compatible desktop personal computer. Only main effects were examined due to the small sample sizes ($n = 82$, excluding 2 internet participants without community of origin responses and n = 92 coffee shop participants). We decided (a priori) to accept a 5% chance of erroneously rejecting the null hypothesis of equality between the urban and rural samples. We defined rural as populations with 50,000 or fewer residents, consistent with the U.S. Census Bureau (2002). The goal of these analyses is to examine differences between sexual minority females raised in urban vis-à-vis rural communities in two independent samples. Although we have two separate samples, we obtained the offline sample to replicate the findings of the

Internet study. Therefore, we do not analyze or comment upon any differences that might exist between these samples in the course of this paper. A between-sample comparison will reported separately, comparing the previously validated sampling design (Mathy et al., 2002) with an offline "sampling as usual" protocol.

Internet Sample Procedures and Participants

Procedures. The Internet sample (Mathy et al., 2002) used a multistage sampling technique to select chat rooms on the Internet and to identify community members of identified chat rooms. Following several months of ethnographic observation, researchers administered questionnaires to community members in a large, easily accessible chat room specifically designated for socializing by lesbian and bisexual females. Researchers operationalized community membership as recognition by others and recognition of others across two or more consecutive visits. The consensus of 3 researchers was required for classification as a community member. The a priori selection criteria required identification of chat rooms that necessitated registration on the host server but permitted free access. In addition, the identified chat rooms were readily identifiable with a major Web search engine.

Researchers invited chat room community members to participate via "Private Mode," a form of online communication visible only to the message's sender and recipient. Eighty-two of 84 eligible females (97.6%) who participated in the ethnographic study agreed to participate in the survey component of the research. We include demographic information for all 84 participants wherever possible. The relatively high response rate reflects the ethnographic origins of the study and the researchers' ability to establish rapport with participants prior to inviting them to complete a questionnaire. Researchers asked potential participants to e-mail a request for a questionnaire to the principal investigator. Upon receipt of the request, the principal investigator sent a questionnaire to the participant via electronic mail. After completing the questionnaire, participants returned it via their e-mail "reply" command. Upon receipt of the completed questionnaire, the principal investigator stripped all identifying information from it. The principal investigator then coached participants how to safeguard the integrity of their confidentiality and to clear the memory of the computer they had been using.

Participants. The data reported here include responses from self-identified lesbian and bisexual females from an easily accessible Internet chat room (n = 84) who were recruited to obtain positivist data designed to complement an ethnographic study of cyberspace communities intended for female sexual minorities. Internet participants included 6 Australians, one Asian, and one woman from Europe. All other Internet participants reported that they reside in North America (United States or Canada). Australian females were included in the data from the Internet sample because the rate and increase of suicide among Australian youth is similar to the U.S. (Desjarlais, Eisenberg, Good, & Kleinman, 1995). One of the participants had emigrated to Canada from Asia, and one had emigrated to the U.S. from Europe. Seventy-five (89.3%) of the Internet participants were white, 2 (2.4%) were African American, 2 (2.4%) were Native American, 3 (3.6%) were Asian and 2 (2.4%) identified as Latina. African American women were underrepresented. This may reflect the disproportionate oppression and poverty in that population, possibly resulting in decreased access to computers and the Internet.

Respondents ranged in age from 15.5 years to 45.2 years ($Md = 21.38$ years; $M = 23.99, SD = 7.24$). Independent t-tests of differences in mean ages for the rural and urban samples were not statistically significant. Eighty-two participants answered the question about the size of the community of their origin. Twenty (21.7%) participants reported that they had grown up in a town of 10,000 people or less. Another 19 (20.7%) indicated they had grown up in a town of 50,000 people or fewer; 15 (16.3%) reported they had been raised in a city of 100,000 people or fewer; another 24 (26.1%) in a city of fewer than one million people, and 14 (15.2%) in a city of one million or more people. Independent sample t-tests for differences in mean ages for rural and urban samples were not statistically significant.

Twenty-four of 84 internet participants (29.3%) reported they had a high school education or less; 32 (39%) had some college education; the remainder (31.7%) had at least a college degree. A total of 56.4% of internet participants indicated their income was at or below the national median. Four of 92 coffee shop participants (4.4%) reported they had a high school education or less; 34 (37%) had some college education and more than half (58.7%) had at least a college degree. About half of the coffee shop participants (50.5%) estimated their income at or below the national median.

Coffee House Sample Procedures and Participants

Procedures. We compiled a comprehensive list of coffee houses in the Twin Cities area. We evaluated coffee houses for geographic, cultural, and financial accessibility. Candidates were nominated by editors and reviewers of small newspapers distributed to Twin Cities coffee houses. We also solicited candidate coffee houses from minority community leaders. We ruled out coffee houses located in areas that were not accessible by public transportation as well as those situated in census tract areas in which the median family income was more than 15% above or below the Twin Cities median. We visited finalist candidates several times at different hours on various days. We eliminated coffee houses in which the clientele appeared culturally homogeneous in age, ethnicity, income, physical or mental abilities, or depicted any particular political ideologies or religious beliefs. For example, we eliminated one candidate coffee house in which a patron was on two separate visits engaged in evangelizing other guests, and we eliminated another candidate coffee house in which two servers brandished potentially offensive tattoos (i.e., the Union Jack flag). In contrast, the selected coffee house is easily accessible by public transportation, a sign above the entrance reads, "Everyone welcome," and the clientele has considerable diversity in age, ethnicity, income, and political affiliation.

The principal investigator approached one of the owners and several employees about the possibility of distributing questionnaires about "Sexual Orientation and Family Origin." With the assent of employees, the owner gave permission to distribute up to 100 questionnaires over 30 days in July and August of 1999. The owner made available a gratis beverage to individuals who completed the survey. Minority sexual orientation was not required for participation. However, we did not use surveys completed by heterosexuals and they did not count toward the 100-questionnaire limit (reasonably) imposed by the owner.

Initially, we approached prospective participants in person in order to pre-screen any difficulties that might arise in the procedure of obtaining or submitting the completed questionnaire. We left blank questionnaires at the barrister's counter, along with manila envelopes into which participants placed the completed surveys. Barristers collected the surveys and kept them in a secure location. Several participants elected to complete the questionnaires when they were not at the coffee house, and returned them separately. The principal investigator received questionnaires by mail at the coffee house until December 1999. Participants returned 92 surveys total out of the 100 distributed, yielding a response rate of 92%.

We should note that the owner advised the principal investigator that she had received complaints from patrons who expressed concerns regarding questionnaire items about suicidal intent and child maltreatment. However, she elected to permit completion of the project because the surveys were confidential and we kept no record of individuals who had requested, completed, or submitted the questionnaires, and informed consent was required for participation. The first page of the questionnaire described the study's purpose and alerted prospective participants that some questions might be "disturbing" to some. The information page of the survey gave prospective participants the telephone number of the principal investigator (an experienced, Master's level psychotherapist), a local telephone crisis line, a national telephone crisis line, and a free walk-in counseling center in the Twin Cities. The principal investigator did not have an institutional affiliation at the time the study was completed. However, the study complied with the American Psychological Association ethical standards for conducting scientific research for publication (APA, 1992). The Kinsey Institute for Sex, Gender, and Reproduction in Bloomington, Indiana approved the study for archival, along with other work by the principal investigator that it has archived. We analyzed the data during the principal investigator's affiliation with the University of Minnesota. The Institutional Review Board at the University of Minnesota authorized analysis and reporting of the archived data.

Participants. All coffee house participants resided in the United States. Eighty-two (90.1%) of the participants were white, 2 (2.2%) were African American, 2 (2.2%) were Native American, 4 (4.4%) were Asian, and 1 (1.1%) was Latina. Ethnicity was missing for one coffee house participant. Participants ranged in age from 16.5 years to 60.0 years ($Md = 29.63$ years; $M = 31.56$, $SD = 10.46$). Twenty (21.7%) participants reported that they had grown up in a town of 10,000 people or fewer. Nineteen (20.7%) indicated they had been raised in a town of 50,000 people or fewer; 15 (16.3%) reported they had grown up in a city of 100,000 people or fewer. Another 24 (26.1%) stated they grew up in a city of fewer than one million people, and 14 (15.2%) had grown up in a city with a population of one million people or more. There was not a statistically significant difference in proportions of participants raised in rural *vis-à-vis* urban areas. Moreover, the coffee house sample had a rural-urban gradient very similar to that of the Internet sample.

RESULTS

Child Maltreatment

Prevalence of child maltreatment differed very little by size of community in which participants were raised (Table 2). *Internet Sample.* In the Internet sample, paternal sexual abuse was reported by 20.0% of urban-raised compared to 3.2% of rural-raised participants ($p = .018$,

TABLE 2. Child Maltreatment (% Yes) by Sizes of Communities in Which Participants Were Raised, Each Sample Separately

	Coffee House			Internet Chat		
	Rural	Urban	χ^2	Rural	Urban	χ^2
Maternal						
Sexual	0	1 (1.9)	1.000[b]	1 (2.2)	1 (2.9)	0.427[b]
Physical	7 (13.0)	5 (13.2)	0.001	8 (17.4)	7 (20.0)	1.407
Neglect	29 (53.7)	15 (39.5)	1.810	14 (30.4)	11 (31.4)	0.346
Psych	14 (25.9)	10 (26.3)	0.002	10 (21.7)	10 (28.6)	1.001
Verbal	21 (38.4)	7 (18.4)	4.413*	9 (19.6)	8 (22.9)	0.078
Spiritual	5 (9.3)	5 (13.2)	0.350	3 (6.5)	6 (17.1)	2.377
NonSexPhy [c]	32 (59.3)	18 (47.4)	1.271	18 (38.3)	15 (42.9)	0.173
Paternal						
Sexual	4 (7.4)	6 (15.8)	1.618	1 (3.2)	7 (20.0)	0.018[b]*
Physical	11 (20.4)	6 (15.8)	0.311	5 (16.1)	8 (22.9)	0.375
Neglect	21 (38.9)	12 (31.6)	0.518	8 (25.8)	12 (34.3)	0.135
Psych	17 (31.5)	13 (34.2)	0.076	8 (25.8)	10 (28.6)	0.499
Verbal	14 (25.4)	10 (26.3)	0.002	8 (25.8)	13 (37.1)	3.104
Spiritual	2 (3.7)	5 (13.2)	0.121[b]	6 (19.4)	2 (5.7)	1.000[b]
NonSexPhy [c]	28 (51.9)	17 (44.7)	0.452	15 (32.6)	19 (54.3)	3.835*

Note.[a]Fisher's Exact Test. [b]p from Fisher's Exact Test because 2 or more cells had expected frequency < 5.*p < .05; [c]Composite of non-sexual and non-physical abuse: any Neglect, Psychological, Verbal or Spiritual Abuse.

Fisher's Exact Test). Participants raised in urban communities also were significantly more likely than those from rural communities (i.e., population < 50,000) to report that they had experienced non-physical and non-sexual forms of paternal abuse (e.g., verbal abuse) as a child or adolescent, χ^2 (df = 1) = 3.84, p = .05. *Coffee House Sample.* In the coffee shop sample, a significant difference in the percent of participants reporting maternal verbal abuse emerged when participants raised in rural regions (38.4%) were compared to those from urban areas (18.4%), χ^2 (df = 1) = 4.41, p = .036.

Suicidality

We found no statistically significant relationships between suicidal behavior and size of community of origin in either the Internet or the

Coffee House samples. *Internet Sample.* Approximately one-third (35.4%) of the lesbian and bisexual women in the Internet sample reported that they had attempted suicide at least once, and about half of the attempters (18.3% of total) indicated that they had made at least two attempts. Percentages of suicide attempters from urban vis-à-vis rural communities (37.1% and 34.0%, respectively) did not differ significantly, χ^2 ($df = 1$) = 0.084, p = n.s. Percentages of repeated suicide attempters from urban vis-à-vis rural communities (17.1% and 19.1%, respectively) also did not differ significantly, χ^2 ($df = 1$) = 0.08, p = n.s. *Coffee House Sample.* Approximately one-fifth of the participants (19.6%) in the Coffee House sample reported at least one suicide attempt and less than half of the attempters (7.6% of the total coffee house sample) attempted two or more times. Approximately the same proportion of coffee house participants with urban (18.4%) and rural (20.4%) origins reported that they had attempted suicide at least once. Nearly identical percentages of both groups (7.9% urban, 7.4% rural) had attempted suicide more than once, (p = 1.00, Fisher's Exact Test).

Self-Disclosure

We evaluated the ages at which sexual minority females from urban and rural communities self-disclosed their sexual preference to (a) another person, (b) a close friend, (c) a family member, and (d) a parent. We conducted independent sample t-tests and the Levene's Test for Equality of Variance. When statistically significant, the latter test indicates that the variance about the means in urban and rural communities was unequal. Therefore, when the Levene's Test was statistically significant, we report (in Table 3) the t-test statistic, its associated degrees of freedom, and its associated probability (*p*-value). *Internet Sample.* In the Internet sample, disclosure to a family member was made at a significantly lower age among urban-raised participants than among those raised in rural communities (17.6 vs. 20.4 years), t ($df = 46.7$) = -2.46, p = .018. Relative to participants from rural communities, lesbian and bisexual women from urban communities self-disclosed their sexual preference to (a) another person, (b) a close friend, and (c) a parent at somewhat but not significantly younger ages. *Coffee House Sample.* However, urban participants in the coffee house sample were younger on average than participants from rural communities by almost 3 years at age of disclosure to another person, t ($df = 89$) = -2.33, p = .022. They were about 3 years younger, on average, when they disclosed their

TABLE 3. Mean Ages of Self-Disclosure and Developmental Milestones by Size of Communities in Which Participants Were Raised, Each Sample Separately

		Coffee House					Internet Chat		
	N	M	SD	t (df)		N	M	SD	t (df)
Told Another Person				−2.33(89)*					−0.70 (79)
Urban	38	18.7	4.1		Urban	34	17.6	4.0	
Rural	53	21.6	7.0		Rural	47	18.3	5.6	
Told a Close Friend				−2.49(87)*					−0.53 (71)
Urban	38	18.9	4.0		Urban	31	18.1	4.0	
Rural	51	21.9	6.8		Rural	42	18.6	4.9	
Told a Family Member				−3.67(67.5)***					−2.46(46.7)*
Urban	32	19.6	3.9		Urban	16	17.6	2.4	
Rural	47	25.1	6.8		Rural	33	20.4	5.5	
Told a Parent				−2.57(53.4)*					−1.29(33)
Urban	27	19.9	3.9		Urban	14	17.9	2.4	
Rural	38	24.1	9.1		Rural	21	19.2	3.4	
Age Preference Questioned				−1.78 (89)					0.61(80)
Urban	37	12.7	5.1		Urban	35	13.4	5.2	
Rural	54	15.3	7.6		Rural	37	12.7	5.3	
Age Certain of Orientation				−2.46 (87)*					−0.71(78)
Urban	36	16.5	4.2		Urban	35	16.6	3.8	
Rural	53	19.9	7.5		Rural	45	17.4	5.1	
Age of Same-Sex Intimacy				−3.15(85)**					−0.83(59)
Urban	37	17.6	5.5		Urban	28	17.2	4.4	
Rural	50	22.4	7.6		Rural	33	18.2	5.4	

*$p < .05$ ** $p < .01$ ***$p < .001$

sexual preference to a close friend, t ($df = 87$) = -2.49, $p = .015$. On average, they were about 5.5 years younger at the time of their disclosure to a family member, t ($df = 67.5$) = -3.67, $p = .000$. Also, relative to peers raised in rural areas, urban Coffee House participants were about 4.2 years younger on average when they told a parent of their same-sex preference, t ($df = 53.4$) = -2.57, $p = .013$.

Psychosexual Developmental Milestones

We also tested for differences in mean ages at which participants (a) first questioned their sexual preference, (b) became certain of their same-sex sexual preference, and (c) engaged in same-sex sexual intimacy. The lower portion of Table 3 reflects the mean age, standard deviation, *t*-statistic, and its degrees of freedom for these developmental milestones. *Internet Sample*. We found no statistically significant differences in mean ages at which participants from rural and urban areas reached these (a-c) psychosexual developmental milestones. *Coffee House Sample*. Compared to peers from rural areas, participants from urban areas were somewhat but not significantly younger when they first questioned their sexual preference and significantly younger than rural peers when they became certain of their same sex preference (16.5 vs. 19.9 years), t ($df = 87$) = -2.46, $p = .016$. Age of first intimacy with a same-sex partner was almost 5 years younger for participants from urban areas when compared to peers raised in rural areas, t ($df = 85$) = -3.15, $p = .002$.

We also examined the proportions of participants who had self-disclosed their sexual orientation in various kinds of relationships. *Internet Sample*. We found that virtually all participants in the Internet sample from urban as well as rural areas had self-disclosed their sexual orientation to another person (97.1% and 100%, respectively). About nine in ten sexual minority females raised in communities of both sizes had self-disclosed their sexual orientation to a close friend (88.6% urban and 89.4% rural, respectively). These differences were not statistically significant. However, fewer than half of the Internet participants raised in urban areas (45.7%) but more than two-thirds of those from rural ones (72.3%) had self-disclosed their sexual orientation to a family member, χ^2 ($df = 1$) = 5.98, $p = .014$. Internet participants who grew up in urban (40.0%) and rural (48.9%) communities did not differ in prevalence of disclosing their sexual orientation to a parent. *Coffee House Sample*. There were no significant urban-rural differences in sexual orientation disclosures among coffee house participants. All participants had self-disclosed their sexual orientation to another person in both urban (100%) and rural (100%) communities and 100% of both groups had disclosed to a close friend. We found that more than nine in ten participants from urban (94.7%) and rural (92.6%) areas had self-disclosed their sexual orientation to a family member. Similarly, more than four-fifths of participants from urban (86.8%) and rural (81.5%) communities had disclosed their sexual orientation to a parent.

Rejection

The survey asked participants about others' reactions to the self-disclosure of their sexual orientation. Response categories fell on an unanchored, seven-point Likert scale that ranged from extreme rejection (1) to extreme acceptance (7), with a midpoint (4) of "neither rejected nor accepted." Statistical analyses yielded no significant differences among either the Internet or Coffee House participants. In fact, all differences fell well within one standard deviation, which ranged from 1.2 to 2.2. *Internet Sample.* Participants from both urban and rural areas in the Internet sample reported that on average they had felt at least somewhat accepted by the first person (mean scores were 5.1 and 4.9, respectively) and first close friend (mean scores were 5.4 and 4.8, respectively) to whom they had disclosed their sexual orientation. On average, Internet participants from both urban and rural settings reported that they felt their family members' and parents' responses were neither particularly accepting nor rejecting. Mean scores of reactions by family members were 3.9 and 4.7 for participants of urban and rural origin, respectively. Mean scores of reactions by parents were 4.0 and 3.8 for participants of urban and rural origin, respectively. *Coffee House Sample.* Very similar results occurred when comparing Coffee House participants from urban and rural communities. On average, reactions following self-disclosure of same-sex attraction to another person and a close friend were somewhat accepting, regardless of the community size of their origin. Upon disclosure to another person, the mean reaction scores for participants in the urban and rural groups were 5.6 and 5.3, respectively. Following disclosure to a close friend, the mean reaction scores for participants of both urban and rural origin were 5.7. Disclosure to a family member by participants of urban and rural origin yielded mean reaction scores of 4.5 and 4.1, respectively. After disclosure to a parent, the mean reaction scores for participants from urban and rural communities were 4.7 and 3.8, respectively.

Victimization

The size of participants' communities of origin did not mediate their reports of verbal abuse, assaults, or threats, regardless of whether or not they knew the perpetrator(s). We obtained this finding in both the Internet and the Coffee House samples. We obtained this result in both samples even when we combined known and unknown perpetrators, pooled assaults by type regardless of whether or not they knew the assailant, and whether or not participants attributed verbal abuse, assaults, or threats to their sexual orientation. Thus, participants from urban and rural communities were at neither greater nor lesser risk of being victims of verbal abuse, assaults, or threats, and independent of whether the perpetrator was a stranger or someone they knew.

DISCUSSION

There is a clear and compelling, inverse relation between heterosexism and size of communities. Rural communities imbue greater solidarity despite individual differences. Moreover, the residents of rural communities are part of a social fabric that Durkheim (1893/1984) referred to as mechanical solidarity. Durkheim argued that divisions of labor associated with social complexity lead to greater individuality and anonymity. The relative dearth of relationships and community members' interdependence reinforces the maintenance of relationships despite differences. This often leaves members of rural communities feeling as if they must project a façade to maintain social harmony. The plethora of potential interpersonal connections in large urban areas makes discomfiting relationships relatively portable and disposable.

Mass media penetrates all areas of society, and members of rural areas are sometimes depicted as "rednecks" that neither know nor care about the world urbanites and suburbanites inhabit. The remonstrance against the effect of rural areas on lesbian, gay male, and bisexual youth who grow up in these communities is itself an "ism"–cultural urbanism–which perceives urban life as preferred, more fulfilling, and more enlightened than rural lifestyles. Despite the greater heterosexism in rural communities, the greater cultural demands for civility outweigh potential engagement in antagonistic interactions. When there is an extensive division of labor, as in large urban areas, occupants of social roles can maintain their anonymity more easily. The solidarity binding residents in smaller communities precludes concealing one's identity. These dynamics constrain the verbal and physical expressions of antipathy in rural areas that might otherwise occur where personal identities are relatively unencumbered by social roles in urban communities.

This paper has challenged the idea that heterosexism negatively affects relationships between sexual minorities and their friends, family, and parents. In contrast to predictions of negative experiences for sexual minorities raised in rural areas, we argued that the close-knit social interactions and extended kin relationships in these areas might provide a source of resilience that buffers against the ostensibly greater risks posed by significantly greater levels of heterosexism. In general, we found virtually no differences between participants raised in rural communities vis-à-vis urban areas. Sexual minority females raised in urban areas were significantly more likely than were peers raised in rural regions to report sexual abuse by their father or primary male caregiver. They were also more likely to report non-sexual and non-physical forms of abuse (e.g., psychological abuse) by their father or primary male caregiver. More participants raised in rural settings than in urban settings reported verbal abuse by mother or primary female caregiver.

We found no differences in suicidality by size of participants' communities of origin. This finding was important because suicidality is strongly associated with child maltreatment. The overall sample size was too small to permit an examination beyond main effects. This precluded an examination of the relation between suicidality and community size controlling for child maltreatment. This would be worth considering in future research with larger samples. Although Corliss, Cochran, and Mays (2003) did not use a larger sample, they did study child maltreatment histories with a nationally representative sample. They found that a significantly greater percentage of sexual minorities than heterosexuals reported histories of child maltreatment. Their sample of sexual minorities was too small to permit an examination beyond the main effects of sexual orientation and child maltreatment. Nonetheless, their study suggested that sexual minorities appear more likely than heterosexuals to have been maltreated as children. We contend that it will be important to determine whether heterosexist environments mediate the child maltreatment experiences of sexual minorities. There are significant relationships between heterosexism and rural-urban gradients as well as heterosexism and the importance of religion. Thus, it is important to consider carefully the causal antecedents as well as psychosocial and social-cultural mechanisms that might mediate or moderate the negative influences of heterosexism in the lives of sexual minorities who grow up in such milieu.

We found that participants raised in urban areas self-disclosed their minority sexuality at significantly younger ages than did those reared in rural areas. The differences between these population size gradients was statistically significant for each type of relationship in which self-disclosure was made, including to (a) another person, (b) a close friend, (c) a family member, or (d) to a parent. Our data revealed that participants raised in rural areas self-disclosed their minority sexuality at significantly older ages relative to their peers reared in urban areas. This is important because delaying the age of self-disclosure seems to be a protective factor (Rotheram-Borus, Rosario, Van Rossem, Reid, & Gillis, R., 1995).

The proportion of participants in rural communities who self-disclosed their sexual orientation to a family member was significantly greater among sexual minority females from rural vis-à-vis urban areas. This finding is important because greater self-disclosure is associated with positive mental health among sexual minority females (Morris, Waldo, and Rothblum, 2001). This suggests that lesbians raised in rural vis-à-vis urban areas may have developed somewhat more mature social skills and interpersonal competencies prior to self-disclosure. Future research may benefit by examining more directly the relation between timing of self-disclosure of sexual preference and the development of social skills and interpersonal competencies among sexual minority females.

The age at which participants achieved sexual developmental milestones was significantly younger among participants raised in urban than in rural settings. Relative to rural participants, the age at which urban participants became certain of their same-sex orientation and the age at which they experienced their first same-sex intimacy occurred several years earlier. The delayed initiation among sexual minority females raised in rural areas may also be a protective factor. Hence, not only do females raised in rural areas appear to wait longer than peers raised in urban areas to disclose their sexual orientation to others, they experience key psychosexual developmental milestones at a significantly older age.

We found no differences in rejection of sexual minority females by any type of relationship in which they had disclosed their sexual orientation. In general, participants felt somewhat accepted by friends and others in relatively distal relationships, regardless of their size of community of origin. On average, participants felt neither especially rejected nor particularly accepted by family members and parents to whom they had disclosed their sexual orientation. We found no relation between rejection and size of community of origin. Rural *vis-à-vis* urban residents were significantly more likely to self-disclose their sexual orientation to a family member.

Growing up in rural areas is not without greater challenges. Nonetheless, sexual minority females raised in rural and urban areas did not report differences in their experiences with verbal abuse, assaults, or threats of violence, whether by strangers or people they knew. The victimization findings in our study do not support the Community Psychology model.

Our strengths-based model considers the personal resilience and family resources that sexual minority females raised in rural areas bring to their psychosexual and psychosocial maturation. We do not deny that heterosexism is significantly greater in rural areas. However, social and family characteristics in rural areas are likely to buffer against the adverse effects of heterosexism. Where we did find differences, sexual minority females raised in urban vis-à-vis rural areas appeared to have more risks associated with poor mental health in adulthood. Moreover, we replicated these findings with a second study prior to publishing these results. Hence, we can be confident that our findings are not an artifact of using the Internet as a research tool (Mathy et al., 2002) or a carefully selected, community-based sample. This suggests closer kinship and friendship networks in rural vis-à-vis urban communities mediate the relation between cultural heterosexism and negative experiences. If heterosexism mediated the relation between relationships and untoward experiences, lesbian and bisexual females who grew up in rural areas would fare significantly worse than those who grew up in urban communities. Clearly, our data would not support this.

LIMITATIONS

Our data from both samples are dependent upon participants' retrospective recall and self-report. Our findings are limited to sexual minority females. The generalizability of our samples is unknown. Although our sampling designs are under investigation and validation, their generalizability generally remains unknown–and perhaps unknowable while same-sex attractions, behaviors, and relationships are socially stigmatized and oppressed. Mathy et al. (2002) have validated the Internet sample with comparisons to the U.S. population, a large stratified random sample drawn from the U.S., and a smaller random sample obtained by the Gallup Poll. The sampling design used to obtain it was more robust than the Gallup Poll's sample, and it yielded a sample with demographics that were as representative of the U.S. population, with the exception of age. Nonetheless, we did not include heterosexuals in our samples and we cannot generalize the findings to males or the entire U.S. female population. Society socializes females to be relatively nurturing and supportive of others (Gilligan, 1982). These characteristics may be more consonant with rural values and constraints on radical individualism. Society socializes males to be relatively individualistic. Hence, it is possible that sexual minority males reared in urban communities have better experiences than peers who grow up in rural areas. This may be an important avenue of further research. Sex-specific research that examines processes that mediate the relation between heterosexism and sexual minorities' experiences in diverse human ecologies may provide keen insights into methods of preventing risks among sexual minority youth.

Although the Internet sample has undergone rigorous validation (Mathy et al., 2002), the Coffee House sample has not. We are in the process of comparing the demographics of the Coffee House sample to census tract data that will determine how representative it is to the area from which it was drawn. Hypothetically, sampling from sexual minority venues in census tract blocks that are representative of a city will yield more representative samples than what researchers historically have obtained with snowball sampling or administering surveys in support groups, therapeutic networks, and social service systems. Until or unless society decreases its stigmatization and oppression of sexual minorities, researchers must find more sophisticated, robust methods of reaching them. Until we reach them and give voice to their experiences, we are all prisoners of the myths and mysterious contradictions perpetuated by stereotypes, ignorance, and naivete.

REFERENCES

Bellah, R. N., Madsen, R., Sullivan, W. M., Swidler, A., & Stipton, S. M. (1985). *Habits of the heart: Individualism and commitment in American life*. New York: Harper & Row.

Corliss, H. L., Cochran, S. D., Mays, V. M. (2003). Reports of parental maltreatment during childhood in a United States population-based survey of homosexual, bisexual, and heterosexual adults. *Child Abuse & Neglect*.

D'Augelli, A. R., & Hart, M. M. (1987). Gay women, men, and families in rural settings: Toward the development of helping communities. *American Journal of Community Psychology, 15(1),* 79-93.

D'Augelli, A. R., & Hershberger, S. L. (1993). Lesbian, gay, and bisexual youth in community settings: Personal challenges and mental health problems. *American Journal of Community Psychology, 21(4),* 421-448.

Desjarlais, R., Eisenberg, L., Good, B., & Kleinman, A. (1995). *World mental health: Problems and priorities in low-income countries*. New York: Oxford University Press.

Durkheim, E. (1893/1984). *The division of labor in society*, with an introduction by L. Coser. Translated by W. D. Halls. New York: Free Press.

Fernald, J. L. (1995). Interpersonal heterosexism. In B. Lott & D. Maluso (Eds.), *The social psychology of interpersonal discrimination*. New York: The Guilford Press.

Gallup Poll (1977). The Gallup opinion index: Political, social, and economic trends. *The Gallup Poll Monthly, 147,* 18.

Gallup Poll (1982). The Gallup report: Political, social, and economic trends. *The Gallup Poll Monthly*, *205*, 6.

Gallup Poll (1996). Do you think homosexual relations between consenting adults should or should not be legal? Unpublished cross-tabulations received via facsimile from M.A. Strausberg, Research Librarian, The Gallup Poll, on September 2, 1998. Princeton, NJ: The Gallup Organization.

Gilligan, C. (1982). *In a different voice*. Cambridge, MA: Harvard University Press.

Hammelman, T.L. (1993). Gay and lesbian youth: Contributing factors to serious attempts or considerations of suicide. *Journal of Gay and Lesbian Psychotherapy, 2* (*1*), 77-89.

Herek, G. M. (1993). The context of antigay violence: Notes on cultural and psychological heterosexism. In L. D. Garnets & D. C. Kimmel (Eds.), *Psychological perspectives on lesbian and gay male experiences*. New York: Columbia University Press.

Hershberger, S.L., & D'Augelli, A.R. (1995). The impact of victimization on the mental health and suicidality of lesbian, gay, and bisexual youths. *Developmental Psychology, 31(1)*, 65-74.

Hershberger, S.L., Pilkington, N.W., & D'Augelli, A.R. (1997). Predictors of suicide attempts among gay, lesbian, and bisexual youth. *Journal of Adolescent Research, 12(4)*, 447-497.

Hugick, L., & Leonard, J. (1991). Do you think homosexual relations between consenting adults should or should not be legal? Sex in America: Mirror of America. *The Gallup Poll Monthly*, 313, 60-73.

Hunter, J. (1990). Violence against lesbian and gay male youths. *Journal of Interpersonal Violence, 5*, 295-300.

Masten, A. S. (2001). Ordinary magic: Resilience processes in development. *American Psychologist, 56*(3), 227-238.

Mathy, R. M., Schillace, M., Coleman, S. M., & Berquist, B. E. (2002). Methodological rigor with internet samples: New ways to reach underrepresented populations. *CyberPsychology & Behavior, 5*(3), 253-266.

Moore, D. W. (1996). Public opposes gay marriages. *The Gallup Poll Monthly*, 318, 19-21.

Morris, J. F., Waldo, C. R., Rothblum, E. D. (2001). A model of predictors and outcomes of outness among lesbian and bisexual women. *American Journal of Orthopsychiatry, 71*(1), 61-71.

Proctor, C.D., & Groze, V.K. (1994). Risk factors for suicide among gay, lesbian, and bisexual youths. *Social Work, 39*, (*5*), 504-513.

Remafedi, G. (1987). Adolescent homosexuality: Psychosocial and medical implications. *Pediatrics, 79(3)*, 331-337.

Remafedi, G., Farrow, J.A., & Deisher, R.W. (1991). Risk factors for attempted suicide in gay and bisexual youth. *Pediatrics, 87(6)*, 869-875.

Remafedi, G., French, S., Story, M., Resnick, M.D., & Blum, R. (1998). The relationship between suicide risk and sexual orientation: Results of a population-based study. *American Journal of Public Health, 88(1)*, 57-60.

Rich, C.L., Fowler, R.C., Young, D., & Blenkush, M. (1986). San Diego suicide study: Comparison of gay to straight males. *Suicide and Life-Threatening Behavior, 16* (*4*), 448-457.

Rotheram-Borus, M.J., Hunter, J., & Rosario, M. (1994). Suicidal behavior and gay-related stress among gay and bisexual male adolescents. *Journal of Adolescent Research, 9(4)*, 498-508.

Rotheram-Borus, M.J., Rosario, M., Van Rossem, R., Reid, H., & Gillis, R. (1995). Prevalence, course, and predictors of multiple problem behaviors among gay and bisexual male adolescents. *Developmental Psychology, 31(1)*, 75-85.

Saad, L. (1997). Majority of Americans unfazed by Ellen's 'coming out' episode. *The Gallup Poll Monthly, 319*, 24-26.

United States Census Bureau (2002). *Statistical abstract of the United States.* Washington, D.C. U.S. Government Printing Office.

The Impact of Religiosity on Lesbian and Bisexual Women's Psychosexual Development: Child Maltreatment, Suicide Attempts, and Self-Disclosure

Robin M. Mathy, MSW, LGSW, MSc, MSt, MA
Marc Schillace

SUMMARY. We examined the relation between religiosity (importance of religion) and child maltreatment, psychosexual development,
self-disclosure of homosexuality and reactions to same with two samples of sexual minority women (Internet $n = 84$, Coffee House $n = 92$)
obtained with block sampling designs. Extremely important religiosity
currently was associated with precocious psychosexual development

Robin M. Mathy is Director of Research and Assistant Professor of Arts & Sciences
at Presentation College in Aberdeen, South Dakota, and is a Licensed Graduate Social
Worker in Minnesota. Mark Schillace is affiliated with the Inter-College Program,
University of Minnesota–Twin Cities.
Address correspondence to Robin M. Mathy (E-mail: math5577@umn.edu).
This work was supported, in part, by a grant from the American Foundation for Addiction Research, as well as a National Institute of Mental Health Supplemental Grant
for an Individual with a Disability (5RO1MH063328) to Robin M. Mathy. The authors
are grateful to Barrie E. Berquist and Sarah M. Coleman for their thorough reviews of
and suggestions on an earlier manuscript.

[Haworth co-indexing entry note]: "The Impact of Religiosity on Lesbian and Bisexual Women's
Psychosexual Development: Child Maltreatment, Suicide Attempts, and Self-Disclosure." Mathy, Robin M.,
and Marc Schillace. Co-published simultaneously in *Journal of Psychology & Human Sexuality* (The
Haworth Press, Inc.) Vol. 15, No. 2/3, 2003, pp. 73-100; and: *Lesbian and Bisexual Women's Mental Health*
(ed: Robin M. Mathy, and Shelly K. Kerr) The Haworth Press, Inc., 2003, pp. 73-100. Single or multiple copies of this article are available for a fee from The Haworth Document Delivery Service [1-800-HAWORTH,
9:00 a.m. - 5:00 p.m. (EST). E-mail address: docdelivery@haworthpress.com].

Digital Object Identifier: 10.1300/J056v15n02_05

and self-disclosure in the Internet sample only. Very important religiosity currently was associated with psychosexual development and self-disclosure of minority sexual orientation at significantly older ages. We discuss these results in the context of arguments that religiosity may be a risk factor for sexual minorities. Although not a risk factor in our samples, religiosity appeared to have lost the protective influence observed in studies of the general population. *[Article copies available for a fee from The Haworth Document Delivery Service: 1-800-HAWORTH. E-mail address: <docdelivery@haworthpress.com> Website: <http://www.HaworthPress.com> © 2003 by The Haworth Press, Inc. All rights reserved.]*

KEYWORDS. Religiosity, lesbian, suicide attempt, child abuse, psychosexual development

Research regarding sexual orientation and suicidal intent emerged from concerns about dramatic increases in rates of youth suicide during the latter half of the 20th century. More than a quarter century ago, Klagsbrun (1976) noted that rates of youth suicide had increased markedly over the preceding decades. Among youth aged 15-24 years, the suicide rate of 11.1 per 100,000 in 1998 was nearly three times (264%) greater than the rate of 4.2 per 100,000 in 1954 (Murphy, 2000; U.S. Bureau of the Census [Census Bureau], 1975). Suicide has been the third leading cause of death in this age group for nearly a decade (Census Bureau, 1994-1999; Murphy, 2000). Youth suicide results in the loss of over one million years of potential life every four years, with each death resulting in a total economic mortality cost of more than a million dollars (Census Bureau, 1999, Tables 140 and 154; cf. Frazier, 1989). Concerns about rising rates of youth suicide subsequently led to the 1989 *Report of the Secretary's Task Force on Youth Suicide*. A polemic about sexual orientation and suicidal behavior ensued when a social work activist suggested in the *Report* that gay and lesbian youth could comprise up to 30 percent of completed suicides in this age group annually (Gibson, 1989).

Researchers have since corroborated relatively high risks of suicide attempts among sexual minority youth (Remafedi, 1999a; Mathy, 2002). More recently, analyses of large, population-based samples have generalized these findings to adult men who have sex with men (Cochran & Mays, 2000; Paul et al., 2002). The relationship between sexual orientation and suicidal intent in population-based studies has been equivocal for female youth and young adult women (Remafedi, 1998; Garofalo, Wolf, Wissow, Woods, & Goodman, 1999; Skegg, Nada-Raja, Dickson, Paul, & Williams, 2003; Wichstrom & Hegna, 2003). However, a number of studies with less rigorous methodological designs have found increased risks of suicide attempts among adult lesbian and bisexual females. Morris, Waldo, and Rothblum (2001) found a relation between sexual orientation and suicide attempts among self-identified lesbian and bisexual females in a large, community-based sample. Researchers using data from another large, community-based sample (Matthews, Hughes, Johnson, Razzano, & Cassidy, 2002) found a relation between sexual orientation and suicide attempts among females with same-sex attraction or activity in the preceding year. Mathy (2002) found a relation between sexual orientation and suicide attempts among self-identified lesbian women as well as gay men in the United States.

Findings of an association between female sexual orientation and suicidal intent have not been limited to the U.S. Kuang, Mathy, Carol, and Nojima (this volume) reported that they found a relation between female sexual orientation and suicide attempts in Taiwan. In their longitudinal study of Norwegian young adults, Wichstrom and Hegna (2003) found that females as well as males had elevated risks for suicide attempts. King et al. (2003) examined the relationship between sexual orientation and mental health in a large, controlled, cross-sectional study in England and Wales. Relative to their heterosexual same-sex peers, lesbians and gay men were significantly more likely to report that they had engaged in self-harm behavior.

Some authors (Gibson, 1989, p. 127) have argued that familial religiosity is a risk factor for suicidal behavior among sexual minorities. This hypothesis would seem to follow logically from the results of national surveys (Gallup Organization, 1977, 1987, 1999), which have consistently demonstrated a clear relationship between respondents' disapproval of homosexuality and the importance they ascribe to religion. Some authors (Collins & Zimmerman, 1983; Strommen, 1993; Gillis, 1998) have suggested that family religiosity predicts negative responses toward gay, lesbian, and bisexual (GLB) family members. In fact, Gillis argued that culturally conservative Christians have been especially effective at characterizing GLB individuals as threats to the "traditional" family. There is empirical evidence that religious doctrines against homosexuality have been devastating for at least some family members of sexual minorities (Lease & Shulman, 2003). However, Lease and Shulman also found that about half (52%) of the family members of

GLB individuals who had reconciled conflicts between religious doctrine and their relative's sexual orientation did so by focusing on their faith's teachings about acceptance and unconditional love.

Researchers often assess religiosity with proxy variables such as frequency of worship service attendance or the importance of religion. Defined in this way, religiosity is an important protective factor for people in the general population. For example, Stack (1983) found a positive relation between church absence and suicide rates from 1954 to 1978. Koenig et al. (1994) found lower rates of psychopathology among individuals who attended church frequently, regardless of Protestant denomination. Stark, Doyle, and Rushing (1983) found a statistically significant (negative) relation between church membership and suicide rates.

Although importance of religion and frequency of worship service attendance are robust indices of religiosity, nationally representative samples obtained by the Gallup Organization have not found a relation between religiosity and major mainstream Christian (i.e., Catholic and Protestant) denominations. Empirical peer-reviewed research (Koenig, George, Meador, Blazer, & Dyck, 1994) also has not found differences in religiosity by levels of conservatism within specific faiths. Although there is a strong relation between right-wing authoritarianism and religious fundamentalism in non-Christian faiths (Hunsberger, 1996), this is also true for Christian denominations (Altemeyer & Hunsberger, 1992). Hence, importance of religion is a good measure of religiosity precisely because it is not associated with particular denominations, political or social conservatism, or authoritarianism.

In this paper, we focus on the "importance of religion" to assess participant's religiosity as well as their perceptions of their parents' religiosity. This indicator of religiosity has been widely used in national surveys, including Gallup Polls and the National Survey on Drug Use and Health [NDDUH] (Office of Applied Studies [OSA], 2003). For example, the OSA asked youth "whether their religious beliefs are a very important part of their lives" (2004). The NSDUH assesses use of cigarettes, alcohol, and illicit drugs in the previous month. The survey found that youth's use of alcohol in the previous month varied significantly by importance of religion to them (27%, not very important; 15%, very important).

The assertion that religion constitutes a risk factor for sexual minority youth (Gibson, 1989, 1992) is inconsistent with other work indicating that religion is a protective factor against suicidal intent for youth and adults in the general population. In fact, in the same volume of the

Report in which Gibson asserted that religion is a risk factor for sexual minority youth, an overview by the National Conference on Prevention and Interventions concluded that, "Religion and family are social contexts in which people are physically, emotionally and psychologically bonded. Religious commitment and strong family ties, in general, provide *protection* from suicide by promoting shared values, strong social interaction and supportive connections with other people" (p. 12; emphasis added). Thus, if we were to accept the assertion that religion constitutes a risk factor for sexual minorities, we would need to obtain empirical evidence that it affects GLB youth (and adults) differently than it does heterosexual youth and adults. However, in counterpoint to the contention that religion is a risk factor for sexual minorities, Carlson (1992) argued that the "data point to a common conclusion: religious belief saves lives, particularly among women and youth" (1992, p. 113).

Thus, it would seem important to examine the role of religiosity (importance of religion) in the lives of sexual minorities. Although religiosity is a protective factor in the general population, its association with heterosexism may imbue risks for sexual minorities. Heterosexism is a major source of social violence in the United States (Fineran, 2002). Perceived discrimination is significantly associated with psychiatric morbidity among lesbian, gay, and bisexual adults in the United States, and it adversely affects their quality of life (Mays & Cochran, 2002). Psychiatric morbidity is associated with increased risks of suicidal intent, and sexual minorities have increased risks for depressive disorders, anxiety, and other stress-related disorders (Cochran & Mays, 2000; Cochran, Sullivan, & Mays, 2003; Gilman, Cochran, Hughes, Ostrow, & Kessler, 2001).

Heterosexist violence may mediate the relation between religiosity and mental health. Religiosity may also exert a positive influence on sexual minorities. We would hypothesize that lesbian and bisexual females who grow up in families in which religion is important may be less likely to be sexually precocious. Sexual precocity may undermine GLB adolescents' abilities to develop social skills needed to self-disclose their sexual orientation to others. Put somewhat differently, we might expect that GLB adolescents who begin sexual exploration at an older age have more advanced cognitive development and hence better formal operations skills. More advanced cognitive and social skills may help sexual minority youth optimize decisions about to whom and when to disclose their sexual orientation, resulting in less rejection and more favorable reactions from others. D'Augelli and Hershberger (1993) found that GLB youth who engage in sexual behavior and self-disclose their sexual orientation to others at older ages are less likely to attempt suicide. Morris, Waldo, and Rothblum (2001) found that social support mediated lesbian and bisexual women's suicidal intent. Self-disclosure is necessary for garnering social support to cope with stressors related to self-awareness and self-acceptance of same-sex attractions, a factor that mitigates sexual minorities' suicidal intent (Rutter & Soucar, 2002) despite increasing the risks for interpersonal rejection by friends and family members.

Schneider, Farberow, and Kruks (1989) found that family problems are associated with gay male suicide attempts. Several studies have found that sexual minorities are at increased risk for family factors associated with suicidal intent. Matthews et al. (2002) found that lesbian and bisexual females, relative to their heterosexual peers, were significantly more likely to report a history of sexual abuse. In a population-based survey of midlife adults, a greater percentage of sexual minorities than heterosexuals reported a history of child maltreatment (Corliss, Cochran, & Mays, 2002). Sexual abuse, physical abuse, and neglect are significant pathways to suicidal behaviors (Shaunesey, Cohen, Plummer, & Berman, 1993; MoⱯcicki, 1995; Wagner, Cole, & Schwartzman, 1995, 1996). Longitudinal, community-based research has found that child maltreatment is associated with youths' suicide attempts even after controlling for age, sex, and symptoms of psychopathology (Johnson et al., 2002).

We are unaware of any studies that have examined the role of religiosity in the relationship between sexual orientation and suicidal intent. Indeed, the dearth of studies on this topic is notable given the assertion that, "Family problems are probably the most significant factor in youth suicide" (Gibson, 1992, p. 103). Hypothetically, families in which religion is very important, relative to others, may be more likely to act out their heterosexism by inflicting maltreatment on their children. Alternatively, one might hypothesize that parents are predisposed to call upon the love and acceptance of their faith when religion is very important, leading them to be less likely to inflict maltreatment on their offspring.

To evaluate the effects of religiosity in families of lesbian and bisexual women, we conducted two studies to answer several questions. First, is there a relationship between importance of religion and suicidal intent or child maltreatment? Second, is there is a relationship between suicidal intent or child maltreatment and participants' perceptions of their parents' religiosity? Third, is religiosity associated with age of self-disclosure or with others' reactions to the self-disclosure of their sexual orientation?

METHODS

We conducted two studies to test the competing hypotheses about the positive vis-à-vis-negative impact of religiosity on sexual minorities. We obtained one of these samples via an Internet chat room ($n = 84$) in the mid to late 1990s and another sample from a coffee house in Minneapolis, Minnesota, in the late 1990s. Published elsewhere is the validation of the design and methodology for the Internet sample (Mathy, Coleman, Schillace, & Berquist, 2002). We have described elsewhere in this volume (see Mathy, Carol, and Schillace) the Sample and the Methods used to conduct the research reported in this paper. We drew the data for these two studies from a research project (Sexual Orientation and Families of Origin [Robin M. Mathy, Principal Investigator]) archived at the Kinsey Institute for Sex, Gender, and Reproduction in Bloomington, Indiana. The Institutional Review Board at the University of Minnesota authorized the analysis of these archived data in the research conducted for this paper.

The survey included 140 items. Only items related to suicidal intent, family religiosity, child maltreatment, psychosexual development, self-disclosure, and others' initial reactions upon self-disclosure are discussed here.

Religiosity. To assess religiosity, we asked participants, "Which of the following best describes your religious orientation? Religion is:" with response categories including: [Extremely important to me] [Very important to me] [Somewhat important to me] [Not important to me]. To assess participants' perceptions of their parents' religiosity, we asked, "If your [MOTHER] [FATHER] were to be asked the following questions, what do you think [SHE] [HE] would answer for [HERSELF] [HIMSELF]?" "Religious orientation? Religion is:" The response categories were [Extremely important to me] [Very important to me] [Somewhat important to me] [Not important to me].

Child Maltreatment. We evaluated child maltreatment by asking participants to complete the statement, "For at least some of my childhood and adolescence, [my mother] [my father] (or primary [female] [male] caregiver) was (INDICATE ALL THAT APPLY)." Response categories included: [Sexually] [Physically] [Emotionally] [Psychologically] [Verbally] [Spiritually] abusive, or [None of the above]. These categories emerged from prior ethnographic research using a grounded theory method designed to determine the meanings participants attributed to labels they ascribed to categories of maltreatment. Sexual and physical abuses are relatively self-explanatory. Verbal abuse was a distinct category. Ethnographic research revealed that emotional abuse is synonymous with neglect (an act of omission). It included behaviors such as repeated or prolonged parental absence without explanation or justification, persistently refusing to acknowledge the participant, and denial or withholding of food, clothing, or requested medical or mental health treatment. Psychological abuses included verbal abuse, such as yelling, shouting, and name-calling. It also included aggressive and intimidating nonverbal behaviors that conveyed contempt, threats, or rejection. Spiritual abuse included references to other worldly sanctions, in a manner intended to elicit fear or pain. All sexual abuse is *ipso facto* physical abuse, and all physical abuse is *ipso facto* psychological abuse. Each category of abuse connotes an act of commission that causes pain or harm. Neglect differs from these in that it is an act of omission that either caused or could have prevented pain or harm to the participant. We scored each abuse or neglect category as a binary variable (yes or no).

Suicidal Intent. To assess suicidal intent, we asked participants to endorse one of the following alternatives: [I have never imagined suicide] [I have imagined suicide, but never seriously considered it] [I have seriously considered suicide, but never attempted it] [I have attempted suicide] and [I have attempted suicide more than once].

Self-Disclosure and Psychosexual Development. We asked participants, "At what age did you first" (a) "*think* you might be attracted," (b) "become *certain* you were attracted," (c) "tell another person of your sexual attraction," (d) "tell a close friend of your sexual attraction," (e) "tell a family member of your sexual attraction," and (f) "tell a parent of your sexual attraction to people of your *own sex?*" We also asked participants, "At what age, if ever, did you first become sexually intimate with a person of your *own sex?*" For each of these items, participants could indicate that the question, "Does not apply to me."

Social Support and Rejection. We asked participants to indicate others responses to their self-disclosure of their sexual orientation. Participants completed the statement, "When I first told [another person] [a close friend] [a family member] [a parent] I am attracted to people of my own sex, I felt:" Each response was scored on a 7-point unanchored Likert scale, ranging from "Extremely rejected" to "Extremely accepted," with a midpoint of, "Neither rejected nor accepted."

Procedure

A more detailed description of the procedure can be found elsewhere (Mathy et al., 2002). The project (Sexual Orientation and Families of

Origin) from which this study's data were drawn are archived at the Kinsey Institute in Bloomington, Indiana. Use of these archived data for the present study was approved by the Institutional Review Board at the University of Minnesota–Twin Cities. Briefly, prospective participants were approached via "private message," seen only by the sender and recipient. They were asked "to participate in a study of sexual orientation and family of origin." Following informed disclosure and assurance of confidentiality, participants were asked to send the author an electronic mail (email) request for a survey. Upon receipt of the request, a survey was sent via email to the sender, with a free encryption program with which to return the completed questionnaire. Submission of the completed questionnaire signified voluntary consent for agreement of participation. The archived data contain no identifying information. All data were analyzed with SPSS 10.0 in a Windows Millennium Edition operating environment, on an IBM compatible personal computer. As conventionally accepted in positivist research, we accepted up to a 5 percent risk of erroneously rejecting the null hypothesis of equality (i.e., $p < .05$). The alternative hypothesis was inequality.

RESULTS

Religiosity and Child Maltreatment

The mean score for importance of religion was significantly lower among Internet-sample participants who had a positive versus negative history of maternal childhood neglect (see Table 1), $t_{(2,80)} = 3.35$, $p < .001$. Participants' perceptions of paternal religiosity were higher, on average, when Internet-sample participants reported a positive versus negative history of paternal spiritual abuse. There were no other statistically significant differences in either the Internet or Coffee House samples.

Maternal Maltreatment. With the exception of maternal sexual abuse, we found statistically significant ($p < .05$) correlations among all maternal abuse categories in both samples. Correlations ranged from .239 (psychological and spiritual abuses) to .688 (neglect and psychological abuse) in the Internet sample, and from .271 (sexual and physical abuses) to .596 (verbal abuse and neglect) in the coffee house sample. Maternal sexual abuse was correlated only with physical abuse ($r = .256$, $p < .05$) and spiritual abuse ($r = .298$, $p < .01$) in the Internet

TABLE 1

	Father							Mother							Participant						
	No			Yes			|t|(2,75)	No			Yes			|t|(2.75)	No			Yes			|t|(2,80)
	N	M	SD	N	M	SD		N	M	SD	N	M	SD		N	M	SD	N	M	SD	
Child Maltreatment (No or Yes) by Mean Importance of Religion to Father, Mother, and Participant in the Internet Sample																					
Maternal																					
Sexual	76	1.25	1.20	1	3.00		1.45	76	1.59	1.20	1	3.00		1.16	81	0.89	1.07	1	0.00		0.83
Physical	65	1.23	1.18	12	1.50	1.38	0.71	65	1.62	1.16	12	1.58	1.51	0.70	70	0.89	1.07	12	0.83	1.12	0.16
Neglect	56	1.38	1.18	21	1.00	1.27	1.22	56	1.63	1.15	21	1.57	1.36	0.86	59	1.07	1.14	23	0.39	0.66	3.35***
Psych	60	1.25	1.20	17	1.35	1.27	0.31	60	1.62	1.15	17	1.59	1.42	0.08	63	1.00	1.11	19	0.47	0.84	1.91
Verbal	59	1.31	1.15	18	1.17	1.43	0.38	60	1.57	1.16	17	1.76	1.39	0.54	62	1.06	1.10	20	0.30	0.73	3.55***
Spiritual	68	1.25	1.20	9	1.44	1.33	0.45	68	1.54	1.19	9	2.11	1.27	1.33	73	0.95	1.07	9	0.33	1.00	1.64
Paternal																					
Sexual	68	1.24	1.17	8	1.38	1.51	0.76	68	1.57	1.18	8	1.75	1.49	0.70	73	0.90	1.10	8	0.75	0.89	0.70
Physical	60	1.18	1.13	16	1.50	1.46	0.43	61	1.59	1.15	15	1.60	1.45	0.98	65	0.89	1.06	16	0.88	1.15	0.95
Neglect	51	1.18	1.14	25	1.40	1.32	0.76	52	1.58	1.21	24	1.63	1.21	0.16	55	0.93	1.09	26	0.81	1.06	0.47
Psych	57	1.18	1.17	19	1.47	1.31	0.94	57	1.60	1.15	19	1.58	1.39	0.05	61	0.85	1.05	20	1.00	1.17	0.53
Verbal	54	1.20	1.14	22	1.36	1.36	0.49	55	1.58	1.17	21	1.62	1.32	0.12	59	0.88	1.05	22	0.91	1.15	0.10
Spiritual	71	1.17	1.16	5	2.40	1.34	2.28*	71	1.56	1.19	5	2.00	1.41	0.78	76	0.87	1.04	5	1.20	1.64	0.67
Child Maltreatment (No or Yes) by Mean Importance of Religion to Father, Mother, and Participant in the Coffee House Sample																					
Maternal																					
Sexual	88	1.33	1.10	1	3.00		1.51	91	1.88	1.14	1	2.00		0.11	90	0.93	1.04	1	3.00		0.06
Physical	77	1.34	1.08	12	1.42	1.31	0.23	80	1.84	1.16	12	2.17	0.94	0.94	79	0.91	1.02	12	1.08	1.17	0.54
Neglect	47	1.32	1.13	42	1.38	1.10	0.26	48	1.77	1.15	44	2.00	1.12	0.97	47	0.74	0.97	44	1.14	1.07	1.84
Psych	66	1.45	1.13	23	1.04	1.02	1.54	68	1.91	1.10	24	1.79	1.25	0.44	67	0.87	1.00	24	1.13	1.12	1.06
Verbal	63	1.46	1.16	26	1.08	0.94	1.63	64	1.80	1.14	28	2.07	1.12	1.07	63	0.86	0.97	28	1.11	1.17	1.07
Spiritual	79	1.42	1.12	10	0.80	0.92	1.68	82	1.82	1.13	10	2.30	1.16	1.24	81	0.88	0.99	10	1.40	1.27	1.53
Paternal																					
Sexual	80	1.36	1.13	9	1.22	0.97	0.36	82	1.83	1.12	10	2.30	1.25	1.24	81	0.93	1.01	10	1.00	1.25	0.21
Physical	73	1.36	1.10	16	1.31	1.20	0.14	75	1.91	1.12	17	1.76	1.25	0.46	74	0.97	1.06	17	0.76	0.90	0.75
Neglect	57	1.40	1.15	32	1.25	1.05	0.63	59	1.98	1.12	33	1.70	1.16	1.16	59	0.90	1.00	32	1.00	1.11	0.45
Psych	60	1.35	1.15	29	1.35	1.05	0.02	62	1.95	1.09	30	1.73	1.23	0.86	61	0.95	0.99	30	0.90	1.13	0.22
Verbal	66	1.44	1.14	23	1.09	1.00	1.41	68	1.96	1.10	24	1.67	1.24	1.07	68	0.93	1.01	23	0.96	1.11	0.12
Spiritual	82	1.33	1.10	7	1.57	1.27	0.55	85	1.92	1.13	7	1.43	1.27	1.10	84	0.89	1.01	7	1.43	1.27	1.33

Note: In Internet sample, *p < .05; ***p < .001; We assumed equal variances unless the Levene's Test for Equality of Variances was statistically significant, p < .05. For maternal maltreatment categories, we could not assume equal variances for physical abuse (importance of religion to mother), df = 2.68; psychological abuse (mother), df = 2.13; neglect (participant), df = 2.68; psychological abuse (mother), df = 2.22; verbal abuse (father), df = 2.24; verbal abuse (participant), df = 2.49. For paternal categories, we could not assume equal variances for psychological abuse (mother), df = 2.27; physical abuse (father), df = 2.19; psychological abuse (mother), df = 2.20; physical abuse (mother), df = 2.34; spiritual abuse (participant), df = 2,4.

Note: In Coffee House sample, under maternal verbal abuse (importance of religion to fathers), the Levene's Test for Equality of Variances was F = 8.66, p < .01. Therefore, equal variances were not assumed and t-test df = 2,58. For paternal verbal abuse (fathers), F = 4.09, p < .05, therefore t-test df = 2,44.

sample, and with physical abuse in the coffee house sample ($r = .271$, $p < .01$).

Paternal Maltreatment. In the Internet sample, we found significant correlations between paternal spiritual, verbal, and psychological abuses and all other categories of abuse, including sexual. These correlations ranged from .252 (verbal and sexual abuse) to .819 (verbal and physical abuse). Paternal sexual abuse was uncorrelated with psychological abuse or neglect in this sample. Paternal sexual abuse was uncorrelated with physical abuse or verbal abuse in the Coffee House sample. In the Coffee House sample, paternal spiritual abuse was not associated with physical abuse or verbal abuse, though it was associated with sexual abuse ($r = .295, p < .01$), neglect ($r = .298, p < .01$), and psychological abuse ($r = .325, p < .01$). Paternal neglect and psychological abuse were associated with all other categories of abuse. Significant correlations in the Coffee House sample ranged from .298 (neglect and spiritual abuse) to .640 (verbal abuse and neglect).

We inspected non-physical and non-sexual abuses to determine whether we needed to collapse any of the maltreatment categories. However, there were no Pearson's correlations greater than .707, which would have resulted in a correlation coefficient (r^2) of .5. If $r^2 = .5$, each variable explains half the variance in the corresponding variable, effectively making redundant the explanatory value of the highly correlated variables.

Religiosity and Suicidal Intent

Participants' religiosity scores did not differentiate suicide attempters ($n = 15$, $M = .60$, $SD = 1.12$) from non-attempters ($n = 67$, $M = .94$, $SD = 1.06$), $t_{(2,80)} = 1.12, p = .27$. Participants' perceptions of their parents' religiosity also did not differentiate attempters from non-attempters. Among suicide attempters, perceived paternal and maternal religiosities averaged scores of 0.60 ($SD = 1.32$) and 1.20 ($SD = 1.37$), respectively. The corresponding mean religiosity scores for non-attempters were 1.29 ($SD = 1.19$) and 1.56 ($SD = 1.17$), respectively.

Religiosity, Psychosexual Development, and Self-Disclosure

Analyses of variance (ANOVA) revealed a statistically significant relation between participants' religiosity and psychosexual development as well as self-disclosure in the Internet sample (see Table 2). Despite the statistically significant F test statistics, closer inspection of

TABLE 2. Psychosexual Development and Self-Disclosure by Importance of Religion

| | Internet Sample | | |
	Father	Mother	Participant
Development			
Might Be	F(3,73) = 0.99	F(3,73) = 2.68	F(3,78) = 3.41*
Certain	F(3,71) = 1.02	F(3,71) = 2.22	F(3,76) = 2.15
Intimate	F(3,53) = 0.76	F(3,52) = 1.13	F(3,57) = 3.22*
Self-Disclosure			
Told Another	F(3,72) = 0.80	F(3,72) = 1.60	F(3,77) = 7.33***
Told Friend	F(3,64) = 0.68	F(3,64) = 2.14	F(3,69) = 3.84*
Told Family	F(3,41) = 0.56	F(3,41) = 0.62	F(3,45) = 3.23*
Told Parent	F(3,27) = 0.72	F(3,27) = 1.08	F(3,31) = 1.27
	Coffee House Sample		
	Father	Mother	Participant
Development			
Might Be	F(3,84) = 2.40	F(3,87) = 1.81	F(3,86) = 1.89
Certain	F(3,82) = 0.79	F(3,85) = 1.92	F(3,84) = 0.27
Intimate	F(3,80) = 0.40	F(3,83) = 2.84*	F(3,82) = 1.99
Self-Disclosure			
Told Another	F(3,84) = 1.13	F(3,87) = 0.98	F(3,86) = 1.75
Told Friend	F(3,82) = 1.31	F(3,85) = 0.97	F(3,84) = 1.79
Told Family	F(3,73) = 0.73	F(3,75) = 2.99	F(3,74) = 0.94
Told Parent	F(3,60) = 0.37	F(3,61) = 2.06	F(3,60) = 0.44

Note. *p < .05; ***p < .001.

these data revealed a curvilinear relationship. Participants for whom religion was most important were the first, on average, to question their sexual orientation ($M = 11.10$, $SD = 4.82$, $n = 10$), followed by participants for whom religion was not at all important ($M = 12.24$, $SD = 4.75$, $n = 42$) and those for whom religion was only somewhat important ($M = 13.00$, $SD = 3.51$, $n = 18$). Post hoc analyses revealed a statistically significant difference between participants for whom religion was not at all important and those who indicated that it was very important ($M = 17.08$, $SD = 7.62$, $n = 12$), $p < .05$. Similarly, participants for whom religion was "extremely important" were, on average, the youngest when they had same-sex intimacy and when they told another person and a family member of their sexual orientation. Conversely, participants for whom religion was very but not extremely important were, on average, the oldest when they (a) questioned their sexual orientation, (b) became certain of it, (c) told another person about it, (d) told a friend about it, and (e) told a family member about it. These results appear in Table 3.

TABLE 3. Importance of Religion by Ages of Psychosexual Development and Self-Disclosure of Sexual Orientation, Internet Sample Only

| Importance | Sexual Development | | Self-Disclosure | | |
	Might Be[a]	Intimate[b]	Another	Friend	Family
Not at All	12.2 (4.8)	17.4 (4.8)	17.6 (4.0)	18.2 (4.2)	19.3 (3.9)
Somewhat	13.0 (3.5)	16.9 (2.3)	16.7 (2.4)	**17.2 (2.1)**	18.4 (2.5)
Very	*17.1 (7.6)*	*22.0 (6.9)*	*23.4 (6.9)*	*19.3 (3.9)*	*26.0 (12.3)*
Extremely	**11.1 (4.8)**	**15.8 (4.2)**	**15.7 (5.7)**	17.6 (1.9)	**17.6 (1.9)**

Notes. [a]Age at which participant first thought she might be attracted to a person of the same sex. [b]Age at which participant first engaged in same-sex intimacy. Levels of religiosity with the youngest ages are bolded. Levels of religiosity with the oldest ages are italicized.

Independent sample *t*-tests did not yield statistically significant differences between levels of religiosity among participants who had versus had not disclosed their sexual orientation to a close friend, a family member, or a parent. However, self-disclosure to another person was associated with level of maternal religiosity in the Internet sample only, $t (2, 74) = -10.31, p < .001$.

We found only one significant ANOVA in the Coffee House sample, $F (3,83) = 2.84, p < .05$. In this sample, there was a linear trend between perceptions of maternal religiosity and mean age at which participants first engaged in same-sex intimacy. Participants who scored mothers as "not at all" on religiosity were the youngest, on average, when they first engaged in same-sex intimacy ($M = 16.79, SD = 5.84$), followed by those who assessed religion as "somewhat" important to their mothers ($M = 18.87, SD 4.96$). Participants who perceived religion to be very important to their mothers were 20.79 years old ($SD = 5.28$), on average, when they had their first same-sex intimacy. Participants who gave their mothers the highest scores on religiosity were, on average, the oldest when they first engaged in same-sex intimacy ($M = 22.54, SD = 8.53$).

Religiosity and Reactions Following Self-Disclosure of Sexual Orientation

In the Internet sample, reactions following self-disclosure of sexual orientation to parents was significantly associated with participants' perceptions of their mothers' religiosity, $F (3,26) = 3.43, p < .05$. However, post hoc analyses revealed no statistically significant pairwise associations. There were no other significant findings in the Internet sample. In the Coffee House sample, reactions following self-disclosure of sexual orientation to a family member were significantly associated with participants' perceptions of mothers' religiosity, F (3,75) = 2.87, $p < .05$. In this sample, there was a significant association between reactions to self-disclosure of sexual orientation to a parent and participants' perceptions of fathers' religiosity. Post hoc tests with Dunnett's C revealed a significant bivariate relationship between the mean religiosity scores for extremely important ($M = 2.82$, $SD = 1.38$) and not at all important ($M = 5.12$, $SD = 1.73$), F (3,66) = 4.80, $p < .01$. Analyses of variance revealed a significant association between the perceived importance of religion to mothers and participants' feelings of acceptance or rejection, F (3,75) = 2.87, $p < .05$. However, post hoc tests with Dunnett's C did not reveal any significant pairwise associations.

DISCUSSION

Limitations

This study had several limitations. First, we did not include males, nor did the sample have females exclusively or predominantly attracted to males. Neither study included a heterosexual control group. Participants in both studies may have been subject to biases endemic to retrospective recall and self-report. Participants' appraisals of their religiosity in the present may have changed considerably since childhood, and participants with precocious sexuality may have begun to attribute more importance to religion as they matured. Our data were drawn from archived cross-sectional studies, so we cannot know the extent to which child maltreatment and adolescent sexuality affected participants' adult religiosity. However, a longitudinal study conducted with data drawn from the National Longitudinal Survey of Youth (Hardy & Raffaeli, 2003; $n = 303$) did not support a bidirectional association between sexual maturity and religiosity. Instead, Hardy and Raffaelli reported that adolescents with higher levels of religiosity were more likely than were peers with lower levels of religiosity to delay onset of sexual involvement (Hardy & Raffaelli, 2003). Chandy, Blum, and Resnick (1996) found that adolescent religiosity was a protective factor against the adverse effects of sexual abuse. There does not appear to be a clear relationship between child maltreatment and adult religiosity.

Participants' appraisals of their parents' religiosity may differ considerably from the actual importance of religion to their parents. Confidentiality and the sampling procedures used in this study precluded direct assessment of parents' actual religiosity. Further, we used only one indicator of religiosity: Importance of religion. Future research might benefit by examining the relation between sexual minorities' development and other aspects of religiosity, such as importance of spirituality or frequency of worship service attendance.

There has been a significant dearth of information about family religiosity in lesbian and bisexual females. Many authors have reported significantly greater difficulties finding or eliciting participation from lesbians than gay males (Young-Bruehl, 1996; Bell, Weinberg, & Hammersmith, 1981). For example, Bell et al. noted they were unable to recruit lesbian respondents from private bars or public places, where they found many of their gay male respondents. In fact, they reported that they obtained most of their lesbian respondents through personal contacts. The Internet provides a medium readily available to researchers and many (if not most) sexual minorities in the United States. This is a valid, reliable, and effective way to locate a heterogeneous sample of difficult-to-reach subjects (Mathy et al., 2002). The Internet and community-owned coffee houses appear to provide less biased sampling venues than community agencies or mental health centers (e.g., D'Augelli & Hershberger, 1993; Hunter, 1990; Rotheram-Borus, Hunter, & Hosario, 1994), support groups and educational milieu (e.g., Schneider, Farberow, & Kruks, 1989), or clinical professional listings (e.g., Kourany, 1987). In fact, researchers have drawn most of the previous community-based samples used in studies of sexual orientation and suicidal intent from such sources. Population-based studies have had difficulty obtaining large enough samples of lesbians, and many have combined lesbian and gay male respondents (Remafedi, 1999a) despite the significant differences between these groups.

Although the Internet sample used in this study was validated previously (Mathy et al., 2002), the validity and reliability of sampling from a community-owned coffee house is unknown, and it constitutes a convenience sample. We elected to use this coffee house dataset in order to verify the findings obtained in the Internet sample. Nonetheless, time-space venue sampling from sites frequented by sexual minorities may be a viable alternative for obtaining a robust sample in the future. Public Health researchers have used this sampling design successfully (Stueve, O'Connell, Duran, San Doval, & Blome, 2001). We would suggest that future studies should include more feminist and lesbian venues, such as lesbian community-owned coffee houses, bookstores, recreational softball leagues, and other social sources commonly frequented by sexual minority women.

Religiosity and Child Maltreatment

The data in Table 1 indicate that child maltreatment was prevalent among the lesbian and bisexual female participants in this study. Although maternal sexual abuse was uncommon ($n = 1$ in each sample), paternal sexual abuse was relatively frequent (9.8% and 10.9% in the Internet and Coffee House samples, respectively). Prior studies have found similar rates of sexual abuse among heterosexual women and sexual minority females (Corliss et al., 2003). Prevalence of physical abuse in our samples was consistent with rates of major physical maltreatment found in Corliss et al.'s study of sexual orientation and child maltreatment among midlife adults. They reported that the percentages of lesbian and bisexual women who acknowledged major physical maltreatment by mothers and fathers were 22.8% and 15.1%, respectively. However, the percentages of lesbian and bisexual women who reported any maternal or paternal physical maltreatment were 32.8% and 27.2%, respectively. We found that 15.7% of our Internet sample and 13% of our Coffee House sample reported maternal physical abuse. The percentages of paternal physical abuse were 31.7% in the Internet Sample and 35.9% in the Coffee House sample. Corliss et al. reported that 38.% of lesbian and bisexual women reported emotional maltreatment by their mothers, and 28.6% acknowledged emotional maltreatment by fathers. We found that 22.9% of participants in the Internet sample and 26.1% of respondents in the Coffee House sample reported maternal psychological abuse. Percentages of participants in these samples who reported maternal verbal abuse were 24.1% and 30.4%, respectively. Paternal psychological abuse was reported by nearly one-fourth (24.4%) of our Internet sample as well as one-third of the Coffee House sample. Over one-fourth of both samples (28.0% Internet, 26.1% Coffee House) reported paternal verbal abuse. The Gallup Poll (Moore, 1995) found that 33% of parents admitted they had verbally abused their children.

We found very high correlations among various forms of abuse, with the exception of maternal sexual abuse. This suggests that lesbian and bisexual females in our study usually experienced more than one form of abuse. The strongest correlation by far was between paternal verbal and physical abuses ($r = .82$), indicating that the occurrence of either form of abuse accounted for approximately two-thirds of the variance in the other. This implies that paternal physical abuse was closely associated with paternal verbal abuse. Thus, clinicians who work with lesbian and bisexual females should be sensitive to their high co-occurrence. It may be easier for some lesbian and bisexual women to acknowledge verbal abuse before disclosing physical abuse. We need further clinical research and better designed studies, particularly with population-based samples, to examine the high co-occurrence of various types of maltreatment in lesbian and bisexual women's childhoods.

Despite the prevalence and co-occurrence of child maltreatment in our lesbian and bisexual women's childhoods, we found that only neglect and verbal abuse were significantly associated with our participants' religiosity–and then only in the more methodologically robust Internet sample (Mathy et al., 2002). It is notable that the mean level of religiosity was higher among participants who had *not* experienced these forms of maltreatment. We found no evidence whatsoever that religiosity was a risk factor for participants. Nor did we find any association between participants' appraisals of their parents' religiosity and their reports of child maltreatment. These results are likely to be surprising to readers who expected religiosity to be a risk factor for sexual minorities. Based on predictions that religiosity poses a risk factor for sexual minorities, we might have expected to find that participants who experienced child maltreatment gave parents higher scores on indices of religiosity than did those who did not experience child maltreatment. However, this was not the case. In fact, where there were statistically significant differences between maltreated participants and their peers (maternal neglect and verbal abuse), importance of religion was a protective factor.

Many sexual minority youth report experiences of child maltreatment. Alas, child maltreatment in the general population is not uncommon. The National Centers for Child Abuse and Neglect reports more than 900,000 cases of substantiated child maltreatment a year, with over half (53.5%) representing cases of neglect (U. S. Department of Health and Human Services, 1998). Perhaps because corporal punishment is socially condoned in the U. S. (Straus, 1994), the typical child abuse scenario begins with a parent who intends to discipline a child and escalates to the point the child is physically harmed, in part because parents have a poor conception of their own strength and the compounding effect of their anger (Zigler & Hall, 1989, p. 57; see also Belsky, 1993). Belsky noted that the disciplinary practices of abusive and nonabusive parents differ. Generally, abusive parents are more likely to rely on physical and aversive methods of control, without an attempt to use inductive reasoning. Feshbach (1998) noted that physically abusive parents score lower on empathy, and parents who are low in empathy are more likely than others to have children with self-regulatory difficulties or other symptoms of maladjustment. Insofar as suicidal and self-destructive behavior are presumed to be developmentally maladaptive (Linehan, 1993), it would seem reasonable to expect that parents who do not (physically) abuse their children would be more likely to have children who do not attempt suicide.

Religiosity and Suicidal Intent

Religiosity was neither a risk nor a protective factor in either of our studies. Religiosity is a common protective factor against suicidal intent in the general population. The absence of a difference in levels of religiosity between attempters and non-attempters may suggest that the protective factor has been lost. The loss of a protective factor may be as serious as acquiring a risk factor. We need further research with better-designed studies, particularly those using use population-based samples, to examine the specific mechanisms that may account for this finding. Although religion does not appear to be either a risk or a protective factor relative to suicidal intent, further research is needed to determine whether the absence of religiosity's protective influence in our studies suggest the loss of a key protective factor among lesbian and bisexual females.

Religiosity, Psychosexual Development, and Self-Disclosure

Participants' religiosity mediated psychosexual development and self-disclosure. However, the relationship between religiosity and each domain was somewhat counter-intuitive. With the exception of disclosure of same-sex attraction to another person, the youngest lesbians to experience significant psychosexual milestones and to disclose their sexual orientation were those for whom religion was most important. However, the oldest lesbians to reach significant psychosexual milestones were those for whom religion was very but not extremely important. Participants for whom religion was either somewhat or not at all important were intermediate between these two groups. Further, parental religiosity did not mediate any of the psychosexual or self-disclosure variables. These findings suggest that there is not a linear relation between religiosity and psychosexual development or self-disclosure.

These findings do not support either the thesis that religiosity is a risk factor nor the thesis that it is a protective factor relative to psychosexual development and self-disclosure among sexual minorities. We would hypothesize that sexual minorities for whom religion is very important are more reserved or cautious than those for whom religion is extremely important. This may be associated with a reluctance to accept doctrinal teachings unconditionally, while simultaneously maintaining a high fidelity to their faith. Conversely, individuals for whom religion is very important may be better able to assimilate or accommodate a sexual orientation discordant with their faith's doctrines. Again, we need additional research regarding the relation between sexual orientation and religiosity to corroborate and reexamine these findings.

Religiosity and Reactions Following Self-Disclosure of Sexual Orientation

We found no evidence that level of religiosity mediated their acceptance or rejection by others upon disclosing their sexual orientation to others (see Table 4). Although we found that participants' perceptions of maternal religiosity yielded statistically significant analyses of variance F tests, post hoc tests of bivariate relationships were negative. We found that participants' perceptions of paternal religiosity had a significant association with self-disclosure to a parent. A post hoc test with Dunnett's C indicated that there was a statistically significant bivariate

TABLE 4. Analyses of Variance for Self-Disclosure of Sexual Orientation by Participants' Religiosity and Perceptions of Each Parents' Religiosity, Each Sample

	Internet Sample		
	Father	*Mother*	*Participant*
Told Another Person	$F(3,70) = 0.82$	$F(3,70) = 2.37$	$F(3,75) = 0.71$
Told a Friend	$F(3,64) = 0.58$	$F(3,64) = 2.40$	$F(3,69) = 0.30$
Told Family Member	$F(3,41) = 0.16$	$F(3,41) = 1.42$	$F(3,45) = 1.10$
Told Parent	$F(3,25) = 0.74$	$F(3,26) = 3.43^*$	$F(3,29) = 0.86$
	Coffee House Sample		
	Father	*Mother*	*Participant*
Told Another Person	$F(3,83) = 0.99$	$F(3,86) = 1.14$	$F(3,85) = 0.48$
Told a Friend	$F(3,82) = 1.02$	$F(3,85) = 0.74$	$F(3,84) = 0.93$
Told Family Member	$F(3,74) = 0.76$	$F(3,75) = 2.87^*$	$F(3,74) = 0.56$
Told Parent	$F(3,66) = 4.80^{**}$	$F(3,67) = 1.69$	$F(3,66) = 0.51$

Note. $^*p < .05$; $^{**}p < .01$.

relationship between the extremes of religiosity (not at all important and extremely important). Closer inspection of these data revealed a linear relationship. Participants who rated paternal religiosity as extremely important were significantly more likely to experience rejection than those who appraised paternal religiosity as not at all important. However, this cross-sectional study does not permit us to determine the direction of the association between paternal religiosity and feelings of rejection upon self-disclosure of sexual orientation to a parent. Participants who felt rejected may be more likely to attribute the poor rejection to fathers' religiosity. Conversely, it is also reasonable to argue that fathers for whom religion is extremely important are more likely to disapprove of their lesbian daughter's sexual orientation. Fathers for whom religion is extremely important may meet the self-disclosure of their daughter's sexual orientation with a reaction that causes lesbian or bisexual daughters to feel rejected. Our data cannot rule out this possibility.

Gibson (1989) may have provided a thesis for which the NCPI (1989) and Carlson (1992) provide an important antithesis. The dialectic synthesis of these two competing hypotheses is this: Religiosity may be a protective factor that provides a buffer against the deleterious effects of maternal neglect and verbal abuse. Religiosity may mediate self-disclosure, though it appears to do so in an inconsistent and counter-intuitive manner. Given our use of convenience samples and the absence of control groups, this finding may represent a sampling artifact. However, the finding occurred in the validated sample, which is more robust than most surveys and just as representative of the U.S. population (Mathy et al., 2002). Because we obtained this finding in the validated Internet sample, we have greater confidence in these results. This confidence leads us to suggest that religiosity mediates psychosexual development and self-disclosure, albeit in unexpected ways. This finding requires further research and corroboration.

The specific mechanisms by which religion exercises its influences are not yet clear. Stark et al. (1983) suggest religious organizations are accessible and provide a source of positive affect and self-esteem. Religion proffers faith in an other-wordly life after death which may help alleviate present suffering. Pescosolido and Georgianna (1989) and Pescosolido (1990) argued that religion is a major social institution through which important aspects of social networks (structure, function, and operation) provide social integration within a larger cultural context. Conceivably, religion may provide an important cultural network in which lesbian, gay male, and bisexual youth enduring the chronic adversity of heterosexism are able to find a positive relationship with a psychosocially competent adult. Masten, Best, and Garmezy (1990) argued such relationships are associated with youth resilience.

In contrast, Gibson (1989) and Herek (1990) essentially argue that religion and religious-based heterosexism undermine sexual minority youths' social integration within their families and communities. Thus, their premise is that religion decreases social integration and simultaneously increases vulnerability to risks of abuse and self-esteem issues, substantially increasing their risks of suicidal behavior. Most significantly, the premise perpetrates the same act of prejudice it purports to reject, despite the previous absence of studies with which to examine the issue empirically. Individuals for whom religion is important comprise communities that are at least as diverse as are those of lesbians, gay men, and bisexual individuals. There are many forms of homophobia, and societal heterosexism does not predict well the behaviors, attitudes, or beliefs of individuals (Young-Bruehl, 1996).

CONCLUSIONS AND IMPLICATIONS

Further research can help us understand the psychological as well as sociological dynamics by which religion functions as a factor potentially increasing resilience among sexual minority youth. Unfortunately, clinical research rarely includes religious variables. In a five-year study of over 2,000 psychiatric articles, only 3% included a variable indicative of religious commitment (Larson, Pattison, Blazer, Omran, & Kaplan, 1986). In a five-year study of over 1,500 abstracts in a clinical journal, only 1% were inclusive of a religious variable (Dowell, Matthews, & Larson, 1993). In a ten-year study of over 600 articles in a family practice journal, only 4% included a religious variable (Craigie, Larson, & Lyons, 1988). Indeed, in most areas of research social science has largely ignored religious effects for the past century (Stark et al., 1983).

Durkheim (1898/1951) argued religion imparts a moral structure that functions to subordinate the individual to collective cultural mores. However, cultural mores proscribe child maltreatment *per se* even as they sanction corporal punishment (Straus, 1994), placing parents at increased risk for "losing control" and inadvertently abusing their child. Theoretically, religion may provide a source of moral restraint (Durkheim, 1898/1951) against child maltreatment. Logically, families in which youth internalize a moral proscription against homosexual behavior are equally likely to internalize a moral proscription against suicidal behavior. In essence, our study may indicate that the risk and protective profiles of religiosity generally cancel out when applied to sexual minorities. Again, however, we should consider finding a loss of a protective influence just as serious as finding another risk factor.

The fact that most parents are not told their youths' sexual orientation (Gagnon & Simon, 1973; Hershberger, Pilkington, & D'Augelli, 1997) logically would seem to make rather unlikely a significant causal relationship between youths' sexual orientation *per se* and child maltreatment. This does not invalidate the fact that some sexual minority youth do indeed experience abuse because of their sexual orientation and their parents' religion. However, heterosexual youth may also experience abuse due to their parents' religion.

From a psychosocial developmental perspective, adolescence is a period of conflict in identity and role confusion (Erikson, 1968). Erikson argued that it is common for youth and young adults to struggle with issues of intimacy and isolation. These issues are common to straight as well as sexually diverse youth. Although Durkheim (1989/1951) proffered the classic functionalist argument that religion is a mechanism of social integration, Piaget (1932) argued that moral reasoning is contingent upon cognitive development. Rates of suicide are relatively low below the age of 15 (Census Bureau, 1994-1999; Murphy, 2000) in part because children generally do not have the cognitive ability (formal operations) to conceptualize death.

Precisely because religion is considered a mechanism of (moral) socialization (Durkheim, 1989/1951) which integrates the individual members of cultures, it may be important to consider the relations among empathy, moral reasoning, and youth suicide. Hypothetically, lesbian, gay male, and bisexual youth who do not attempt suicide, despite pervasive cultural heterosexism, may have higher moral reasoning skills. Gagnon and Simon (1973) argued it is critical for sexual minority individuals to accept themselves by integrating their self-concept with perceptions of the prevailing moral order. Sexual minority youth who have (a) reached formal operations and who (b) have superior moral reasoning skills may more effectively integrate initially disparate self-concepts of their sexual orientation (i.e., internalized heterosexism) with their perceptions of morality as well as religious beliefs. Empathy, prosocial moral reasoning, and perhaps temperament may provide an integral developmental pathway linking the ecological subsystems (individual, family, community, society, and worldviews). Nonetheless, variables assessing cognitive and moral development are conspicuously absent in research concerning sex, sexual orientation, and suicidal behavior.

Much more research is needed to link the different ecological levels together. The present study has demonstrated that we cannot presume to predict individual behavior by knowledge of cultural factors associated with heterosexism. Similarly, we cannot predict individual responses with sociological variables. Thus, we must integrate our conceptual frames to link individuals to their social contexts without expanding individual variability to explain social problems and without reducing cultural variability to predict individual psychopathology. Put somewhat differently, individual differences do not account for social problems, nor do the social phenomena defined as "problems" enable us to equate individual diversity with psychopathology. With this in mind, longitudinal research from lifespan and ecological developmental perspectives may help decrease the psychological and social costs of child maltreatment and the economic mortality cost and potential years of life lost to youth suicide.

Researchers have for too long focused on the woes of lesbian, gay, bisexual, and transgender youth. This may reflect professionals' discomfort with non-heterosexual youth or perhaps their discomfort with attitudes and beliefs about non-heterosexual youth. However, *most* sexual minority youth do not attempt suicide. Therefore, it would seem more practical, feasible, and productive to begin focusing more attention on the resilience of sexual minority youth who do well, rather than reexamining and reemphasizing the risk factors associated with a minority sexual orientation. An omnipresent focus on risks deprives resilient sexual minority youth of the opportunity to teach all of us how to marshal diverse resources under adverse circumstances in oppressive environments.

REFERENCES

Altemeyer, B., & Hunsberger E. (1992). Authoritarianism, religious fundamentalism, quest, and prejudice. *International Journal for the Psychology of Religion, 2*(2), 113-133.

Azar, B. (2000). A web of research. *Monitor on Psychology, April*, 42-43.

Bell, A., Weinberg, M. S., & Hammersmith, S. K. (1981). *Sexual preference: Its development in men and women*. Bloomington, IN: Indiana University Press.

Belsky, J. (1993). Etiology of child maltreatment: A developmental-ecological analysis. *Psychological Bulletin, 114*(3), 413-434.

Briere, J. (1992). Types and forms of child maltreatment. *Child abuse trauma, theory and treatment of the lasting effects.* Newbury Park, CA: Sage.

Burke, S. K. (2000). In search of lesbian community in an electronic world. *CyberPsychology & Behavior: The Impact of the Internet, multimedia, and virtual reality on behavior and society, 3*(4), 591-604.

Carlson, A. C. (1992). The decline of religion and family causes teen suicide. In M. Biskup (Ed.), *Suicide: Opposing viewpoints.* San Diego, CA: Greenhaven Press.

Chandy, J. M., Blum, R. W., & Resnick, M. D. Female adolescents with a history of sexual abuse: Risk outcome and protective factors. *Journal of Interpersonal Violence, 11*, 503-518.

Cochran, S. D., & Mays, V. M. (2000). Lifetime prevalence of suicide symptoms and affective disorders among men reporting same-sex sexual partners: Results from NHANES III. *American Journal of Public Health, 90*(4), 573-578.

Cochran, S. D., Sullivan, J. G., & Mays, V. M. (2003). Prevalence of mental disorders, psychological distress, and mental services use among lesbian, gay, and bisexual adults in the United States. *Journal of Consulting & Clinical Psychology, 71*(1), 53-61.

Collins, L., & Zimmerman, N. (1983). Homosexual and bisexual issues. In J. C. Hansen, J. D. Woody, & R. H. Woody (Eds.), *Sexual issues in family therapy* (pp. 82-100). Rocville, MD: Aspen.

Conceptual Foundations Workgroup, Workshop on Suicide & Sexual Orientation, Atlanta, GA. (1995). Recommendations for a research agenda in suicide and sexual orientation. *Suicide and Life-Threatening Behavior, 25(Supplement)*, 82-88.

Corliss, H. L., Cochran, S. D., Mays, V. M. (2002). Reports of parental maltreatment during childhood in a United States population-based survey of homosexual, bisexual, and heterosexual adults. *Child Abuse & Neglect, 26*, 1165-1178.

Craigie, F. C., Larson, D. B., Lyons, J. S. (1988). A systematic analysis of religious variables in the *Journal of Family Practice. Journal of Family Practice, 27*(5), 509-513.

D'Augelli, A. R., & Hershberger, S. L. (1993). Lesbian, gay, and bisexual youth in community settings: Personal challenges and mental health problems. *American Journal of Community Psychology, 21*(4), 421-448.

Desjarlais, R., Eisenberg, L., Good, B., & Kleinman, A. (1995). *World mental health: Problems and priorities in low-income countries.* New York: Oxford University Press.

Dowell, E. H., Matthews, D. A., & Larson, D. B. (1993). No room at the inn?: Neglect of religious variables by clinical epidemiologists. *Clinical Research, 41*, 516A.

Durkheim, E. (1898/1951). *Suicide: A study in sociology.* New York: Free Press.

Erickson, E. H. (1968). *Identity, youth, and crisis.* New York: Norton.

Feshbach, N. D. (1987). Parental empathy and child adjustment/maladjustment. In N. Eisenberg & J. Strayer (Eds.), *Empathy and its development.* New York: Cambridge University Press.

Fineran, S. (2002). Sexual harassment between same-sex peers: Intersection of mental health, homophobia, and sexual violence in schools. *Social Work, 47*(1), 65-74.

Frazier, S. H. (1989). Introduction and overview: Magnitude of the problem. *Report of the Secretary's task force on youth suicide* (Vol. 1) (DHHS Publication No. ADM 89-1621). Washington, DC: U.S. Government Printing Office.

Gallup Poll. (1977). The Gallup opinion index: Political, social, and economic trends. *The Gallup Poll Monthly, 147,* 18.

Gallup Poll. (1987). The Gallup report: Political, social, and economic trends. *The Gallup Poll Monthly, 258,* 13.

Gallup Poll. (1999). [Question 35: Do you think homosexual relations between consenting adults should or should not be legal?] Unpublished contingency tables: Author.

Garfinkel, H. (1967). *Studies in ethnomethodology.* Englewood Cliffs, NJ: Prentice-Hall.

Garofalo, R., Wolf, R. C., Wissow, L. S., Woods, E. R., & Goodman, E. (1999). Sexual orientation and risk of suicide attempts among a representative sample of youth. *Archives of Pediatrics & Adolescent Medicine, 153*(5), 487-493.

Geertz, C. (1973). Thick description: Toward an interpretive theory of culture. *The interpretation of cultures.* New York: Basic Books.

Gibson, P. (1989). Gay male and lesbian youth suicide. In M. Feinleib (Ed.), *Report of the Secretary's task force on youth suicide* (Vol. 3) (pp. 110-142) (DHHS Publication No. ADM 89-1623). Washington, DC: U.S. Government Printing Office.

Gillis, J. R. (1998). Cultural heterosexism and the family. In C. J. Patterson & A. R. D'Augelli (Eds.), *Lesbian, gay, and bisexual identities in families.* New York: Oxford University Press.

Gilman, S. E., Cochran, S. D., Mays, V. M., Hughes, M., Ostrow, D., & Kessler, R. C. (2001). Risk of psychiatric disorders among individuals reporting same-sex sexual partners in the National Comorbidity Survey. *American Journal of Public Health, 91*(6), 933-939.

Giovannoni, J. (1989). Definitional issues in child maltreatment. In D. Cicchetti & V. Carlson (Eds.), *Child maltreatment: Theory and research on the causes and consequences of child abuse and neglect* (pp. 3-37). New York: Cambridge University Press.

Hardy, S. A., & Raffaelli, M. Adolescent religiosity and sexuality: An investigation of reciprocal influences. *Journal of Adolescence, 26*(6), 731-740.

Herek, Gregory M. (1993). The context of antigay violence: Notes on cultural and psychological heterosexism. In L. D. Garnets & D. C. Kimmel (Eds.), *Psychological perspectives on lesbian and gay male experiences.* New York: Columbia University Press.

Hunsberger, B. (1996). Religious fundamentalism, right-wing authoritarianism, and hostility toward homosexuals in non-Christian religious groups. *International Journal for the Psychology of Religion, 6*(1), 39-49.

Hunter, J. (1990). Violence against lesbian and gay male youths. *Journal of Interpersonal Violence, 5,* 295-300.

King, M., McKeown, E., Warner, J., Ramsay, A., Johnson, K., Cort, C., Wright, L., Blizard, R., & Davidson, O. (2003). Mental health and quality of life of gay men and lesbians in England and Wales: Controlled, cross-sectional study. *British Journal of Psychiatry, 183,* 552-558.

Klagsbrun, F. (1976). *Too young to die.* Boston: Houfton Mifflin.

Linehan, M. M. (1993). *Cognitive-behavioral treatment of borderline personality disorder.* New York: Guilford.

Koenig H. G., George, L. K., Meador, K. G., Blazer, D. G., & Dyck, P. B. (1994). Religious affiliation and psychiatric disorder among Protestant baby boomers. *Hospital and Community Psychiatry, 45*(6), 586-596.

Kourany, R. F. C. (1987). Suicide among homosexual adolescents. *Journal of Homosexuality, 13*(4), 111-117.

Larson, D. B., Pattison, E. M., Blazer, D. G., Omran, A. R., & Kaplan, B. H. (1986). Systematic analysis of research on religious variables in four major psychiatric journals, 1978-1982. *American Journal of Psychiatry, 143*(3), 329-334.

Lease, S. H., & Shulman, J. L. (2003). A preliminary investigation of the role of religion for family members of lesbian, gay male, or bisexual male and female individuals. *Counseling and Values, 47,* 195-209.

Masten, A. S., Best, K. M., & Garmezy, N. (1990). Resilience and development: Contributions from the study of children who overcome adversity. *Development & Psychopathology, 2*(4), 425-444.

Mathy, R. M. (2002). On reliability and cultural competence in studies of sexual minority suicidality. *American Journal of Public Health, 12*(1), 1.

Mathy, R. M. (2002). Suicidality and sexual orientation in five continents: Asia, Australia, Europe, North America, and South America. *International Journal of Sexuality and Gender Studies, 7*(2/3), 215-225.

Mathy, R. M., Bigner, J. J., & Leicht, N. E. (in press). Methodological Rigor with Internet Samples: New Ways to Reach Underrepresented Populations. In R. M. Mathy & M. Haga (Eds.), *Out on the Prairie.* Minneapolis: New Diversity Press.

Mathy, R. M., Leicht, N. E., & Bigner, J. J. (in press). Lesbian and Bisexual Females Raised in Rural Versus Urban Communities: Child Abuse, Suicide Attempts, Self-disclosure, Rejection, and Victimization." In R. M. Mathy & M. Haga (Eds.), *Out on the Prairie.* Minneapolis: New Diversity Press.

Mays, V. M., & Cochran, S. D. (2002). Mental health correlates of perceived discrimination among lesbian, gay, and bisexual adults in the United States. *American Journal of Public Health, 91*(11), 1869-1876.

Moore, D. W. (1995). Three million children victims of physical abuse last year: Another one million children victims of sexual abuse. *The Gallup Poll Monthly, 363,* 4-15.

Mo∇cicki, E. K. (1995). Epidemiology of suicidal behavior. *Suicide and Life-Threatening Behavior, 25*(1), 22-35.

Murphy, S. L. (2000). Final data for 1998. *National Vital Statistics Reports, 48*(11), 26 (DHHS Publication No. PHS 2000-1120). Hyattsville, MD: National Center for Health Statistics.

National Conference on Prevention and Interventions. (1989). Summary of the national conference on prevention and interventions in youth suicide. In M. Feinleib (Ed.), *Report of the Secretary's task force on youth suicide* (Vol. 3) (pp. 5-19) (DHHS Publication No. ADM 89-1623). Washington, DC: U.S. Government Printing Office.

Office of Applied Studies. (2003). *Results from the 2002 National Survey on Drug Use and Health: National findings* (DHHS Publication No. SMA 03-3836, NHSDA Series H-22). Rockville, MD: Substance Abuse and Mental Health Services Administration.

Pescosolido, B. A. (1990). The social context of religious integration and suicide: Pursuing the network explanation. *The Sociological Quarterly, 31*(3), 337-357.

Pescosolido, B. A., & Georgianna, S. (1989). Durkheim, suicide, and religion: Toward a network theory of suicide. *American Sociological Review, 54*(1), 33-48.

Piaget, J. (1932). *The moral judgment of the child.* New York: Harcourt Brace.

Remafedi, G., French, S., Story, M., Resnick, M., & Blum, R. (1998). The relationship between suicide risk and sexual orientation: Results of a population-based study. *American Journal of Public Health, 88*(1), 57-60.

Remafedi, G. (1999a). Suicide and sexual orientation: Nearing the end of controversy? *Archives of General Psychiatry, 56,* 885-886.

Remafedi, G. (1999b). Sexual orientation and youth suicide. *Journal of the American Medical Association, 282,* 1291-1292.

Rotheram-Borus, M. J., Hunter, J., & Rosario, M. (1994). Suicidal behavior and gay-related stress among gay and bisexual male adolescents. *Journal of Adolescent Research, 9*(4), 498-508.

Rubin, A., & Babbie, E. (1997). *Research Methods for Social Work, 3rd* ed. New York: Brooks/Cole.

Schneider, S. G., Farberow, N. L., & Kruks, G. N. (1989). Suicidal behavior in adolescent and young adult gay men. *Suicide and Life-Threatening Behavior, 19*(4), 107-122.

Shaunesey, K., Cohen, J. L., Plummer, B., & Berman, A. (1993). Suicidality in hospitalized adolescents: Relationship to prior abuse. *American Journal of Orthopsychiatry, 63*(1), 113-119.

Skell, K., Nada-Raja, S., Dickson, N., Paul, C., & Williams, S. Sexual orientation and self-harm in men and women. *American Journal of Psychiatry, 160*(3), 541-546.

Stack, S. (1983). The effect of the decline in institutionalized religion on suicide, 1954-1978. *Journal for the Scientific Study of Religion, 22*(3), 239-252.

Stark, R., Doyle, D. P., & Rushing, J. L. (1983). Beyond Durkheim: Religion and suicide. *Journal for the Scientific Study of Religion, 22*(2), 120-131.

Straus, M. A., & Donnelly, D. A. (1994). Beating the Devil out of Them: Corporal Punishment in American Families. New York: Lexington Books.

Strommen, E. F. (1993). You're a what?: Family member reactions to the disclosure of homosexuality. In L. D. Garnets & D. C. Kimmel (Eds.), *Psychological perspectives on lesbian & gay male experiences.* New York: Columbia University Press.

Stueve, A., O'Donnell, L. N., Duran, R., San Doval, A., & Blome, J. (2001). Time-space sampling in minority communities: Results with young Latino men who have sex with men. *American Journal of Public Health, 91*(6), 922-926.

U. S. Bureau of the Census. Series B 149-166. Death rate, for selected causes: 1900 to 1970. *Historical statistics of the United States: Colonial times to 1970.* White Plains, NY: Kraus International.

U. S. Bureau of the Census. 1994-1999. *Statistical abstract of the United States: Annual.* Washington, DC: U.S. Government Printing Office.

U. S. Department of Health and Human Services. (1998). *Child maltreatment 1998: Reports from the States to the National Child Abuse and Neglect Data System.* Washinton, DC: U.S. Government Printing Office.

Wagner, B. M., Cole, R. E., & Schwartzman, P. (1995). Psychosocial correlates of suicide attempts among junior and senior high school youth. *Suicide & Life-Threatening Behavior, 25*(3), 358-372.

Wagner, B. M., Cole, R. E., & Schwartzman, P. (1996). Comorbidity of symptoms among junior and senior high school suicide attempters. *Suicide & Life-Threatening Behavior, 26*(3), 300-307.

Wichstrom, L., & Hegna, K. (2003). Sexual orientation and suicide attempt: A longitudinal study of the general Norwegian adolescent population. *Journal of Abnormal Psychology, 112*(1), 144-151.

Young-Bruehl, E. (1996). *The anatomy of prejudices*. Cambridge, MA: Harvard University Press.

Zigler, E., & Hall, N. W. (1989). Physical child abuse in America: Past, present, and future. In D. Cicchetti & V. Carlson (Eds.), *Child maltreatment: Theory and research on the causes and consequences of child abuse and neglect*. New York: Cambridge University Press.

Lesbians in Psychotherapy:
Relationship of Shame
and Attachment Style

G. Beverly Wells, PhD

SUMMARY. Using self-report measures, this study explored the relationship of attachment style and internalized shame among 100 self-identified lesbians. The participants were in the highest stage of lesbian identity integration (Cass's model, stage 6, synthesis) and were in ongoing interpersonal psychotherapy. Compared to earlier research on a non-clinical national sample of 317 self-identified lesbians, this sample of mid-life lesbians (predominantly European-American and college educated) reported higher levels of secure attachment and lower (non-clinical) levels of internalized shame. Collectively, scores of the four attachment styles predicted 43% of the variability in internalized shame. Secure attachment significantly predicted reduced shame. This article in-

G. Beverly Wells is affiliated with the West Coast Institute and Family Services.

Address correspondence to G. Beverly Wells, 125 Brompton Avenue, San Francisco, CA (E-mail: doctorbev@earthlink.net).

This research is based in part on a presentation given at the Second Annual Conference on Attachment and Psychopathology, Toronto, Canada, in 1998. It is an extension of the author's dissertation research, *Effects of Adult Attachment Style and Lesbian Identity Integration on Internalized Shame*. A related article coauthored with Nancy Dowling Hansen appears in *Journal of Homosexuality* 45(1), 2003. The article is entitled "Lesbian Shame: Its Relationship to Identity Integration and Attachment."

[Haworth co-indexing entry note]: "Lesbians in Psychotherapy: Relationship of Shame and Attachment Style." Wells, G. Beverly. Co-published simultaneously in *Journal of Psychology & Human Sexuality* (The Haworth Press, Inc.) Vol. 15, No. 2/3, 2003, pp. 101-116; and: *Lesbian and Bisexual Women's Mental Health* (ed: Robin M. Mathy, and Shelly K. Kerr) The Haworth Press, Inc., 2003, pp. 101-116. Single or multiple copies of this article are available for a fee from The Haworth Document Delivery Service [1-800-HAWORTH, 9:00 a.m. - 5:00 p.m. (EST). E-mail address: docdelivery@haworthpress.com].

Digital Object Identifier: 10.1300/J056v15n02_06

cludes a discussion of theoretical and practical implications of the find-ings. *[Article copies available for a fee from The Haworth Document Delivery Service: 1-800-HAWORTH. E-mail address: <docdelivery@haworthpress.com> Website: <http://www.HaworthPress.com> © 2003 by The Haworth Press, Inc. All rights reserved.]*

KEYWORDS. Lesbians, psychotherapy, shame, attachment, mental health

Attachment theory provides a way to better understand attachment styles and their relationship to affect regulation and interpersonal psy-chotherapy (Bowlby, 1973, 1988; Schore, 2003). Its usefulness is two-fold. First, attachment theory focuses on how early life experiences affect the development of internal working models of the self and oth-ers, which ultimately influence subsequent relationships throughout the lifespan. Secondly, attachment theory provides a frame to help us exam-ine the potential implications of the therapeutic relationship on attach-ment style and regulation of affect. Many approaches recognize the importance of the therapeutic relationship in developing secure attach-ment, yet empirical data on psychotherapy and the relationship of shame and attachment style among stigmatized groups, such as lesbi-ans, is scarce.

In a prior study, Wells and Hansen (2003) found that 317 non-clinical lesbians revealed high levels of both dismissing attachment and inter-nalized shame despite having reached the highest levels of lesbian iden-tity integration. This led to the central concern of this study. What would be the relationship of shame and attachment among a similar clinical sample of lesbians who were in ongoing interpersonal psycho-therapy?

The earlier study (Wells & Hansen, 2003) provided support that les-bians, like other marginalized groups, suffer wide-ranging effects of stigma, including internalized shame and difficulties in developing a positive identity (Kaufman & Raphael, 1996). They further discovered that even lesbians who had established the highest levels of lesbian identity integration still suffered from high levels of internalized shame. Lesbian identity integration refers to the integration of one's affectional and sexual orientation into overall personal identity (Bohan, 1996). Both this study and the earlier study (Wells & Hansen, 2003) applied Cass's congruency model (1979, 1984), the most widely cited model in empirical research (Cass, 1984; Chapman & Brannock, 1987; Levine, 1997). Stages of Cass's model parallel models for other stigmatized groups, such as racial identity models.

One implication of Cass's model is that effects of stigma are experienced to a lesser degree as lesbian identity integration increases. Prior research with 317 self-identified lesbians supports this view in that lesbians at stages 4, 5, and 6 reported lower internalized shame than those in earlier stages of lesbian identity formation (Wells & Hansen, 2003). To control for this variable, the current study was limited to lesbians at stage 6 (synthesis), the highest level of identity integration.

Another possible consequence of stigma is the experience of shame (Kaufman, 1996; Kaufman & Raphael, 1996). Being seen as *different* is one potent source of shame. Often, being *lesbian* is renounced as being *sick* and *unnatural*. Embedded in these judgments are expressions of intense shame about one's identity. Shame is deeply connected to self-esteem, identity, and close relationships (Kaufman, 1996; Levine, 1997; Schore, 2003; Wells & Hansen, 2003). Feelings of internalized shame often lead to a desire to hide and become distrustful of others as in the lesbian experience below.

> *I felt flushed and queasy after coming out to my family. Mom burst out with, "You can't be one of those horrible people!" I wanted the floor to swallow me up.* (Beverly Wells, personal interview, August 31, 2003)

Helen Block Lewis (1987) has spoken of shame as "an inevitable response to loss of love" (p. 30), i.e., that "losing someone to whom one is attached . . . feels like a loss of self-esteem" (p. 32). Elaborating further, Lewis (1987) states that shame is the affective experience in which "one accepts the loss of the other as if it were a loss in the self" (p. 32). An empirical study of the depressive disorders suggests that "negative self-esteem" forms the foundation of all types of depression and that shame is the affective-cognitive state of low self-esteem (Prosen, Clark, Harrow, & Fawcett, 1983). Finally, low self-esteem and shame are associated with a wide variety of problems for which individuals, regardless of gender and sexual orientation, seek psychotherapy (Jacoby, 1994; Nathanson, 1992; Tangney, Burggraf, & Wagner, 1995).

Much has been written about shame and its importance in early attachment relationships and in identity formation (e.g., Lewis, 1971; Basch, 1985; Kaufman, 1996; Schore, 2003). Kaufman (1996) speaks of shame binds, specifically when the need for a secure bond with the parent is unmet, resulting in an internalized bind between shame and relationship distress. Kaufman (1996) stated that shame may become so pervasive that "one's identity becomes based on shame" (p. 108).

Schore (2003) refers to shame-induced misattunement with the primary caregiver. Patterns of such misattunement create "a belief that one's affective needs generally are unacceptable and shameful" (Basch, 1985, p. 35). Internalized shame becomes associated with an expectation of painful affect that the individual is unable to modulate, resulting in conscious avoidance of painful affect (Lewis, 1971). This pattern may contribute to what has come to be known as a dismissing attachment style. Recently, Cook (1994; 2000) has examined internalized shame using an empirical approach.

Kaufman and Raphael (1996) also have described how lesbians and gay men may be at higher risk for developing internalized shame due to familial misattunement and marginalized status in society. An earlier study provided preliminary support for this belief. Applying Cook's (1994) empirical approach, Wells (1996) found that self-identified lesbians, gay men, and bisexuals combined scored significantly higher on internalized shame than did self-identified heterosexual men and women. More recently, a non-clinical sample of 317 self-identified lesbians (Wells & Hansen, 2003) revealed an overall mean shame score of 48.9 (SD = 14.3), close to the cut-off score of 50 for clinically significant shame scores (Cook, 1994), providing further evidence to support this expectation. However, internalized shame has not yet been examined in a stage 6 sample of lesbians in ongoing psychotherapy.

The second variable of interest in this study was attachment style, specifically the disproportionate percentage of dismissing (avoidant) attachment style scores among this same national non-clinical sample of lesbians (Wells & Hansen, 2003). Individuals with this adaptive attachment pattern deal with the anxieties of close relationships through emotional distancing. Such isolating behavior impacts all close relationships including the relationship with oneself (Siegel, 1999). Naturally intense emotions may become muted or "flattened," leaving the individual feeling distant from one's own feelings.

Bowlby's (1988) internal working model of attachment extends basic views of self and others to interpersonal relationships throughout the lifespan, while more recent studies (Siegel, 1999; Schore, 2003) have linked shame and affect dysregulation to the development of insecure attachment patterns. Although the existing research with lesbian samples (Greenfield & Thelen, 1997; Ridge & Feeney, 1998) has revealed differing frequencies of insecure attachment styles (anxious-ambivalent vs. avoidant styles), Wells and Hansen's (2003) non-clinical sample of lesbians revealed 49% with secure attachment style and 51% with insecure attachment styles. Of those with insecure attachment, 45% were classified with a dismissing style. High levels of internalized shame, as expected, were more closely associated with insecure styles of all kinds.

Daniel Siegel (1999) suggested that early secure attachment helps the individual develop the capacities for (a) knowing oneself over time, (b) social cognition, i.e., empathy and the ability to understand others, (c) flexibility resulting from the ability to weigh options before acting, and (d) emotion regulation, e.g., the ability to soothe oneself and to be soothed by others. Since interpersonal and other psychodynamic therapies are hypothesized to provide a base upon which secure attachment may develop, this study asks the question, "Would lesbians in ongoing psychotherapy reveal more participants with secure attachment styles?" In Wells and Hansen's (2003) non-clinical sample of 317 lesbians, each insecure attachment style was positively related to internalized shame ($p < .001$) while secure attachment was negatively related to internalized shame: (r (317) $= -.51, p < .001$).

Based on Bowlby's (1979) earlier work, Bartholomew (1990) proposed a model of adult attachment characterized by two underlying dimensions: model of the self (either positive or negative) and model of others (either positive or negative). These dimensions produce four possible attachment styles: secure (positive self and other), preoccupied (negative self, positive other), dismissing (positive self, negative other), and fearful (negative self and other). To maintain consistency with the Wells and Hansen (2003) study, this research applied Bartholomew's model of adult attachment, which has been supported by previous research (e.g., Bartholomew & Horowitz, 1991; Diehl, Elnick, Bourbeau, & Labouvie-Vief, 1998; Horowitz, Rosenberg, & Bartholomew, 1993).

One such study (Bartholomew & Horowitz, 1991) examined the relationships between attachment styles and personal insecurity, sociability, and interpersonal problems. Individuals with preoccupied and fearful styles (both representing negative self dimensions) responded similarly to measures of personal insecurity. The two groups classified as avoidant in close relationships (fearful and dismissing, both representing negative other dimensions) had difficulties in becoming close to and relying on others. Individuals with a preoccupied attachment style (negative self, positive other) tended to blame themselves for perceived rejections by others. In contrast, persons with a dismissing style (positive self, negative other) minimized the importance of others experienced as rejecting, thereby deflecting the hurt, and appeared to maintain higher self-esteem.

In their sample of 317 non-clinical lesbians (mean age = 39.9, SD = 11.1) Wells and Hansen (2003) found, as expected, that secure attachment was negatively related to internalized shame ($r = -.51, p < .001$) whereas the insecure attachment styles were positively related to shame: fearful attachment ($r = .57, p < .001$); preoccupied attachment ($r = .33, p < .001$); and dismissing attachment ($r = .19, p < .001$). As a participant's insecure attachment score increased, her score on internalized shame increased as well.

The final concern of this study was to examine the relationship of the four attachment style scores to the variability in shame scores to determine statistical significance of both collective and individual predictors. Among their non-clinical participants, Wells and Hansen (2003) found that although collectively their predictors (four attachment styles plus lesbian identity stage) explained a statistically significant (40%) amount of the variability in shame ($R^2 = .40, F(5, 311) = 42.5, p < .001$), only three of the five individual predictors were statistically significant at the ($p < .001$) level: secure, fearful, and preoccupied. Scores on dismissing attachment and lesbian identity integration, however, did not individually predict internalized shame.

The goals of the current study were to determine (a) if a similar sample of lesbians in ongoing interpersonal psychotherapy would reveal more participants with secure attachment and fewer with dismissing attachment style, and thus, a greater percentage with a positive self-view than the previous non-clinical sample, (b) if levels of internalized shame would be lower (in the non-clinical range) for this sample than in the non-clinical sample, and (c) statistical significance of predictor variables (shame and attachment), both collectively and individually. The literature suggests that lesbians in ongoing interpersonal psychotherapy would reveal an increase in secure attachment and a decrease in internalized shame, whereas secure attachment (hypothesized to increase the ability to regulate affect) would be the individually significant predictor variable.

METHOD

Participants and Procedures

Participants were 100 self-identified lesbians, ranging in age from 35 to 55 years (mean age = 49.5) who had been in ongoing individual interpersonal psychotherapy from 3 to 10 years (mean years = 6), with sessions averaging once a week. Participants had initially sought psychotherapy for "relationship issues." The participants were volunteers. They were employed in professional careers and resided in California. All participants had completed some college education, ranging from 2 to 6 years (mean years = 4). Their predominant ethnicity was European-American (70%) with 15% Latin-American, 10% African-American, and 5% Asian- American. Most (60%) were in a partnered relationship, and 55% reported an annual income between $30,000 and $55,000.

To generate a sample of participants who were (a) middle-aged, (b) had a minimum of an eighth grade English reading level, (c) had been in individual interpersonal psychotherapy for a minimum of 3 years for "relationship issues," (d) believed that they had accepted and integrated their identity as a lesbian into their life as a whole, and (e) were willing "to explore feelings associated with how they, as self-identified lesbians, experience themselves and their relationships," the author contacted psychotherapists in Northern California who posted or distributed a flyer announcing the study and its purpose to prospective participants in their clinical practice. Prospective participants who expressed interest in the study were given questionnaire packets by their therapists. Participants returned the packets to the author in the stamped, self-addressed envelope provided.

Instructions and a background questionnaire appeared first in the packet, followed by the three other questionnaires in counterbalanced order (Self-identity Questionnaire, Levine, 1997; Internalized Shame Scale, Cook, 1994; and the Relationship Styles Questionnaire, Griffin & Bartholomew, 1994). Analyses of Variance to test for order effects were not statistically significant. The author sent a summary of the results to each participant who requested this information.

INSTRUMENTS

Self-Identity Questionnaire (SIQ)

The Self-Identity Questionnaire (Brady & Busse, 1994; Levine, 1997), based on an earlier measure (Cass, 1984), is an inventory of 45 randomly-ordered items. Participants rated each item as either true or false. Three of the items serve as validity checks. Identity stage designation was derived from the other 42 items, which include six subsets of 7 questions each. Each subset represents one stage in Cass's model. Each true response is added and the subset containing the most points represents the participant's stage designation. Levine's (1997) participant results were as follows: stage 4 (identity acceptance), 31%; stage 5 (identity pride), 21%; and stage 6 (identity synthesis), 40%. Stages 1 through 3 (identity confusion, comparison, and tolerance) comprised the final 8%.

Internal consistency coefficients for subsets varied from .58 (stage 5) to .80 (stage 1) (Levine, 1997). Brady and Busse (1994) and Levine (1997) found that the SIQ appears to offer a valid assessment for lesbians in the higher stages of identity development. Levine's (1997) sample of 118 self-identified, mid-life (mean = 31.4, range from 18 to 56), educated, predominately European-American lesbians revealed a positive relationship between high SIQ scores and high self-esteem. SIQ stage was used as a continuous variable for correlational analyses. A similar procedure was used in the analysis of this study.

Internalized Shame Scale (ISS)

The 30-item ISS (Cook, 1994) was developed to assess "internalized shame" and "shame-based identity" concepts. It contains 24 items that measure shame in each of the two scales and a 6-item subscale to reduce response set bias. Each item (e.g., I feel like I am somehow defective as a person) is rated on a 5-point Likert scale from 0 (never) to 4 (almost always). When the item ratings are added, they result in a total shame score ranging from 0 to 96.

Cronbach's *alpha* was .95 and the 7-week test-retest reliability was .84 for the total shame score (Cook, 1994). Convergent validity data revealed significant positive correlations between the total shame score and the Janis-Fields Feelings of Inadequacy Scale ($r = .81$), the Multiscore Depression Inventory's Alienation subscale ($r = .74$), and the Bell Object Relations and Reality Testing Inventory's Alienation subscale ($r = .67$) (Cook, 1994). Discriminate validity data revealed significant negative correlations between the total shame score and the Coopersmith Self-Esteem Scale ($r = -.52$) and the Tennessee Self-Concept Scale total score ($r = -.66$) (Cook, 1994). Likewise, the ISS shame score was found to be unrelated to the Marlowe-Crowne Social Desirability Scale ($r = .16$) (Cook, 1994).

Relationship Styles Questionnaire (RSQ)

The RSQ includes 30 phrases consistent with four attachment patterns: secure, fearful, preoccupied, and dismissing (Griffin & Bartholomew,

1994). Participants are asked to identify how they typically feel in their adult romantic relationships using 30 statements (e.g., I worry I will be hurt if I allow myself to become too close to others) and a 5-point Likert scale from 1 (not at all like me) to 5 (very much like me). Likert ratings are added together for the four items associated with each of the fearful or preoccupied patterns and for the five items associated with each of the secure or dismissing patterns. The additional 12 items were included to obscure the nature of the questionnaire. Scores are then standardized to provide comparisons (1 to 5), and the category with the highest score indicates the attachment style. Categorical attachment style was used only to compare this sample's distribution with prior research. Otherwise, consistent with the findings of Fraley and Waller (1998), continuous scores were used in all analyses to better capture the dimensional nature of attachment.

Wells and Hansen (2003) found Cronbach *alphas* similar to previous studies: .48 for secure, .80 for fearful, .68 for preoccupied, and .70 for dismissing. These internal consistency coefficients are probably related to the small number of items ($n = 4$ or 5) contained on each of the four subscales. Fraley and Shaver (1997) reported test-retest coefficients of $r = .65$ over a 3-week period. Convergent validity of the RSQ was revealed with the Relationship Questionnaire (Dutton, Saunders, Starzomski, & Bartholomew, 1994), interview ratings (Griffin & Bartholomew, 1994), the Adult Attachment Scale (Holtzworth-Munroe, Stuart & Hutchinson, 1997), and measures of relationship quality, emotional experience, and relationship dynamics (Fraley & Shaver, 1997). The underlying two dimensions (self-model and other-model, anxiety and avoidance) of the four attachment styles were confirmed through various analyses (Griffin & Bartholomew, 1994). Despite modest psychometric properties, the RSQ is the only multi-item adult attachment scale that provides continuous scores for each of Bartholomew's four attachment patterns. To maintain consistency with the earlier non-clinical study, the author selected it for use in this study.

RESULTS

Of the 128 packets the author received, 100 were selected for inclusion in this study. Of those excluded, 5 were incomplete and the remaining 23 were at stages earlier than stage 6. To control for the variable of lesbian identity development, the study included only those 100 competed packets in which the participants were classified as stage 6 (synthesis), the highest stage of lesbian identity integration.

One goal of this study was to describe the attachment styles to determine if the mid-life lesbians in ongoing psychotherapy would reveal similar or different attachment patterns compared to the earlier non-clinical sample, in particular, to determine if there would be an increase in proportion of participants with secure attachment style. Of the 100 participants, attachment styles were classified as follows: 58% secure; 28% dismissive; 6% fearful; and 8% preoccupied, revealing a positive self-view in 86% of the sample and a negative self-view in 14% of the sample.

Compared to the non-clinical lesbians (Wells & Hansen, 2003), this sample revealed more lesbians with secure attachment (58%, a majority) whereas the earlier non-clinical sample was found to have 49%, just under half of the sample. In this study, only 28% were found to have a dismissing attachment style whereas the non-clinical sample revealed 45% with dismissing attachment, almost twice as many as in this study. Both studies revealed lower percentages of the other two insecure styles compared with dismissing: fearful (6% current study, 3% earlier study); and preoccupied (8% current study, 3% earlier study). Both studies revealed more dismissing attachment compared to other insecure styles. However, this study differs from the earlier non-clinical one in that it revealed a greater number of lesbians with a secure attachment style.

Whether the higher percentage of those with secure attachment is related to their participation in ongoing interpersonal therapy needs to be supported by further research. Theoretically, providing a "secure base" through interpersonal psychotherapy would be expected to support an increase in secure attachment. As shown in Table 1, the highest variable intercorrelations appear between RSQ fearful ($r = -.43, p < .001$) and RSQ secure. This is consistent with Bartholomew's model in which the two attachment styles are polar opposites, with fearful combining both negative self and negative other whereas secure combines both positive self and positive other dimensions.

The overall mean shame score for this sample was 45.9 (SD = 10.3), within the standard deviation range (mean $= 33$, SD = 16) (Cook, 1994) for non-clinical adult females and significantly lower than the mean shame score (mean = 53, SD = 19) for female alcoholics (Cook, 1994). A t-test comparison between these samples revealed that the lesbians in this sample reported significantly less shame than Cook's (1994) clinical sample, t (277) = 2.08, $p < .05$. This is in contrast to Wells and Hansen's (2003) earlier non-clinical sample of lesbians, whose mean

TABLE 1. Correlations Among the Variables: Shame Scores and RSQ Attachment Styles (N = 100)

Variable	1	2	3	4	5
1. ISS shame score	1.00	−.36***	.04	.33***	.22**
2. RSQ secure attachment		1.00	−.09	−.43***	−.19*
3. RSQ dismissing attachment			1.00	.27**	−.11
4. RSQ fearful attachment				1.00	.26**
5. RSQ preoccupied attachment					1.00

* $p < .05$, ** $p < .01$, *** $p < .001$

Note. ISS = Internalized Shame Scale (Cook, 1994); RSQ = Relationship Styles Questionnaire (Griffin & Bartholomew, 1994).

shame score (48.9), was close to the clinically significant cut-off shame score of 50 (Cook, 1994).

The final goal of this study was to examine the four attachment style scores and their relationship to the variability in shame scores to determine statistical significance of both collective and individual predictors. Taken together, the four attachment style predictors explained a statistically significant amount (43%) of the variability in shame ($p <$ .001). As shown in Table 2, only one of the individual predictors was statistically significant: secure ($\beta = -.26, p < .001$). This finding is consistent with Bowlby's construct of attachment (1988) and Kaufman's (1996) affect theory, which predicts that individuals with secure attachment would obtain significantly lower internalized shame scores than would those with insecure attachment. Results are also consistent with implications of the literature (Siegel, 1999; Schore, 2003) that individuals with secure attachment would be better able to regulate affect.

DISCUSSION

This sample of 100 middle-aged, educated, predominately European-American self-identified lesbians were all classified at the highest level of lesbian identity integration, having reached Cass's stage 6, synthesis. The investigator selected this group to control the variable of lesbian identity integration. However, future studies should expand on this sample by seeking participants who are at earlier stages of lesbian identity development and who also are in ongoing psychotherapy.

TABLE 2. Multiple Regression Analysis for Predicting Levels of Internalized Shame (N = 100)

Predictor Variables	B	SE B	β
Secure Attachment	−3.78	1.51	−.26**
Dismissing Attachment	−.35	1.31	.03
Fearful Attachment	2.17	1.21	.19
Preoccupied Attachment	1.68	1.36	.12

** $p < .01$

Note. $R^2 = .43$, $F(4/95) = 5.39$, $p < .001$

Compared to the earlier study of non-clinical self-identified lesbians (Wells & Hansen, 2003), this sample of lesbians in ongoing psychotherapy revealed ISS shame scores (mean = 45.9) within the high normative range for non-clinical females whereas the earlier study of lesbians, (98% at stage 4, identity acceptance or higher; 58% at stage 6, synthesis) scored (mean = 48.9) very near the cut-off score for clinical females (50 for affective disorders; 53 for alcoholics) (Cook, 1994). If, as Kaufman and Raphael (1996) suggest, lesbians seek psychotherapy to address issues related to shame and stigma, which affect how they see themselves in relationship to significant others, interpersonal psychotherapy may contribute to a reduction in stigma-induced internalized shame. More studies of lesbians who have completed or are in ongoing psychotherapy would help to determine whether there is further support for this notion.

As expected from the earlier study of non-clinical lesbians, secure attachment was found to be negatively related to shame. Also, among these lesbians in ongoing psychotherapy, 58% (a clear majority) were classified with secure attachment compared with 49% secure (just under half) in the earlier non-clinical study. Similar to the earlier study, of the three insecure styles, dismissing attachment was the most prevalent style, with considerably fewer (28%) in the current study compared to almost half (45%) in the non-clinical study. As in the earlier study, the four attachment styles collectively contributed a statistically significant amount of the variability in shame (40% in the earlier study; 43% in the current study). However, unlike the earlier study, only one predictor variable, secure attachment style, was individually significant in explaining variability in shame (β = −.26, p < .001), a finding consistent with Bowlby's construct of attachment (1988) and Kaufman's affect theory (1996) that individuals with secure attachment would obtain significantly lower internalized shame scores than would those with any style of insecure attachment.

Although attachment styles among psychotherapy clients have been associated with different patterns of interpersonal problems, the efficacy of short-term dynamic therapy to treat these problems has had the poorest prognosis with individuals with dismissing attachment style (Horowitz et al., 1993). However, among this sample with a mean of six years in interpersonal psychotherapy, secure attachment style predominated. These findings suggest that it may take longer for psychotherapists to establish a therapeutic alliance with their lesbian clients, who have been stigmatized by families and society, and who have adopted a dismissing attachment style. Providing acceptance and support consistently over time within a safe therapeutic alliance can be a powerful therapeutic intervention, one that provides secure-base priming. Such priming for secure attachment experiences and capacities through interpersonal psychotherapy may help lesbians with dismissing attachment to better modulate intense emotions and manage interpersonal relationships without activating extreme avoidant behaviors.

LIMITATIONS

This study extends our knowledge of the relationship between shame and attachment patterns among lesbians and provides preliminary implications for the effect of interpersonal psychotherapy on attachment style and shame. Some cautions are important to keep in mind, however. First, all data came from self-report measures. As such, response set could be operating to cloud the real relationships between variables. Secondly, participants were predominantly European-American and college educated. Future research should include a larger sample size containing greater diversity.

Although the findings of this study suggest that ongoing psychotherapy may have a positive influence on the development of secure attachment and reduction of internalized shame, further research with lesbians who have completed at least 3 years of interpersonal therapy is needed to determine whether these findings can be generalized to lesbians, as a group. A longitudinal study of lesbians would provide even more data on attachment style and internalized shame.

Finally, correlational analyses do not determine causal relationships. Future research using structural equation modeling may aid us in understanding whether early misattunement leads to a shame-based identity which, in turn, influences adult attachment style or if early misattunement helps form an enduring attachment style, which contributes to a shame-based identity within a society which stigmatizes lesbians. Future research should attempt to operationalize the concept of stigma directly and then investigate its relationship to internalized shame and attachment.

Despite these reservations, the present study suggests that college educated mid-life lesbians who have reached the highest level of lesbian identity integration and are in ongoing psychotherapy for a minimum of 3 years, experience non-clinical levels of internalized shame, and the majority has developed a secure attachment style. Although much remains to be learned about internalized shame, psychotherapy, and adult attachment for lesbians, this study has been an attempt to shine more light on a less visible corner of the psychological literature.

REFERENCES

Bartholomew, K. (1990). Avoidance of intimacy: An attachment perspective. *Journal of Social and Personal Relationships, 7*, 148-178.

Bartholomew, K. & Horowitz, L. (1991). Attachment styles among young adults: A test of a four-category model. *Journal of Personality and Social Psychology, 61*, 226-244.

Bartholomew, K., & Shaver, P. (1998). Methods of assessing adult attachment: Do they converge? In J. Simpson & W. Rhodes (Eds.) *Attachment theory and close relationships* (pp. 25-45). New York: Guilford.

Basch, M.F. (1985). Interpretation: Toward a developmental model. In A. Goldberg (Ed.) *Progress in self psychology, 1, 33-42*. New York: Guilford.

Bohan, J (1996). *Psychology and sexual orientation: Coming to terms*. New York: Routledge.

Bowlby, J.(1973). *Attachment and loss: Vol. 2. Separation, anxiety and anger*. New York: Basic Books.

Bowlby, J. (1988). *A secure base: Parent-child attachment and healthy human development*. New York: Basic Books.

Brady, S. & Busse, W. (1994). The gay identity questionnaire: A brief measure of homosexual identity formation. *Journal of Homosexuality, 26*, 1-22.

Cass, V. (1979). Homosexual identity formation: A theoretical model. *Journal of Homosexuality, 4*, 219-235.

Cass, V. (1984). Homosexual identity formation: Testing a theoretical model. *The Journal of Sex Research, 20*, 143-167.

Cass, V. (1996). Sexual orientation identity formation: A Western phenomenon. In R. Cabaj & T. Stein (Eds.) *Textbook of homosexuality and mental health* (pp. 227-252). Washington, D.C.: American Psychiatric Press.

Chapman, B., & Brannock, J. (1987). Proposed model of lesbian identity development: An empirical examination. *Journal of Homosexuality, 14*, 69-80.

Cook, D. (1994). *Internalized shame scale.* Menomonie, WI: Channel Press.

Crocker, J., & Major, B. (1989). Social stigma and self-esteem: The self-protective properties of stigma. *Psychological Review, 96*, 608-630.

Diehl, M. Elnick, A., Boubeau, L., Lebouvic-Vief, G. (1998). Adult attachment styles: their relations to family context and personality. *Journal of Personality and Social Psychology, 74*, 1656-1669.

Dutton, D., Saunders, K., Starzomski, A., & Bartholomew, K. (1994). Intimacy-anger and insecure attachment as precursors of abuse in intimate relationships. *Journal of Applied Social Psychology, 24*, 1367-1386.

Fraley, R., & Shaver, P. (1997). Adult attachment and the suppression of unwanted thoughts. *Journal of Personality and Social Psychology, 73*, 1080-1091.

Fraley, R., & Waller, N. (1998). Adult attachment patterns: A test of the topological model. In J. Simpson & W. Rhodes (Eds.) *Attachment theory and close relationships* (pp.77-104). New York: Guilford.

Griffin, D., & Bartholomew, K. (1994). Models of the self and other: Fundamental dimensions underlying measures of adult attachment. *Journal of Personality and Social Psychology, 67*, 430-445.

Greenfield, S., & Thelen, M. (1997). Validation of the fear of intimacy scale *14*, 707-716.

Holtzworth-Munroe, A., Stuart, G., & Hutchinson, G. (1997). Violent versus nonviolent husbands: Differences in attachment patterns, dependency, and jealousy. *Journal of Family Therapy, 11*, 314-331.

Horowitz, L., Rosenberg, S., & Bartholomew, K. (1993). Interpersonal problems, attachment styles, and outcome in brief dynamic psychotherapy. *Journal of Consulting and Clinical Psychology, 61*, 549-560.

Jacoby, M. (1994). *Shame and the origins of self-esteem.* New York: Routledge.

Kaufman, G. (1996). *The psychology of shame: The theory and treatment of shame-based syndromes* (2nd ed.). New York: Springer.

Kaufman, G., & Raphael, L. (1996). *Coming out of shame: Transforming gay and lesbian lives.* New York: Doubleday.

Levine, H. (1997). A further exploration of the lesbian identity development process and its measurement. *Journal of Homosexuality, 343*, 67-78.

Lewis, H. B. (1971). *Shame and guilt in neurosis.* New York: International University Press.

Lewis, H.B.(1987). The role of shame and depression over the lifespan. In H.B. Lewis (Ed.) *The role of shame in symptom formation* (pp. 29-50). Hillsdale, NJ: Erlbaum.

Nathanson, D. (1992). *Shame and pride: Affect, sex and birth of the self.* New York: Norton.

Prosen, M., Clark, D., Harrow, M., & Fawcett, J. (1983). Guilt and conscience in major depressive disorders. *American Journal of Psychiatry, 140*, 839-844.

Ridge, S., & Feeney, J. (1998). Relationship history and relationship attitudes in gay males and lesbians: Attachment style and gender differences. *Australian and New Zealand Journal of Psychiatry, 33,* 848-859.

Schore, Allan (2003). *Affect regulation and repair of the self.* New York: Norton.

Shaver, P., Collins, N., & Clark, C. (1996). Attachment styles and internal working models of self and relationship partners. In G. Fletcher & J. Fitness (Eds.) *Knowledge structures in close relationships: A social psychological approach* (pp. 25-61). Mahwah, NJ: Erlbaum.

Siegel, Daniel (1999). *The developing mind: How relationships and the brain interact to shape who we are.* New York: Guilford.

Tangney, J., Burggraf, S., & Wagner, P. (1995). Shame-proneness, guilt-proneness, and psychological symptoms. In J. Tangney & K. Fischer (Eds.) *Self-conscious emotions: The psychology of shame, guilt, embarrassment and pride.* New York: Guilford.

Wells, G.B. (1996, June). *Adult Attachment styles and internalized shame.* Paper presented at the annual meeting of the Society for Research in Adult Development,

Wells, G.B., & Hansen, N. (2003). Lesbian shame: Its relationship to identity integration and attachment. *Journal of Homosexuality, 45(1),* 93-110.

Mental Health Implications of Same-Sex Marriage: Influences of Sexual Orientation and Relationship Status in Canada and the United States

Robin M. Mathy, MSW, LGSW, MSc, MSt, MA
Shelly K. Kerr, PhD
Barbara A. Lehmann, PhD

SUMMARY. Marriage is a mental health protective factor and homosexuality is sometimes a risk factor. The combined effect of these factors on mental health was examined in this study. We conducted a secondary

Robin M. Mathy is Director of Research and Assistant Professor of Arts & Sciences at Presentation College in Aberdeen, South Dakota, and is a Licensed Graduate Social Worker in Minnesota. Shelly K. Kerr is Assistant Director and Training Director at the University of Oregon Counseling and Testing Center. Barbara A. Lehmann is Assistant Professor of Social Work and Director of the Women's Resource Center at Augsburg College.

Address correspondence to Robin M. Mathy (E-mail: math5577@umn.edu).

This article was supported by a grant from the American Foundation for Addiction Research and an NIMH Research Supplement for an Individual with a Disability (Gearald A. August, PhD, Principal Investigator) to the first author.

The authors express gratitude to Marc Schillace for research assistance. Conversations with Susan Cochran and Gary Remafedi have been helpful in developing this paper.

[Haworth co-indexing entry note]: "Mental Health Implications of Same-Sex Marriage: Influences of Sexual Orientation and Relationship Status in Canada and the United States." Mathy, Robin M., Shelly K. Kerr, and Barbara A. Lehmann. Co-published simultaneously in *Journal of Psychology & Human Sexuality* (The Haworth Press, Inc.) Vol. 15, No. 2/3, 2003, pp. 117-141; and: *Lesbian and Bisexual Women's Mental Health* (ed: Robin M. Mathy, and Shelly K. Kerr) The Haworth Press, Inc., 2003, pp. 117-141. Single or multiple copies of this article are available for a fee from The Haworth Document Delivery Service [1-800-HAWORTH, 9:00 a.m. - 5:00 p.m. (EST). E-mail address: docdelivery@haworthpress.com].

Digital Object Identifier: 10.1300/J056v15n02_07

analysis of an international, cross-sectional survey completed in 2000 ($N =$ 7,616). We examined risks of suicide ideations and attempts, behavioral problems, and treatment histories for male and female participants from Canada and the United States. We found significant relations between sexual orientation and suicidality in all four gender-country groups. We found significant associations between relationship status and suicidality for men but not women in both countries. Behavioral problems and treatment histories were equivocal. We discuss the mental health implications of these findings for same-sex marriage. *[Article copies available for a fee from The Haworth Document Delivery Service: 1-800-HAWORTH. E-mail address: <docdelivery@haworthpress.com> Website: <http://www.HaworthPress.com> © 2003 by The Haworth Press, Inc. All rights reserved.]*

KEYWORDS. Marriage, homosexual, bisexual, attempted suicide, service utilization

Recent legal and political events have focused public attention on the issue of same-sex marriage. Public discourse regarding this issue has focused on religious and political themes. In response to the American Psychological Association Council of Representatives (1998) call for the use of psychological knowledge to "inform the current public and legal debate on same-sex marriage," this paper will examine the issue of same-sex marriage from a psychological perspective. First, we present a review of judicial and legal cases relevant to same-sex marriage. Second, we review the limited mental health literature on this topic. Finally, we discuss research conducted to determine whether relationship status mediates the association between sexual orientation and suicidality, behavioral problems, or treatment histories.

Same-sex marriage is not a new debate. In *Baker v. Nelson*, two men sued for a marriage license in Minnesota in 1971 (Eskridge, 1996; McCloud, 2004). Their suit was unsuccessful. Instead, a judge allowed one man to adopt the other in order to create a legal relationship (McCloud, 2004). Most recently, the Massachusetts Supreme Judicial Court ruled in *Goodridge v Department of Public Health* that the government "failed to identify any constitutionally adequate reason for denying civil marriage to same-sex couples. In their majority opinion, justices wrote that marriage "anchors an ordered society by encouraging stable relationships over transient ones and confers enormous private and social advantages." The opinion goes on to describe marriage as "a deeply personal commitment to another human being and a highly public celebration of the ideals of mutuality, companionship, intimacy, fidelity, and family." "The decision whether and whom to marry is among life's momentous acts of self-definition" (Goodridge v. Department of Public Health, 2004). Quickly following the Massachusetts decision, the Ohio Senate passed an extremely restrictive piece of legislation prohibiting same-sex unions. In addition to prohibiting same-sex marriage, this legislation also prohibited state employees from receiving benefits for domestic partners (Washington Times, 2004).

Massachusetts was not the first state to adjudicate same-sex marriage issues. In *Baehr v. Miike* (1993) the Hawaii Supreme Court ruled that the state could not deny same-sex partners the right to marry. This decision led to an amendment to the state constitution in 1998, restricting marriage to heterosexual couples. Alaska subsequently amended its constitution to prohibit same-sex marriage. In fact, the Hawaii Supreme Court decision created a firestorm of state legislative proposals designed to enact laws that prohibit same-sex marriage and forbid recognition of same-sex marriages performed in other states. The federal government subsequently adopted the Defense of Marriage Act (DOMA) in 1996. The Act authorizes states to ignore same-sex marriages performed in other states and defines marriage as a union between a man and a woman (Bender, Leone, Stalcup, Barbour, & Roleff, 1998; CNN.com, 2004).

Same-sex marriage is an international as well as domestic issue. Denmark became the first country to recognize same-sex partners by creating a domestic partner registry in 1989. In 2000, the Netherlands became the first country to permit same-sex couples actually to marry. Belgium followed in 2003. The Canadian provinces of Ontario and British Columbia began to allow same-sex marriage in the same year (McCloud, 2004).

In contrast to the religious and political cacophony concerning same-sex marriage, there is a paucity of scientific literature examining psychological issues relevant to same-sex marriage. Researchers only recently have begun to explore the topic of lesbian and gay families (Peplau & Spalding 2003; Savin-Williams & Esterberg, 2000), and Garnets and Kimmel (2003) have recommended further study to examine the problems in lesbian and gay relationships that may be caused by social prejudice and lack of social recognition.

Brzuzy (1998) posited that DOMA "codifies prejudice against gay men and lesbians" (p. 330). Brzuzy argues that a public policy that denies legal marriage rights to same-sex couples perpetuates negative attitudes toward lesbians and gay men. The continued internalization of negative social attitudes is directly relevant to the mental health of lesbians and gay men. A minority stress model would suggest that lesbians' and gay men's mental health may be negatively influenced by environmental stressors such as discrimination and social oppression (Garnets & Kimmel, 2003). Placido (1998) examined the impact of environmental stressors and found that negative events and internalized homophobia are associated with psychological distress among lesbian and bisexual women. Researchers have found that internalized homophobia is correlated with depression (Placido, 1998; Shildo, 1994) and poor self-esteem (Gonsiorek, 1993; Placido 1998). Numerous studies have concluded that a positive lesbian or gay identity is associated with healthy psychological adjustment (Herek & Glunt, 1995; Leserman et al., 1994; Miranda & Storms, 1989; Savin-Williams, 1989; Schmitt & Kurdek, 1987). Some research has found an association between disclosure of one's sexual orientation and relationship satisfaction among lesbians (Berger, 1990; Caron & Ulin, 1997). Other research has found an association between internalized homophobia and relationship instability among gay men (Meyer & Dean, 1998).

Society's invalidation of same-sex relationships can affect the most basic activities in the daily lives of lesbians and gay men. One study found that clerks in shopping malls provided slower service to same-sex couples than to heterosexual couples (Walters & Curran, 1996). Another study (Jones, 1996) found that hotels were significantly less likely to reserve rooms for same-sex couples than they were for heterosexual couples. A prohibition against same-sex marriage denies lesbians and gay men important benefits. Examples include (a) rights of survivorship for pensions and Social Security (ACLU, 1998; Bender et. al, 1998; Eskridge, 1996), (b) joint tax returns (ACLU, 1998; Bender et. al, 1998), (c) bereavement and sick leave to care for a partner (ACLU, 1998), (d) health insurance policies (Bender et. al, 1998; Eskridge, 1996), (e) the right to make important health care decisions involving one's partner (ACLU, 1998; Eskridge, 1996), and (f) the right to claim human remains upon a partner's death (Eskridge, 1996). These legal protections influence the mental health of lesbians and gay men. In a resolution adopted by the American Psychological Association (1998), the absence of access to the benefits provided by legal marriage "constitutes a significant psychosocial stressor for lesbians, gay men, and their families." The APA supports legislation that would provide to same-sex couples the legal benefits obtained with marriage.

The legal benefits of marriage and the symbolic commitment represented by marriage may be important to the perceived quality of lesbian relationships. Bryant and Demian (1994) found that lesbians' relationship quality is significantly associated with such factors as relationship commitment and executing legal protections (e.g., powers of attorney and wills). Kurdek (1998) found that commitment can pose a barrier that makes it difficult to end a relationship. Examples of these barriers include the psychological, emotional, or financial costs associated with ending a relationship. These barriers may compel married couples to work toward resolving relationship problems rather than simply dissolving the relationship (Peplau & Spalding, 2003).

Relationship status itself may be relevant to the mental health of lesbians and gay men. Classic social theorists (Durkheim, 1966) and contemporary researchers (Kreitman, 1988; Kposowa, 2000; Popoli, Sobelman, & Kanarek, 1989; Smith, Mercy, & Conn, 1988) have substantiated the hypothesis that marriage protects people against suicidal behavior. Smith, Mercy, and Conn (1988) found that married individuals in every age and sex group have the lowest suicide rates. Others (Kposowa, 2000) found that marital status is associated with decreased mortality only among men. In either case, prohibitions against same-sex marriage appear to deprive sexual minorities of marriages' protective influences despite the increased mental health risks posed by greater oppression and social stigma experienced by gay men, lesbians, and bisexuals (Cochran & Mays, 2000; Mays & Cochran, 2001).

There is a clear and compelling relation between sexual orientation and suicide ideation as well as attempts (McDaniel, Purcell, D'Augelli, 2001; Mathy, 2002). Individuals with bisexual and homosexual orientations appear to have different risks than do heterosexuals for acquiring stress-related disorders (Jorm et al., 2002). Using a community based sample, Jorm et al. compared heterosexual, bisexual, and homosexual participants on sexual orientation by measures of psychopathology and risks for decreased mental health. They found that bisexuals, on average, had the worst mental health of the three groups, although the homosexual participants also reported significantly greater distress than heterosexuals.

Hypothetically, therefore, we would expect the combined effects of sexual orientation and relationship status to be greater than the main effect of either alone. A plethora of recent research has substantiated a significant relation between sexual orientation and stress-related disorders (Cochran & Mays, 2000a; Cochran & Mays, 2000b; Gilman, Cochran, Mays, Hughes, Ostrow, & Kessler, 2001; Mays & Cochran, 2001; Mays, Yancey, Cochran, Weber, & Fielding, 2002). In other words, research has substantiated that marriage is a protective factor against suicidality, the primary cause of which is psychopathology (Cochran & Mays, 2000). Simultaneously, same-sex attraction, behavior, and identities are significant risk factors for suicidality (McDaniel et al., 2001; Mathy, 2002) and psychopathology (Cochran et al., 2000; Cochran & Mays, 2000a; Cochran & Mays, 2000b). However, the reasons for this are unclear.

The preceding discussion suggests that living in a heterosexist society without the protections of marriage puts sexual minorities at increased risk for suicidality and self-perceived mental health problems. To examine this hypothesis, we used an existing dataset (Cooper, Scherer, & Mathy, 2001; Cooper, Griffin-Shelley, & Delmonico, 2001; Mathy, 2001; Cooper, Morahan-Martin, Mathy, & Maheu, 2002; Mathy, 2002b; Mathy, 2002c; Mathy, 2002d) to examine the risks of suicidality, behavioral problems, and treatment utilization associated with sexual orientation and relationship status.

METHOD

Procedure

These data were drawn from a large dataset ($N = 40,935$) used in a number of previously published peer-reviewed articles (Cooper, Scherer, & Mathy, 2001; Cooper, Griffin-Shelley, Delmonico, & Mathy, 2001; Cooper, Morahan-Martin, Mathy, & Maheu, 2002; Mathy, 2002a; Mathy, 2002b; Mathy, 2001). The data reported here have not been published previously. The specific sampling design has been discussed elsewhere (Cooper, Scherer, & Mathy, 2001). The dataset includes the combined samples of a selected random sample ($n = 7,544$) and a convenience sample ($n = 33,391$). These data were gathered in June 2000 via the Website of a major news organization. We eliminated 6.5% of the convenience sample and 6.8% of the selected random sample to maintain the integrity and reliability of the sample. Elimination of these cases reduced the sample size to 38,204 (94.6% of original combined samples). For the purposes of the study reported here, we used the selected random sample to obtain participants from the U.S. We used the combined samples for the Canadian sample. Prior research has demonstrated that differences between the samples are negligible (Cooper, Scherer, & Mathy, 2001).

Participants

Participation was voluntary. Prior to beginning the survey, participants were required to give their informed consent and acknowledge that they were aged 18 years or older. Agreement to participate in the study and acknowledgment of majority age status were required to gain access to the questionnaire. Our sample included Canadian men ($n = 923$; 90.36% heterosexual; 17.8% married) and women ($n = 259$; 84.56% heterosexual; 29.73% married) as well as United States men ($n = 5,385$; 90.70%; 46.78% married) and women ($n = 1,049$; 84.56% heterosexual; 33.93% married). Race and ethnicity of participants was not assessed because the survey was designed for international administration. Racial and ethnic groups vary widely cross-culturally. The absence of universal terms and the presence of contradictory concepts generally obviate the inclusion of ethnic and racial subgroup analyses in most cross-cultural survey research. For example, "Indian" has different meanings for residents of India and North America.

Our final sample was not representative of all users of the Web site in June 2000. We cannot generalize the results to all Internet users. Although a national sample, it is not representative of the U.S. population. However, this community-based sampling design enabled us to gather a large and heterogeneous, community-based sample from a nonclinical source that is entirely independent of formal or informal organizations and institutional infrastructures. Participation did not rely upon knowing any other person (as in snowball methods), membership in any organization (as in social or recreational activities), or potentially confounding educational structures (as in university support groups).

Instrument

The principal investigators of the study from which our data are drawn have appended elsewhere their 76-item instrument (Cooper & Griffin-Shelly et al., 2002). All measures are categorical. Our key variables include current sexual orientation and relationship status. We based sexual orientation on participants' self-identification as "lesbian," "bisexual," or "heterosexual/straight." We used participants self-identified relationship status as "married," "committed," or "single." Self-reported history of suicide ideations and suicide attempts were provided as "yes" or "no" responses to, "I have had serious thoughts of suicide," and, "I have made a serious suicide attempt or gesture." Self-identified history of mental health difficulties was based solely upon participants' yes or no response to, "In the past, I have excessively used or had difficulties controlling use of (check all that apply) [Alcohol] [Drugs] [Gambling] [Sex] [Food] [Spending]." We report only alcohol, drugs, gambling, and sex in this paper. These were chosen because they frame an underlying addictive component that can be associated with impulsivity and compulsivity associated with addictions and problem behaviors. Self-reported history of psychotherapy and psychiatric medication were assessed by yes or no response to, "In the past, I have been in psychotherapy," "I am currently in psychotherapy," "In the past, I have been on medications for a psychiatric condition," and, "I am currently on medications for a psychiatric condition."

RESULTS

We conducted analyses of variance (ANOVA) to assess the association between sexual orientation as the independent variable with 3 categories (heterosexual, bisexual, and lesbian/gay) and the variables in each of 3 outcome domains. These domains included suicidality (suicide attempts and ideations), behavioral problems (alcohol, drugs, sex, gambling), and treatment history (psychiatric medications in past or present, and psychotherapy in the past or present). Each outcome domain had 2 categories (yes or no). Significant associations were found between sexual orientation and suicidal ideation ($F = 6.045$, $p < .01$) and attempts ($F = 4.285$, $p < .05$); past behavioral problems with sex ($F = 4.728$, $p < .01$); and past psychotherapy ($F = 6.451$, $p < .01$) for Canadian women (Table 1). Post-hoc tests using Scheffe's revealed that Canadian lesbians endorsed suicidal ideation and attempts significantly more than did Canadian heterosexual females. Lesbians also reported higher participation in past psychotherapy than did heterosexual females. Bisexual women endorsed past behavioral problems with sex significantly more than did heterosexual women.

Significant associations were found between sexual orientation and suicidal ideation ($F = 4.293$, $p < .05$) and attempts ($F = 8.340$, $p < .01$), past behavioral problems with sex ($F = 6.097$, $p < .01$), and past difficulties with gambling ($F = 4.792$, p. $< .01$) for Canadian men (Table 2). Scheffe's post-hoc tests revealed that a significantly greater percentage of Canadian bisexual men, relative to heterosexual same-sex peers, en-

TABLE 1. Analyses of Variance for Proportion of Canadian Female Sample with Positive History of Suicidality, Behavioral Problems, or Mental Health Treatment by Sexual Orientation, Mean (*M*) and Standard Deviation (*SD*)

	Heterosexual n = 219		Lesbian n = 10		Bisexual n = 30			
	M	SD	M	SD	M	SD	F(2,256)	Post-hoc[e]
Suicidality								
Ideation	.15	.36	.50	.53	.30	.47	6.05**	L>H
Attempt	.06	.25	.30	.48	.13	.35	4.29*	L>H
Behavioral Problem								
Alcohol	.15	.36	.20	.42	.23	.43	0.82	
Drugs	.07	.26	.10	.32	.17	.38	1.50	
Sex	.11	.30	.20	.42	.30	.47	4.73**	B>H
Gambling	.02	.13	.10	.32	.00	.00	2.03	
Treatment History								
PsychMed[a]	.14	.35	.30	.48	.23	.43	1.62	
PsychHx[b]	.12	.33	.50	.53	.23	.43	6.45**	L>H
PsychRx[c]	.06	.25	.00	.00	.03	.18	0.54	
PsychTx[d]	.04	.19	.00	.00	.03	.18	0.19	

Notes.*P < .05; **P < .01; ***P < .001; [a]Past Psychiatric Medication; [b]Past Psychotherapy; [c]Current Psychiatric Medication; [d]Current Psychotherapy; [e]L = lesbian, B = bisexual, H = heterosexual.

dorsed suicidal ideation and suicide attempts. A significantly greater percentage of bisexual men than gay men also reported suicide attempts. A significantly greater percentage of bisexual men than either gay or heterosexual men reported past behavioral problems with sex and gambling.

We found that U.S. women's sexual orientation and suicide ideation were significantly associated (F = 14.460, p < .001), as were attempts (F = 7.651, p < .01); past behavioral problems with alcohol (F = 4.721, p < .05), drugs (F = 6.561, p < .01), and sex (F = 6.701, p < .01); past psychotherapy (F = 8.863, p < .001) and current psychotherapy (F = 4.222, p < .01). Scheffe's post-hoc tests revealed that a significantly greater percentage of U.S. bisexual women, relative to their U.S. heterosexual peers, reported suicide ideation and attempts. A significantly greater percentage of bisexual women than heterosexual same-gender peers reported past behavioral problems with alcohol, drugs, and sex. A significantly greater percentage of U.S. lesbians than either heterosex-

TABLE 2. Analyses of Variance for Proportion of Canadian Male Sample with Positive History of Suicidality, Behavioral Problems, or Mental Health Treatment by Sexual Orientation, Mean (*M*) and Standard Deviation (*SD*)

	Heterosexual n = 834		Gay n = 52		Bisexual n = 37			
	M	SD	M	SD	M	SD	F(2,934)	Post-hoc[e]
Suicidality								
Ideation	.15	.36	.19	.40	.32	.47	4.29*	B>H
Attempt	.04	.20	.06	.24	.19	.40	8.34***	B>H, B>G
Behavioral Problem								
Alcohol	.20	.40	.13	.34	.24	.44	0.90	
Drugs	.11	.32	.06	.24	.19	.40	1.85	
Sex	.14	.32	.04	.19	.30	.46	6.10**	B>G, B>H
Gambling	.04	.20	.00	.00	.14	.35	4.79**	B>G, B>H
Treatment History								
PsychMed[a]	.08	.27	.13	.34	.11	32	1.22	
PsychHx[b]	.10	.30	.15	.36	.19	.40	2.30	
PsychRx[c]	.05	.22	.04	.19	.08	.28	0.43	
PsychTx[d]	.03	.16	.02	.14	.03	.16	0.08	

Notes.*P < .05; **P < .01; ***P < .001; [a]Past Psychiatric Medication; [b]Past Psychotherapy; [c]Current Psychiatric Medication; [d]Current Psychotherapy; [e]G = gay, B = bisexual, H = heterosexual.

ual or bisexual peers reported that they had participated in psychotherapy (see Table 3).

Among U.S. men, there were significant associations between sexual orientation and suicidal ideation (F = 18.69, p < .001) and attempts (F = 13.79, p < .001); and past psychiatric medication (F = 8.23, p < .001), past psychotherapy (F = 17.82, p < .001), current psychiatric medication (F = 7.20, p < .01), and current psychotherapy (F = 10.70, p < .001). Scheffe's post-hoc tests revealed that a significantly greater percentage of U.S. gay men than heterosexual peers reported suicidal ideation and attempts. Relative to their heterosexual male peers, a significantly greater percentage of gay males reported that they had a history positive for past and current use of psychiatric medication and past and current participation in psychotherapy. Relative to heterosexual men, a signifi-

TABLE 3. Analyses of Variance for Proportion of U.S. Female Sample with Positive History of Suicidality, Behavioral Problems, or Mental Health Treatment by Sexual Orientation, Mean (*M*) and Standard Deviation (*SD*)

	Heterosexual $n = 887$		Lesbian $n = 46$		Bisexual $n = 116$			
	M	*SD*	*M*	*SD*	*M*	*SD*	*F(2,1046)*	*Post-hoc*[e]
Suicidality								
Ideation	.22	.41	.26	.44	.44	.50	14.46***	B>H
Attempt	.10	.30	.20	.40	.21	.41	7.65**	B>H
Behavioral Problem								
Alcohol	.13	.33	.20	.40	.22	.42	4.72**	B>H
Drugs	.08	.27	.09	.29	.18	.39	6.56***	B>H
Sex	.10	.30	.09	.29	.22	.41	6.70***	B>H
Gambling	.02	.13	.02	.15	.03	.16	0.25	
Treatment History								
PsychMed[a]	.19	.39	.30	.47	.25	.44	2.77	
PsychHx[b]	.22	.41	.46	.50	.31	.47	8.86***	L>H
PsychRx[c]	.09	.28	.15	.36	.12	.33	1.58	
PsychTx[d]	.05	.22	.11	.31	.11	.32	4.22*	B>H

Notes.*P < .05; **P < .01; ***P < .001; [a]Past Psychiatric Medication; [b]Past Psychotherapy; [c]Current Psychiatric Medication; [d]Current Psychotherapy; [e]L = lesbian, B = bisexual, H = heterosexual.

cantly greater percentage of bisexual men reported suicidal ideation and attempts, higher levels of past and current use of psychiatric medication, and past and current participation in psychotherapy (see Table 4).

Analyses of variance performed on Canadian women (see Table 5) revealed only a significant association between relationship status and past behavioral problems with alcohol (F = 3.722, p < .05). A Scheffe's post-hoc test revealed that Canadian women who were single were significantly more likely to report problems with alcohol use than were women in committed relationships. For Canadian men (see Table 6), significant associations were found between relationship status and suicidal ideation (F = 6.723, p < .01) and attempts (F = 3.435, p < .05). Scheffe's post-hoc tests revealed that single men reported significantly higher rates of suicidal ideation and attempts than did married men.

Among U.S. women (see Table 7), we found a significant association between relationship status and suicidal ideation (F = 4.385, p < .05); past behavioral problems with sex (F = 4.309, p < .05); and past psychiatric medication (F = 4.615, p < .01), past psychotherapy (F = 3.783, p <

TABLE 4. Analyses of Variance for Proportion of U.S. Male Sample with Positive History of Suicidality, Behavioral Problems, or Mental Health Treatment by Sexual Orientation, Mean (*M*) and Standard Deviation (*SD*)

	Heterosexual n = 4,884		Gay n = 344		Bisexual n = 206			
	M	SD	M	SD	M	SD	F(2,5431)	Post-hoc[e]
Suicidality								
Ideation	.12	.32	.20	.40	.23	.42	18.69***	G>H, B>H
Attempt	.04	.20	.09	.29	.09	.29	13.79***	G>H, B>H
Behavioral Problem								
Alcohol	.18	.38	.19	.40	.19	.40	0.33	
Drugs	.12	.32	.15	.36	.16	.36	2.92	
Sex	.14	.35	.15	.36	.20	.40	2.60	
Gambling	.03	.18	.02	.15	.03	.18	0.65	
Treatment History								
PsychMed[a]	.08	.28	.13	.34	.15	.35	8.23***	G>H, B>H
PsychHx[b]	.13	.33	.23	.42	.20	.40	17.82***	G>H, B>H
PsychRx[c]	.04	.19	.07	.26	.07	.26	7.20**	G>H, B>H
PsychTx[d]	.02	.15	.05	.22	.06	.24	10.70***	G>H, B>H

Notes.$^*P < .05$; $^{**}P < .01$; $^{***}P < .001$; [a]Past Psychiatric Medication; [b]Past Psychotherapy; [c]Current Psychiatric Medication; [d]Current Psychotherapy; [e]G = gay male, B = bisexual, H = heterosexual.

.05) and current psychotherapy (F = 4.636, p < .01). Scheffe's post-hoc testing revealed that single women were significantly more likely to report suicidal ideation than were married women. Single women were significantly more likely to report current participation in psychotherapy than were married or committed women. Women in committed relationships were significantly more likely to report past behavioral problems with sex and past participation in psychotherapy than were married women. Women in committed relationships and single women were significantly more likely than were married women to report past use of psychiatric medication.

We found among U.S. men (see Table 8) a significant association between relationship status and suicidal ideation (F = 26.946, p < .001) and attempts (F = 10.232, p < .001); past behavioral problems with drugs (F = 5.246, p < .01), sex (F = 8.710, p < .001), and gambling (F = 3.012, p < .05). We also found among U.S. men a significant association between relationship status and past psychiatric medication (F = 4.242,

TABLE 5. Analyses of Variance for Proportion of Canadian Female Sample with Positive History of Suicidality, Behavioral Problems, or Mental Health Treatment by Relationship Status, Mean (*M*) and Standard Deviation (*SD*)

	Married n = 77		Lesbian n = 78		Bisexual n = 104			
	M	*SD*	*M*	*SD*	*M*	*SD*	*F(2,256)*	Post-hoc[e]
Suicidality								
Ideation	.16	.37	.14	.35	.22	.42	1.15	
Attempt	.05	.22	.08	.27	.11	.31	0.87	
Behavioral Problem								
Alcohol	.13	.34	.09	.29	.23	.42	3.72*	S>C
Drugs	.05	.22	.08	.27	.12	.32	1.19	
Sex	.12	.32	.12	.32	.15	.36	0.39	
Gambling	.01	.11	.01	.11	.03	.17	0.41	
Treatment History								
PsychMed[a]	.12	.32	.12	.32	.22	.42	2.60	
PsychHx[b]	.13	.34	.14	.35	.17	.38	0.36	
PsychRx[c]	.04	.20	.04	.19	.09	.28	1.30	
PsychTx[d]	.04	.20	.04	.19	.03	.17	0.09	

Notes.*$P < .05$; **$P < .01$; ***$P < .001$; [a]Past Psychiatric Medication; [b]Past Psychotherapy; [c]Current Psychiatric Medication; [d]Current Psychotherapy; [e]M = married, C = committed, S = single.

$p < .05$), past psychotherapy ($F = 10.867$, $p < .001$), current psychiatric medication ($F = 3.966$, $p < .05$), and current psychotherapy ($F = 3.059$, $p < .05$). Scheffe's post-hoc testing revealed that, relative to married men in the U.S., a significantly greater percentage of single men as well as men in committed relationships reported suicidal ideation and attempts. Men in committed relationships and single men were significantly more likely than were married men to report problems with drugs and sex. Single men were significantly more likely to report problems with gambling than were married men. Single men were significantly more likely to report past use of psychiatric medication than were married men or men in committed relationships. Single men and those in committed relationships were significantly more likely than others to report past participation in psychotherapy. Single men also were significantly more likely to report current use of psychiatric medication than were married men. See Table 8 for results pertaining to U.S. men.

TABLE 6. Analyses of Variance for Proportion of Canadian Male Sample with Positive History of Suicidality, Behavioral Problems, or Mental Health Treatment by Relationship Status, Mean (*M*) and Standard Deviation (*SD*)

	Married *n* = 331		Committed *n* = 232		Single *n* = 374			
	M	*SD*	*M*	*SD*	*M*	*SD*	$F_{(2,934)}$	Post-hoc[e]
Suicidality								
Ideation	.11	.31	.16	.36	.21	.40	6.72**	S>M
Attempt	.02	.15	.06	.25	.06	.24	3.44**	S>M
Behavioral Problem								
Alcohol	.16	.37	.21	.41	.22	.42	2.00	
Drugs	.09	.29	.13	.34	.12	.33	0.11	
Sex	.15	.35	.14	.35	.14	.35	4.93	
Gambling	.05	.22	.02	.13	.06	.23	2.79	
Treatment History								
PsychMed[a]	.06	.24	.09	.29	.09	.29	1.61	
PsychHX[b]	.07	.26	.12	.32	.13	.33	2.89	
PsychRx[c]	.05	.21	.06	.24	.05	.22	0.32	
PsychTx[d]	.02	.13	.03	.16	.04	.19	1.23	

Notes.*P < .05; **P < .01; ***P < .001; [a]Past Psychiatric Medication; [b]Past Psychotherapy; [c]Current Psychiatric Medication; [d]Current Psychotherapy; [e]M = married, C = committed, S = single.

Hierarchical logistic regressions (Table 9) revealed a significant improvement in goodness of fit when the combined effects of relationship status and sexual orientation were used to predict suicide attempts among Canadian and U.S. males. Among Canadian males, the addition of sexual orientation (-2LL = 350.54) at step 2 to relationship status (-2LL = 359.38) at step 1 significantly increased the goodness of fit for a model predicting suicide attempts, $\chi^2_{(2)} = 8.84$, $p < .05$. Among U.S. males, the addition of sexual orientation (-2LL = 2002.42) to relationship status (-2LL = 2019.00) significantly improved the goodness of fit for a model predicting suicide attempts, $\chi^2_{(2)} = 16.58$, $p < .01$. Thus, the combined effects of sexual orientation and relationship status were a better prediction of men's suicide attempts than was either variable alone.

Hierarchical logistic regression also revealed that the combined effects of relationship status and sexual orientation significantly in-

TABLE 7. Analyses of Variance for Proportion of U.S. Female Sample with Positive History of Suicidality, Behavioral Problems, or Mental Health Treatment by Relationship Status, Mean (*M*) and Standard Deviation (*SD*)

	Married *n* = 887		Committed *n* = 46		Single *n* = 116			
	M	*SD*	*M*	*SD*	*M*	*SD*	F(2,1046)	Post-hoc[e]
Suicidality								
Ideation	.19	.39	.26	.44	.28	.45	4.39*	S>M
Attempt	.09	.29	.13	.34	.12	.33	1.36	
Behavioral Problem								
Alcohol	.12	.33	.16	.37	.14	.44	1.37	
Drugs	.08	.27	.10	.30	.09	.29	0.55	
Sex	.08	.27	.15	.36	.11	.32	4.31*	C>M
Gambling	.02	.14	.01	.11	.02	.15	0.56	
Treatment History								
PsychMed[a]	.15	.36	.23	.42	.23	.42	4.62**	C>M, S>M
PsychHx[b]	.19	.39	.27	.44	.26	.44	3.78*	C>M
PsychRx[c]	.08	.27	.09	.29	.11	.32	1.15	
PsychTx[d]	.04	.21	.04	.21	.09	.29	4.64**	S>M, S>C

Notes.*P < .05; **P < .01; ***P < .001; [a]Past Psychiatric Medication; [b]Past Psychotherapy; [c]Current Psychiatric Medication; [d]Current Psychotherapy; [e]M = married, C = committed, S = single.

creased the goodness of fit in a model predicting suicide ideations among U.S. males and females. The addition of sexual orientation at step 2 (-2LL = 4116.90) to relationship status at step 1 (-2LL = 4139.86) significantly improved the goodness of fit in predicting suicide ideation in U.S. females, $\chi^2_{(2)} = 22.97, p < .01$. Similarly, the addition of sexual orientation at step 2 (-2LL = 1129.64) to relationship status at step 1 (-2LL = 1152.34) significantly improved the goodness of fit in predicting suicide ideation in U.S. females, $\chi^2_{(2)} = 22.70, p < .01$.

DISCUSSION

Review of Key Findings

The present study demonstrated a statistically significant relationship between sexual orientation and (a) suicidality (ideation and attempts), (b) behavioral problems with alcohol, drugs, gambling, and sex, and

TABLE 8. Analyses of Variance for Proportion of U.S. Male Sample with Positive History of Suicidality, Behavioral Problems, or Mental Health Treatment by Relationship Status, Mean (*M*) and Standard Deviation (*SD*)

	Married n = 2,519		Committed n = 1,100		Single n = 1,815			
	M	*SD*	*M*	*SD*	*M*	*SD*	*F(2,5431)*	*Post-hoc*[e]
Suicidality								
Ideation	.09	.29	.15	.35	.17	.37	26.95***	C>M, S>M
Attempt	.03	.18	.06	.24	.06	.23	10.23***	C>M, S>M
Behavioral Problem								
Alcohol	.17	.38	.18	.38	.19	.40	1.58	
Drugs	.10	.31	.14	.34	.13	.34	5.25**	C>M, S>M
Sex	.13	.34	.18	.39	.14	.35	8.71***	C>S, C>M
Gambling	.03	.17	.03	.18	.04	.20	3.01*	S>M
Treatment History								
PsychMed[a]	.08	.28	.08	.27	.11	.31	4.24*	S>M, S>C
PsychHx[b]	.11	.32	.16	.37	.15	.36	10.87***	C>M, S>M
PsychRx[c]	.04	.19	.03	.18	.05	.22	3.97*	S>M
PsychTx[d]	.02	.15	.02	.14	.03	.18	3.06*	

Notes.*$P < .05$; **$P < .01$; ***$P < .001$; [a]Past Psychiatric Medication; [b]Past Psychotherapy; [c]Current Psychiatric Medication; [d]Current Psychotherapy; [e]M = married, C = committed, S = single.

(c) intervention with past and current psychiatric medication and psychotherapy. We also found a significant association between relationship status and (a) suicidality, (b) behavioral problems with alcohol, drugs, gambling, and sex, and (c) intervention with past and current psychiatric medication and psychotherapy.

Closer examination of the data reveals differences among U.S. and Canadian men and women. For women in both the U.S. and Canada, there was a relationship between sexual orientation and suicidal ideation and suicide attempts. Canadian lesbians were more likely to report suicidality than were Canadian heterosexual women, whereas U.S. bisexual women were more likely to report suicidality than were heterosexual women. For women in both the U.S. and Canada, there was also a significant relationship between sexual orientation and past behavioral problems with sex as well as prior participation in psychotherapy. A significantly greater percentage of Canadian and U.S. lesbians than peers reported participation in past psychotherapy. Canadian and U.S.

TABLE 9. Goodness of Fit in Predicting Suicidality with Relationship Status and Sexual Orientation

Improvement in Goodness-of-Fit

Canadian Males

	Ideation				Attempt			
	-2LL	X2	df	p	-2LL	X2	df	p
Constant	820.883				366.996			
Relationship	808.246	12.64	2	.002***	359.376	7.62	2	.022*
Orientation	803.061	5.19	2	.075	350.539	8.84	2	.012*

Canadian Females

	Ideation				Attempt			
	-2LL	X2	df	p	-2LL	X2	df	p
Constant	242.291				145.766			
Relationship								
Orientation	232.686	9.605	2	.008**	139.863	5.903	2	.052

U.S. Males

	Ideation				Attempt			
	-2LL	X2	df	p	-2LL	X2	df	p
Constant	4193.849				2039.913			
Relationship	4139.862	53.987	2	.000***	2019.002	20.911	2	.000***
Orientation	4116.895	22.967	2	.000***	2002.419	16.584	2	.000***

U.S. Females

	Ideation				Attempt			
	-2LL	X2	df	p	-2LL	X2	df	p
Constant	1161.304				746.061			
Relationship	1152.337	8.967	2	.011*				
Orientation	1129.640	22.696	2	.000***	732.945	13.117	2	.001***

Notes.*$p < .05$, **$p < .01$, ***$p < .001$

bisexual women were more likely to report behavioral problems with sex. For U.S. women, there was also relationship between sexual orientation and past behavioral problems with alcohol and drugs (bisexual women reporting greater problems than did heterosexual women) and participation in current psychotherapy (bisexual women reporting higher rates than heterosexual women).

For both Canadian and U.S. men, sexual orientation was associated with suicidal ideation and attempts. Canadian bisexual men were more likely to report suicidality than were Canadian heterosexual men or gay men. However, U.S. gay men were more likely to report suicidality than were heterosexual men. Sexual orientation was also associated with behavioral problems with sex and gambling for Canadian men, with bisexual men being more likely to report these problems than were heterosexual or gay men. For U.S. men, sexual orientation was also associated with past and current psychiatric medication and past and current psychotherapy. U.S. gay and bisexual men were more likely to report past and current use of psychiatric medication and past and current participation in psychotherapy than were heterosexual men.

For U.S. women, we found a significant relationship between relationship status and suicidal ideation, behavioral problems with sex, past use of psychiatric medication, and participation in past and current psychotherapy. Single women were more likely to report suicidal ideation, current participation in psychotherapy, and past use of psychiatric medication than were married women. Single women also were more likely to report current participation in psychotherapy than were women in committed relationships. Women in committed relationships were more likely to report past participation in psychotherapy and past use of psychiatric medication than were married women. However, we found that only behavioral problems with alcohol were significantly associated with relationship status among Canadian women. Single Canadian women were more likely to report problems with alcohol than were women in committed relationships.

For U.S. and Canadian men, relationship status was significantly associated with suicidal ideation and attempts. Single Canadian men were more likely to report suicidality than were married men, whereas U.S. single men and those in committed relationships were more likely to report suicidality than were their married peers. U.S. men's relationship status also was significantly associated with behavioral problems with drugs, sex, and gambling, past and current use of psychiatric medication, and past and current participation in psychotherapy. Men in committed relationships and single men were more likely to report problems with drugs and sex than were married men, and single men were more likely to report problems with gambling than were married men. Single men were more likely to report past use of psychiatric medication than were married or committed men, and they were more likely to report current use of psychiatric medication than were married men. Single and committed men were more likely to have participated in previous therapy than were married men.

Finally, the combined effects of sexual orientation and relationship status significantly improved the goodness of fit in predicting suicide attempts among males in both Canada and the U.S. The combined effects of these variables significantly improved the goodness of fit in predicting suicide ideation among U.S. females and males. This suggests that the protective main effects of relationship status and the risky main effects of sexual orientation have a combined effect that is greater than either effect by itself. Canadian females were the only group for which we did not find the combined effects to increase the goodness of fit in predicting either suicide ideation (both genders in U.S.) or suicide attempts (males in both countries). However, this may have been the result of a relatively small sample size. There was an adverse main effect of sexual orientation on suicide ideations ($p < .01$), and the adverse main effect of sexual orientation on suicide attempt neared significance ($p = .052$).

Conclusions and Implications

Researchers often make an erroneous assumption that marital status is irrelevant to the study of sexual orientation. This is an error, particularly in the study of female sexual orientation. Bell and Weinberg (1978) noted that a number of researchers had found that about one-fifth of sexual minorities have been in heterosexual marriages. Their study found that 20% of white gay males and 13% of black gay males had been in heterosexual marriages. They also found that 35% of white lesbian females and 47% of black lesbian females had been heterosexually married.

Studies of sexual orientation consistently find that at least half of sexual minority females identify as bisexual vis-à-vis lesbian (Diamond, 1998, 2000, 2003). Particularly given Diamond's findings of considerable fluidity in the self-identified sexual orientation of young adult females, it may be fruitful to explore the ways in which societal expectations about marriage and reproduction affect women's narratives about their same-sex sexual experiences across the lifespan. Marriage serves, in part, to legitimize ostensibly "normal" heterosexual relationships. In doing so, it also serves to stigmatize putatively "abnormal" non-heterosexual relationships. Sexual minority females must create a personal narrative that makes meaning out of their experiences while coming out and exploring (Coleman, 1981) their psychosexual development in a patriarchal and heterosexist culture. Research that excludes relationship status from studies of sexual orientation reifies precisely those cultural, social, and perhaps political processes that obfuscate the importance of relationships in sexual minority females' lives.

More specific to the issue of same-sex marriage, our findings indicate that there is an association between relationship status and mental health for women and men in the United States. Consistent with results of previous studies (Smith, Mercy, and Conn, 1988), married individuals constituted the smallest percentage of participants who reported suicidality. Married individuals also constituted the smallest percentage of participants who reported behavioral problems and past use of medication and psychotherapy. Women and men in committed relationships were more likely to report problems than were married peers of the same sex. Whereas the mental health of participants in committed relationships fared better than single participants, married participants were the least likely to report mental health problems. Marriage appears to act as a protective factor against these problems. Interestingly, Canadian women and men reported fewer mental health problems than did the U.S. participants in this study. In the few areas in which relationship status was significantly associated with mental health problems, single Canadian participants reported more difficulties than did their married or committed peers.

Mr. George W. Bush announced on February 24 his support for "an amendment to our Constitution defining and protecting marriage as a union of a man and a woman as husband and wife." Mr. Bush's position became clear with a February 6 statement that, "Marriage is a sacred institution between a man and a woman" and a similar assertion on February 24 that, "Marriage cannot be severed from its cultural, religious and natural roots without weakening the good influence of society." Same-sex unions were socially accepted until the 13th century, at which time religious orders declared them immoral. In fact, same-sex marriage rituals had been condoned for more than 3,000 years in Africa, Asia, Egypt, Greece, Mesopotamia, and a number of indigenous cultures in North America (Boswell, 1994). Boswell discovered and translated dozens of liturgies in Greek, Latin, Slavic, and Russian that had sanctified same-sex unions.

The day after Mr. Bush proposed a constitutional amendment defining marriage as the exclusive purview of one man and one woman, the Executive Board of the American Anthropological Association (2004) responded:

> The results of more than a century of anthropological research on households, kinship relationships, and families, across cultures and through time, provide no support whatsoever for the view that either civilization or viable social orders depend upon marriage as an exclusively heterosexual institution. Rather, anthropological research supports the conclusion that a vast array of family types,

including families built upon same-sex partnerships, can contribute to stable and humane societies.

Our findings go a bit further. Not only do we agree that "same-sex partnerships can contribute to stable and humane societies," our data suggest that the failure to support same-sex marriage imposes public health risks and deprives an oppressed minority group of the protective benefits of marriage.

The prohibition of same-sex marriage also has adverse consequences for heterosexuals. As noted above, a sizable minority of gay male, lesbian, and bisexual individuals has been married. Their heterosexual partners must also endure the anguish of separation and divorce (Kaye, 2000). However, gay men who have entered into heterosexual unions most frequently indicate they married because it "seemed natural" (65.4%) or because they "wanted children and family life" (65.4%) (Higgins, 2002, p. 24). Supporting same-sex marriage would help these marriages "seem natural" and allow same-sex partners to fulfill a desire for "children and family life" without subjecting heterosexual partners and themselves to the adverse consequences of divorce. Bruce and Kim (1992) found that marital disruptions were associated with a high prevalence of major depression in men as well as women. Separated and divorced individuals are significantly more likely to attempt suicide than their married or never-married peers (Petronis, Samuels, Moscicki, Anthony, 1990). Divorce is significantly associated with the incidence of both medical as well as psychiatric problems (Segraves, 1985). Theoretically, same-sex marriage will reduce the deleterious effects of divorce and increase the positive influence of marriage. Further research is needed to study the relations between same-sex marriage and mental health as well as the effects of divorce among homosexual or bisexual individuals married to heterosexual partners.

This research has a number of limitations. Although the database from which we drew our sample has been validated and found to be robust (Cooper et al., 2001), it is not a nationally representative sample. The data obtained for this study reflects participants' retrospective recall. Additionally, some of the samples are small. The database was formed in June 2000, using a cross-sectional design that provides a snapshot in time. It therefore precludes any assessment of causality. Replication of this study with nationally representative samples would help determine whether the inclusion of participants' relationship status and sexual orientation could reliably increase the prediction of suicidality and psychopathology.

REFERENCES

American Anthropological Association Executive Board (2004). Statement on marriage and the family from American Anthropological Association. Downloaded March 2, 2004, from http://aaanet.org/press/ma_stmt_marriage.htm.

American Civil Liberties Union. (1998). Prohibitions against same-sex marriage are unconstitutional. In D. Bender, R. Leone, B. Stalcup, S. Barbour, and T. L., Roleff (Eds.) *Gay Marriage*, pp. 12-17. San Diego, CA: Greenhaven Press, Inc.

American Psychological Association. (1998). Legal benefits for same-sex couples.

Bell, A. P., & Weinberg, M. S. (1978). *Homosexualities: A study of diversity among men and women.* New York: Simon & Schuster.

Bender, D., Leone, R., Stalcup, B., Barbour, S., and Roleff, T. L. (Eds.) *Gay Marriage.* San Diego, CA: Greenhaven Press, Inc.

Boswell, J. (1994). *Same-sex unions in premodern Europe.* New York: Knopf.

Bruce, M. L., & Kim, K. M. (1992). Differences in the effects of divorce on major depression in men and women. *American Journal of Psychiatry, 149*(7), 914-917.

Brzuzy, S. (1998). Public policy interventions to prejudice. In Hecht, M. (Ed.), *Communicating prejudice*, pp. 326-333. Thousand Oaks, CA: Sage.

Bryant, A. S. & Demian. (1994). Relationship characteristics of American gay and lesbian couples: Findings from a national survey. *Journal of Gay and Lesbian Social Services, 1*, 101-117.

Caron, S. L. & Ulin, J. (1997). Closeting and the quality of lesbian relationships. *Families in Society, 78*, 587-600.

Cochran, S. D., Keenan, C., Schober, C., & Mays, V. M. (2000). Estimates of alcohol use and clinical treatment needs among homosexually active men and women in the U.S. population. *Journal of Consulting & Clinical Psychology, 68(6)*, 1062-1071.

Cochran, S. D., & Mays, V. M. (2000a). Lifetime prevalence of suicide symptoms and affective disorders among men reporting same-sex sexual partners: Results from NHANES III. *American Journal of Public Health, 90(4)*, 573-578.

Cochran, S. D., & Mays, V. M. (2000b). Relation between psychiatric syndromes and behaviorally defined sexual orientation in a sample of the US population. *American Journal of Epidemiology, 151(5)*, 516-523.

Coleman, E. (1982). Developmental stages of the coming out process. *Journal of Homosexuality, 7(2-3)*, 31-43.

Cooper, A., Griffin-Shelley, E., Delmonico, D. L., & Mathy, R. M. (2001). Online sexual problems: Assessment and predictive variables. *Sexual Addiction & Compulsivity, 8(3/4)*, 267-285.

Cooper, A., Scherer, C., & Mathy, R. M. (2001). Overcoming methodological concerns in the investigation of online sexual activities. *CyberPsychology & Behavior, 4(4)*, 437-447.

Cooper, A., Morahan-Martin, J., Mathy, R. M., & Maheu, M. (2002). Toward an increased understanding of user demographics in online sexual activities. *Journal of Sex & Marital Therapy, 28*, 105-129.

Diamond, L. M. (1998). Development of sexual orientation among adolescent and young adult women. *Developmental Psychology, 34*(5), 1085-1095.

Diamond, L. M. (2000). Sexual identity, attractions, and behavior among young sexual-minority women over a 2-year period. *Developmental Psychology, 36(2),* 241-250.

Diamond, L. M. (2003). Was it a phase? Young women's relinquishment of lesbian/bisexual identities over a 5-year period. *Journal of Personality & Social Psychology.*

Durkheim, E. *Suicide.* (1966). New York: Free Press.

Eskridge, W. N. (1996). *The Case for Same-Sex Marriage: From Sexual Liberty to Civilized Commitment.* New York: The Free Press.

Garnets, L. D. & Kimmel, D. C. (Eds.) (2003). *Psychological Perspectives on Lesbian, Gay, and Bisexual Experiences.* New York: Columbia University Press.

Gilman, S. E., Cochran, S. D., Mays, V. M., Hughes, M., Ostrow, D., & Kessler, R. C. (2001). Risk of psychiatric disorders among individuals reporting same-sex sexual partners in the National Comorbidity Survey. *American Journal of Public Health, 91(6),* 933-939.

Gonsiorek, J. (1993). Mental health issues of lesbian and gay adolescents. *Journal of Adolescent Health Care, 9,* 114-122.

Herek, G. M. & Glunt, E. K. (1995). Identity and community among gay and bisexual men in the AIDS era: Preliminary findings from the Sacramento Men's Health Study. In G. M. Herek & B. Greene (Eds.), *AIDS, Identity, and Community: The HIV Epidemic and Lesbians and Gay Men,* pp. 55-84. Newbury Park, CA: Sage Publications.

Higgins, D. J. (2002). Gay men from heterosexual marriages: Attitudes, behaviors, childhood experiences, and reasons for marriage. *Journal of Homosexuality, 42(4),* 15-34.

Hillary Goodridge & others [FN1] vs. Department of Public Health & another [FN2], SJC-08860.

Jones, D. A. (1996). Discrimination against same-sex couples in hotel reservation policies. *Journal of Homosexuality, 31,* 153-59.

Jorm, A. F., Korten, A. E., Rodgers, B., Jacomb, P. A., & Christensen, H. (2002). Sexual orientation and mental health: Results from a community survey of young and middle-aged adults. *British Journal of Psychiatry, 180,* 423-427.

Kaye, B. (2000). *Gay husbands/straight wives: A mutation of life.* Bloomington, IN: 1st Books.

Kposowa, A.J. (2000). Marital status and suicide in the National Longitudinal Mortality Study. *Journal of Epidemiology and Community Health, 54,* 254-261.

Kreitman, N. (1988). Suicide, age, and marital status. *Psychological Medicine, 18,* 121-128.

Kurdek, L. A. (1998). Relationship outcomes and their predictors: Longitudinal evidence from heterosexual married, gay cohabiting, and lesbian cohabiting couples. *Journal of Marriage and the Family, 60,* 553-568.

Leserman, J., DiSantostefano, R., Perkins, D. O., & Evans, D. L. (1994). Gay identification and psychological health in HIV-positive and HIV-negative gay men. *Journal of Applied Social Psychology, 24,* 2193-2208.

Mathy, R. M. (2001). A nonclinical comparison of transgender identity and sexual orientation: A framework for multicultural competence. *Journal of Psychology & Human Sexuality, 13(1),* 31-54.

Mathy, R. M. (2002a). On reliability and cultural competence in studies of sexual minority suicidality. *American Journal of Public Health*, 92(12), 1883.

Mathy, R. M. (2002b). Transgender identity and suicidality in a nonclinical sample: Sexual orientation, psychiatric history, and compulsive behaviors. *Journal of Psychology & Human Sexuality, 14(4).*

Mathy, R. M. (2002c). Suicidality and sexual orientation in five continents: Asia, Australia, Europe, North America, and South America. *International Journal of Sexuality and Gender Studies, 7*(2-3), 215-225.

Mathy, R. M. (2002d). Homosexual related legislation does not reduce suicidal intent in sexual minority groups. *BMJ (British Medical Journal), 325,* 1176.

Mays, V. M., & Cochran, S. D. (2001). Mental health correlates of perceived discrimination among lesbian, gay, and bisexual adults in the United States. *American Journal of Public Health, 91*(11), 1869-1876.

Mays, V. M., Yancey, A. K., Cochran, S. D., Weber, M., & Fielding, J. E. (2002). Heterogeneity of health disparities among African American, Hispanic, and Asian American women: Unrecognized influences of sexual orientation. *American Journal of Public Health, 92*(4), 632-639.

McCloud, J. (2004). The battle over gay marriage. *Time Magazine*, February 16, 2004.

McDaniel, J., S., Purcell, D., & D'Augelli, A. R. (2001). The relationship between sexual orientation and risk for suicide: Research findings and future directions for research and prevention. *Suicide & Life-Threatening Behavior, 31*(1,Suppl), 84-105.

Meyer I. & Dean, L. (1998). Internalized homophobia, intimacy, and sexual behavior among gay and bisexual men. In G. M. Herek (Ed.), *Stigma and Sexual Orientation: Understanding Prejudice Against Lesbians, Gay Men, and Bisexuals*, pp. 160-186. Thousand Oaks, CA: Sage.

Miranda, J. & Storms, M. (1989). Psychological adjustment of lesbians and gay men. *Journal of Counseling and Development*, 68, 41-45.

Ohio Senate bans gay "marriage." (2004). The Washington Times, January 23, 2004.

Peplau, L. A. & Spalding, L. R. (2003). The close relationships of lesbians, gay men, and bisexuals. In L. D. Garnets & D. C. Kimmel (Eds.), *Psychological Perspectives on Lesbian, Gay, and Bisexual Experiences*, pp. 449-474. New York: Columbia University Press.

Petronis, K. R., Samuels, J. F., Moscicki, E. K., & Anthony, J.D. An epidemiological investigation of potential risk factors for suicide attempts. *Social Psychiatry & Psychiatric Epidemiology, 25*(4), 193-199.

Placido, J. (1998). Minority stress among lesbians, gay men, and bisexuals: A consequence of heterosexism, homophobia,and stigmatization. In G. M. Herek (Ed.), *Stigma and Sexual Orientation: Understanding Prejudice Against Lesbians, Gay Men, and Bisexuals*, pp. 138-159. Thousand Oaks, CA: Sage.

Popoli, G., Sobelman, S., & Kanarek (1989). Suicide in the state of Maryland. *Public Health Report, 104,* 298-301.

Savin-Williams, R. C. (1989). Coming out to parents and self-esteem among gay and lesbian youth. *Journal of Homosexuality, 18,* 1-35.

Savin-Williams, R.C. and Esterberg, K. G. (2000). Lesbian, gay, and bisexual families. In Demo, D. H., Allen, K. R. & Fine, M. A. (Eds.), *Handbook of Family Diversity*. New York: Oxford University Press (pp. 197-215).

Schmitt, J. P. & Kurdek, L. A. (1987). Personality correlates of positive identity and relationship involvement in gay men. *Journal of Homosexuality, 13*, 101-109.

Segraves, R. T. Divorce and health problems. *Medical Aspects of Human Sexuality, 19*(7), 152-164.

Shildo, A. (1994). Internalized homophobia: Conceptual and empirical issues in measurement. In B. Greene & G. M. Herek (Eds.), *Lesbian and Gay Psychology: Theory, Research, and Clinical Applications*, pp. 176-205. Thousand Oaks, CA: Sage.

Smith, J. C., Mercy, J.A., & Conn, J. M. (1988). Marital status and the risk of suicide. *American Journal of Public Health, 78*, 78-80.

States determine marriage laws (2004). CNN.com LAW CENTER. January 13, 2004.

Walters, A. S. & Curran, M. (1996). Excuse me sir? May I help you and your boyfriend?: Salespersons' differential treatment of homosexual and straight customers. *Journal of Homosexuality, 31*, 135-152.

A Review of Lesbian Depression and Anxiety

Shelly K. Kerr, PhD
Alice M. Emerson, PhD

SUMMARY. The Surgeon General's first report on mental health identified depression and anxiety as significant mental health issues that disproportionately affect women. Research indicates that lesbians experience depression at rates that parallel those of the general female population, suggesting that depression is an important mental health issue for lesbians. Given the high rate of comorbidity between depression and anxiety disorders, it is likely that many depressed lesbians have struggled with problems related to anxiety as well. This paper reviews literature pertaining to lesbians and depression including incidence rates, risk factors, suicidality and treatment approaches, and stress and anxiety that may also contribute to the experience of depression among lesbians. *[Article copies available for a fee from The Haworth Document Delivery Service: 1-800-HAWORTH. E-mail address: <docdelivery@haworthpress.com> Website: <http://www.HaworthPress.com> © 2003 by The Haworth Press, Inc. All rights reserved.]*

Shelly K. Kerr is Assistant Director and Training Director at the University Counseling and Testing Center, University of Oregon. Alice M. Emerson is affiliated with Washington State University.

Address correspondence to Shelly K. Kerr, University Counseling and Testing Center, 1590 East 13th Avenue, University of Oregon, Eugene, OR.

[Haworth co-indexing entry note]: "A Review of Lesbian Depression and Anxiety." Kerr, Shelly K., and Alice M. Emerson. Co-published simultaneously in *Journal of Psychology & Human Sexuality* (The Haworth Press, Inc.) Vol. 15, No. 4, 2003, pp. 143-162; and: *Lesbian and Bisexual Women's Mental Health* (ed: Robin M. Mathy, and Shelly K. Kerr) The Haworth Press, Inc., 2003, pp. 143-162. Single or multiple copies of this article are available for a fee from The Haworth Document Delivery Service [1-800-HAWORTH, 9:00 a.m. - 5:00 p.m. (EST). E-mail address: docdelivery@haworthpress.com].

Digital Object Identifier: 10.1300/J056v15n04_01

KEYWORDS. Review, lesbian, depression, anxiety

The first Surgeon General's report on mental health (2000) identified depression and anxiety as major mental health problems in the United States that disproportionately affect women. Women are 2 to 4 times as likely to become depressed as are men (American Psychiatric Association, 1994; Blazer, Kessler, McGonagle, & Swartz, 1994; McGrath, Keita, Strickland, & Russo, 1990; Sprock & Yoder, 1997). McGrath et al. (1990) identified several risk factors that lead to increased rates of depression among women, including marital status, parenting of young or several children, poverty, victimization, biochemical and hormonal factors, personality traits that stem from gender role socialization, and ruminative coping styles. Women also are at increased risk for most anxiety disorders (American Psychiatric Association, 1994; Kessler et al., 1994; Lewinshohn, Gotlib, Lewinsohn, Seeley, & Allen, 1998). There is little theoretical or empirical literature that examines possible reasons for this gender difference. Hypothesized risk factors for women include genetics (Kendler, Neale, Kessler, Heath, & Eaves, 1992), higher levels of emotionality (Joiner & Blalock, 1995), and environmental factors (Kendler et al., 1992). Based on results from the National Comorbidity Survey, it also appears that women are more likely than men to have comorbid disorders (Kessler et al., 1994), including comorbid depression and anxiety (Joiner & Blalock, 1995).

Despite validating mental health care as a legitimate area of focus and emphasizing the special mental health needs of women, the Surgeon General's report made no mention of the unique issues facing lesbians as a special population. The Institute of Medicine (IOM), a component of the National Academy of Sciences, noted that the mental and physical health of lesbians has not been adequately addressed even as women's health has received more attention in recent years. In its report on lesbian health, the IOM called for an increase in research and education focusing on the mental and physical health of lesbians (Solarz, 1999). However, research on the mental health of lesbians has been sparse (Bradford, Ryan, & Rothblum, 1994).

Rothblum's (1990) review examined risk factors and the role of therapy for depressed lesbians. The paucity of research on this topic led her to describe depression among lesbians as "unresearched" and "invisible." While still underrepresented, a few studies have emerged focusing specifically on lesbians and some reviews addressing depression among women in general mention lesbians as a distinct subgroup of women with special risk factors and treatment issues (McGrath et al., 1990; Sprock & Yoder, 1997). However, stress and anxiety among lesbian women continues to be invisible in the literature. In her search of PsycLIT and Sociofile databases for the previous five years, Tait (1997) found no literature related to stress among lesbians. The present authors' review of literature yielded six studies related to stress or anxiety, one study that identified anxiety as a consequence of victimization, and one study exploring disclosure and occupational stress.

This paper will build upon Rothblum's (1990) review to discuss research related to depression among lesbians. Given the high rate of comorbidity and overlap between depression and anxiety (Barbee, 1998; Copp, Schwiderski, & Robinson, 1990; Joiner & Blalock, 1995; Katon & Roy-Byrne, 1991; Kendler, Neale, Kessler, Heath, & Eaves, 1992; Wittchen, Essau, & Krieg, 1991), and the role of stress and anxiety in increasing vulnerability to depression (Barbee, 1998; Reinherz et al., 1999), this paper will also review literature pertaining to lesbians' experience of stress and anxiety. The review will examine the prevalence of these problems among lesbians, risk factors and mediating variables for depression and anxiety among lesbians, and consequences and coping strategies related to these mental health problems.

DEPRESSION

Prevalence of Depression

Reported rates of depression among lesbians range from 33% (Bradford et al., 1994) to 66% (Trippett, 1994), depending upon the research methodology and instrumentation used to obtain data. Some research studies use more open-ended and subjective questions, such as asking whether participants have ever experienced a "long depression or sadness" (Bradford et al., 1994), whether they had been "seriously or clinically depressed" in the past (Lehmann, Lehmann, & Kelly, 1998) or experienced any of a list of mental health problems (Trippett, 1994). Although McGrath et al. (1990) indicated that subclinical depressive symptoms are correlated with clinical depression, one cannot be certain that research participants endorsing some depressive symptoms on a checklist actually meet the criteria for a depressive disorder diagnosis. Other data are based on participant responses to standardized depression inventories such as the Center for Epidemiological Studies Depression Scale, CES-D (Herek, Gillis, & Cogan, 1999; Luhtanen, 2003;

Oetjen & Rothblum, 2000; Otis & Skinner, 1996), the Composite International Diagnostic Interview Short Form (Cochran, Sullivan, & Mays, 2003), the General Contentment Scale (Ayala & Coleman, 2000), or the Depression scale of the MMPI-2 (Griffith, Myers, Cusick, & Tankersley, 1997). Another complication in comparing depression research is the heterogeneity (e.g., major depressive disorder, dysthymic disorder, adjustment disorder with depressed mood) and overlap (e.g., double depression consisting of major depression that occurs in the presence of dysthymic disorder) of depressive disorders and distinguishing between symptoms of depression and a cluster of symptoms, or syndrome, that suggests the presence of a DSM diagnosis of a depressive disorder (McGrath et al., 1990). The broad range of definitions of depression and the variety of measurement tools must be considered as one evaluates the research on the prevalence of depression among lesbians.

Rogers, Emanuel, and Bradford (2003) conducted a chart review for 223 lesbian and bisexual women who presented for services at a health clinic in Boston. Their conclusions were based on clients' self-report and clinicians' assessment of clients' problems. Depressive symptoms were reported by 85% of the women. Rogers et al. reported a discrepancy between self-reported symptoms of depression and diagnoses made by clinicians, noting that only 39% of the lesbian and bisexual women in this study were actually diagnosed with a mood disorder despite the high percentages reporting depressive symptoms. However, 44% of the sample diagnosed with an adjustment disorder probably included women with depressive symptoms as well.

Bradford et al. (1994) surveyed 1,925 lesbians for a national health care survey and provided one of the most extensive looks at lesbian mental health. Their sample consisted primarily of Caucasian lesbians (88%), with 6% of the sample identifying as African-American and 4% as Latina. Eighty percent of the participants were between 25 and 44 years old and 69% had a college degree. A response rate of 42% leaves room to wonder about the demographic characteristics and mental health concerns of those who chose not to participate in the study.

More than one-third of the women in the National Health Care Survey said they had experienced a "long depression or sadness" in the past, 11% reported being currently depressed, and 11% indicated that they were currently being treated for depression (Bradford et al., 1994). Other research includes a sample of 53 lesbians in which 49% reported having been seriously or clinically depressed in the past (Lehmann et. al., 1998) and a survey of 503 lesbian women in which 66% said they had experienced depression (Trippett, 1994). Lesbians, aged 55 and older, were least likely to report problems with depression (Bradford et al., 1994), consistent with research showing that rates of depression decrease with age (Blazer et al., 1994; Jorm, 2000). Luhtanen's (2003) study that included 168 lesbian and bisexual women yielded contradictory results. This sample of women scored in the lower range on the CES-D, below the cutoff score for clinical depression. However, their return rate of 10% limits the generalizability of these results.

Variation in the way that depression is defined and measured complicates attempts to compare rates between lesbians and the general female population. Comparisons of rates of depression between lesbian and heterosexual women yield mixed results. Analysis of data from the MacArthur Foundation National Survey of Midlife Development in the United States (Cochran, Sullivan, and Mays, 2003) found no significant differences by women's sexual orientation group (lesbian and bisexual vis-à-vis heterosexual) for meeting diagnostic criteria for major depression. Bradford et al. (1994) concluded that lesbians in their sample reported depression rates comparable to studies of heterosexual women that also had used broad measures of depression. Additionally, no significant differences in levels of depression were found between heterosexual and lesbian females who had experienced intimate partner abuse (Tuel & Russell, 1998). However, a study of sexually abused and non-sexually abused heterosexual and lesbian women found that heterosexual women were significantly more depressed than lesbian women, regardless of abuse history (Griffith et al., 1997).

Using the CES-D, Cochran and Mays (1994) found higher rates of depression for lesbians than women in general, and elevated levels of depressive symptoms among African-American lesbians ($n = 505$, aged 18-60, median 15 years of education). Symptomatic HIV-infected gay and bisexual men reported the highest level of depressive distress, but distress among women, including lesbians and bisexuals, did not differ significantly from these men or from asymptomatic HIV-infected men. Women reported significantly more distress than did HIV-negative gay men or men with an unknown HIV-status was unknown. Lesbian and bisexual women and symptomatic HIV-infected men reported significantly more somatic complaints than did the other three groups. Cochran and Mays found that the mean CES-D score (13.6) for the African-American lesbian and bisexual women in their sample was higher than the published mean for African-Americans (9.9-11.5). Separate mean scores for men ($M = 12.8$) and women ($M = 14.7$) in this study were also noted to be higher than means for African American men ($M = 9.8$) and women ($M = 12.8$) reported in other studies. Thirty-eight percent of the African-American lesbian and bisexual women scored higher than the CES-D cutoff score that identifies individuals at risk for clinical depression. The authors indicated that this percentage is higher than another set of studies of African-American women in which 26% of the women were classified as being at risk for clinical depression (Cochran & Mays, 1994).

Risk Factors for Depression

Relationship status has been correlated with depression among lesbians. Ayala and Coleman's (2000) study of self-identified lesbians in Western Canada found that lesbians in romantic relationships were significantly less depressed than lesbians who were not in relationships. Oetjen and Rothblum (2000) also found that being in a primary relationship was linked to lower levels of depression, while single lesbians who were not dating tended to be more depressed. Although lesbians' satisfaction with their relationships did not correlate with depression, satisfaction with relationship status appeared to be related to depression. Lesbians who were more satisfied with their relationship status (i.e., being single or partnered) were less likely to be depressed.

Hate and bias crime victimization has been identified as negatively influencing the mental health of lesbians (Herek, Gillis, & Cogan, 1999; Herek, Gillis, Cogan, & Glunt, 1995; Otis & Skinner, 1996). Herek et al. (1999) found that one-fifth of the women in a survey of 1,170 lesbian and bisexual women had been adult victims of a hate crime based on sexual orientation. Another study of 499 lesbians in two Southern cities (Otis & Skinner, 1996) revealed a high percentage of participants who perceived hate motivated crimes, including threats or verbal abuse (57%), theft or vandalism (35%), sexual assaults by men (12%), and physical assaults (17%).

Otis and Skinner (1996) found no significant difference in the rates of depression (based on responses to the CES-D) for gay and lesbian hate crime victims and victims of non-hate motivated crimes. When victimization did affect depression among lesbians, sexual assault, physical attack, and threats or verbal abuse were most likely to lead to increased levels of depression (Otis & Skinner, 1996). In contrast, Herek et al. (1995) and Herek et al. (1999) concluded that victims of hate and bias crimes were significantly more depressed than either non-victims or victims of non-hate crimes. It is possible that length of time since the hate crime may be a mediating variable that affects depression rates among lesbian hate crime victims. Victims of hate crimes committed within five years prior to the Herek et al. (1999) survey reported significantly more depressive symptoms on the CES-D than did lesbians and gay men who (a) were not victims of any crime, (b) had been victims of non-hate or bias crime, or (c) had been victims of hate crimes that occurred more than five years before the study was conducted. Otis and Skinner (1996) found that additional mediating variables for lesbian hate crime victimization were self-esteem and external stress. Higher levels of self-esteem appeared to serve as a buffer against depression after hate crime victimization. This finding is consistent with the results of Grossman and Kerner's (1998) study of lesbian and gay male adolescents aged 14-21 years old, who were primarily African-American and Latino/a. Self-esteem emerged as a strong predictor of degree of emotional distress for females. Otis and Skinner's definition of external stress included the degree to which lesbians believed they have "dealt successfully with irritating hassles," effectively coped with changes in their lives, were confident that they could handle personal problems, and were able to control the way they spent their time. Lesbian hate crime victims who reported greater external stress also reported greater levels of depression.

The presence or absence of social support has been evaluated as a potential risk factor leading to psychological maladjustment, including depression. Zea, Reisen, and Poppen (1999) examined the role of social support for Latina lesbians and found that both social support and identification with the Latino/a gay and lesbian community were associated with lower levels of depression. Ayala and Coleman's (2000) study of lesbians in Western Canada revealed that perceptions of low social support from friends, measured on the Perceived Social Support Scale, were significantly and moderately correlated with higher levels of depression as measured by the Generalized Contentment Scale. Lesbians' perceptions of low family social support were also significantly, although more weakly, correlated with higher levels of depression. Robinson and Garner (1995) concluded that depression is associated with smaller social networks and dissatisfaction with perceived availability of support and that having a confidante can provide a buffering effect against depression. Using Procidano and Heller's (1983) Perceived Social Support Scale and Derogatis's (1983) Symptom Checklist 90-4, Kurdek and Schmitt (1987) examined the impact of social support on psychopathology for married ($n = 44$), cohabitating heterosexual ($n = 35$), gay male ($n = 50$), and lesbian couples ($n = 56$). Relative to married couples and cohabiting heterosexual couples, lesbian and gay male couples perceived more support from friends than from family. The difference in perceptions of support from family and friends did not appear to negatively influence lesbian or gay male couples' psychological adjustment. Across all groups, individuals who scored high on perceived emotional support from friends reported fewer psychopathology symptoms over the previous seven-day period. Kurdek and Schmitt (1987) noted, however, that their sample was comprised of couples who were already relatively well-adjusted and fairly satisfied with their relationships.

Kurdek (1988) continued to examine the relationship between social support and psychological adjustment for lesbians and gay men using the Social Support Questionnaire (SSQ; Sarasonson, Levine, Basham, and Sarason, 1983) and the Global Severity Index of the Symptom Checklist-90-Revised (Derogatis, 1983). When family members were collectively identified as support providers, participants ranked them in descending order: (a) friends, (b) partner, (c) family, and (d) coworkers. Kurdek (1988) found that relatively high scores of psychological adjustment for lesbians and gay men were significantly related to (a) frequent support from friends, (b) frequent support from partner, (c) a high total number of supporters, and (d) most strongly to higher satisfaction with support. The study also revealed that lesbian (but not gay male) couples who showed relatively large and significant differences in their reports of satisfaction with support were more likely to report low relationship quality. Most recently, Grossman, D'Augelli, and Hershberger (2000) examined social support networks of lesbian, gay, and bisexual adults, aged 60 and over. Based on self-rating mental and emotional health on a continuum from very poor to excellent, Grossman et al. found that greater satisfaction with the support received by participants was correlated with relatively high ratings of mental and emotional health.

Based on the Social Support Questionnaire (Sarason et al., 1983) Otis and Skinner (1996) found that when victimization was correlated with increased depression, reports of having no support were correlated with higher depression scores on the CES-D for the previous year. As expected, increased partner support was associated with lower depression scores. This relationship was stronger for lesbians than gay men. The authors were surprised to find that increases in the number of situations (14 possible) in which friends might be relied on to provide support was associated with increased depression scores for gay men and lesbian women. Otis and Skinner present a "commiseration hypothesis," which suggests that simply talking to more people about a problem may not lead to developing problem-solving skills that would reduce depressive symptoms. This hypothesis is consistent with Robinson and Garber's (1995) review, in which they suggested that support network size *and* the quality of the support provided are both important factors for individuals with depression.

There are mixed results related to whether self-disclosure of one's lesbian identity affects depression. Oetjen and Rothblum (2000) found no significant correlation between self-disclosure in any context (e.g., work, family, friends) and depression as measured by the Center for Epidemiological Studies Depression Scale (CES-D). Ayala and Coleman (2000) found a significantly low to moderate correlation between self-disclosure and depression, with lesbians who disclosed their sexual orientation to more people being less likely to be depressed than lesbians who disclosed to few or no people. Although they did not specifically address depression in their study of 499 lesbians, Jordan and Deluty (1998) examined the link between disclosure of sexual orientation and "positive affectivity." The researchers defined positive affectivity as a mood state that encompasses happiness and satisfaction. The construct of positive affectivity is negatively correlated with measures of depressive symptoms and diagnoses (Clark, Watson, & Mineka, 1994). Women who more widely disclosed their lesbian orientation expressed significantly more positive affectivity than women who disclosed more narrowly (Jordan & Deluty, 1998). Jordan and Deluty also noted that higher levels of self-disclosure were correlated with higher levels of receiving support and that disclosure to friends was the best predictor of overall support. This correlation was significant, but not particularly strong.

In contrast to gay men, internalized homophobia did not significantly increase depression levels for lesbian hate crime victims in the Otis and Skinner (1996) study. This is surprising in light of the authors' findings that self-esteem mediated depression. One might intuitively expect internalized homophobia to be linked to self-esteem. However, the way in which these constructs were measured may account for this lack of connection between self-esteem and internalized homophobia. Self-esteem was measured using Rosenberg's (1965) scale, whereas internalized homophobia was assessed from participants' responses to only one question: "I feel stress or conflict with myself because of my sexual orientation." This question only taps into the most obvious and conscious awareness of internalized homophobia and does not elicit information about more subtle evidence of internalized homophobia.

Luhtanen's (2003) study of 168 lesbian and bisexual women found that rejection of negative stereotypes and positive sexual minority identity were significant predictors of level of depression. Eliason and Morgan (1998) examined differences between women whose lesbian identities were defined politically or nonpolitically. Nonpolitical definitions were based on the personal meaning of sexuality (e.g., being in love with a woman), whereas political definitions were based on identifying as part of an oppressed group. Politically identified lesbians were significantly more likely to report depression; however, 50% of non-politically identified women also reported depression. Nonpolitically identified lesbians had higher self-esteem scores (albeit not statistically significant), a trend suggesting that self-esteem may be acting as a mediating variable. Higher levels of depression among politically identified lesbians could be interpreted in two ways. It is possible that a political lesbian identity increases one's risk for becoming depressed. Half of the nonpolitically identified lesbians reported depression. Therefore, a non-political identity does not necessarily translate into a low rate of depression. Secondly, as Eliason and Morgan noted, it is also possible that some women may have developed a political lesbian identity during treatment for mental health problems. This may have occurred as they developed insights into the effects of membership in two oppressed groups.

STRESS AND ANXIETY

Prevalence of Stress and Anxiety

As sparse as the literature is pertaining to depression among lesbians, stress and anxiety among lesbians is even less researched. As a result, it is difficult to draw many conclusions about the extent to which lesbians experience significant levels of stress or have symptoms of DSM anxiety diagnoses. As noted for the depression literature, studies that examine stress and anxiety among lesbians use differing definitions and instrumentation to measure symptoms. Some researchers ask participants to identify whether they have experienced "constant anxiety or fear" or were "worried and nervous" (Bradford et al., 1994). Others ask participants to rate the degree of stress felt in relation to several listed items (Bernhard & Applegate, 1999). Instruments used include the Composite International Diagnostic Interview Short Form (Cochran, Sullivan, & Mays, 2003), a standardized anxiety scale, the State-Trait Anxiety Inventory (Jordan and Deluty, 1998), stress-related items from Derogatis' Symptom Checklist-90 (Tait, 1997), and the Occupational Stress Inventory (Driscoll, Kelley, & Fassinger, 1996). An early study that included both gay men and lesbians used the neuroticism scale on the Eysenck Personality Inventory (Miranda & Storms, 1989).

The Bradford et al. (1994) large-scale study of 1900 lesbians revealed that 11% percent of the participants in this study reported "constant anxiety or fear" previously, 7% reported "constant anxiety or fear" currently, and 7% were currently being treated for "constant anxiety or fear." When asked how often participants were "so worried or nervous" that they could not do "necessary things," 18% endorsed "often" and 38% endorsed "sometimes." Although women aged 55 and older were least likely to report "constant anxiety or fear," they were more likely to report frequent worrying than were younger lesbians. Rogers, Emanuel, and Bradford's (2003) study of 223 lesbian and bisexual women in Boston also found that a large percentage (79%) of their sample reported symptoms of anxiety. A striking discrepancy was found between client self-report and clinician diagnosis, with less than 4% of the sample being diagnosed with anxiety disorders. However, another 9% of the sample was diagnosed with post-traumatic stress disorder. It is also likely that some of the 44% of the sample diagnosed with an adjustment disorder also included women reporting anxious symptoms.

Research that compares rates of stress and anxiety between lesbian and heterosexual women yields mixed results. Analyzing data from the MacArthur Foundation National Survey of Midlife Development in the United States, Cochran, Sullivan, and Mays (2003) found that a significantly higher prevalence of lesbian than heterosexual women met the diagnostic criteria for generalized anxiety disorder. However, there were no significant differences between those groups for panic disorder.

Tait (1997) found lesbian and heterosexual female participants in her research to be similar in their levels of stress. Using a snowball method of sampling, Tait measured stress levels among 29 lesbian women and 77 heterosexual females using 25 items from the Derogatis' Symptom Checklist-90. The two groups appeared to be relatively similar in terms of educational level, personal income, and age. The majority of both groups were Caucasian (97% lesbians, 80% heterosexual females). Mean scores on the symptom checklist revealed that both groups had experienced "a little bit of stress" in the previous six months, with no significant differences between the groups. The 25 stress checklist items were analyzed separately to determine which symptoms were most frequently reported. The lesbian sample endorsed the symptom "feeling low in energy or slowed down," followed by "blaming yourself for things," "feeling blue," "feeling tense or keyed up," and "easily hurt feelings." The heterosexual sample endorsed the symptom "feeling tense or keyed up," followed by "feeling low in energy or slowed down," "blaming yourself for things," "headaches," and "easily hurt feelings." The most intensely experienced symptom reported by both groups was "feeling tense or keyed up." Finally, Tait analyzed three clusters of symptoms (depression and anxiety, somatic illness, and interpersonal problems) and found that lesbian participants endorsed all of the depression and anxiety symptoms, six of nine somatic symptoms, and nine of ten interpersonal problems more frequently than the heterosexual female participant. These differences were statistically non-significant, but the sample size was small.

Bernhard and Applegate (1999) surveyed a convenience sample of 179 self-identified lesbians and 79 heterosexual women in a large midwestern city. The majority of the sample was Caucasian (86%), with 14% of the participants being persons of color, mostly African-American. This was a highly educated sample, with 43% of the participants having a college education and 36% having a graduate school education. The researchers used a general measure of mental health and found no differences between lesbian and heterosexual participants in terms of overall mental health. Participants were found to be in generally good mental health. They also found no differences between lesbian and heterosexual women in the degree of distress reported when participants were asked to evaluate their overall level of stress using the categories of none, little, moderate, and extreme. However, when participants rated 18 items on a 4-point Likert scale according to the degree of stress they felt in relation to each item, lesbians were significantly more likely than heterosexual women to report stress related to sexual identity and emotional problems. It seems that lesbian participants, when asked outright, did not perceive themselves to be particularly stressed. However, when specific items were analyzed, lesbians endorsed higher levels of stress than did their heterosexual counterparts.

Jordan and Deluty (1998) examined anxiety among lesbians using the Trait scale of the State-Trait Anxiety Inventory and found that their sample of lesbians was more anxious than the original normative sample that included both men and women. The authors noted that lesbians' scores on this instrument were comparable to another study in which women were experiencing "stressful and potentially anxiety-producing situations associated with pain."

Risk Factors for Anxiety

The earliest known study that examined stress among lesbians (Gillow & Davis, 1987) asked 142 lesbians to identify their primary stressors. Descriptive statistics revealed that (a) 27% of the women listed job-related stressors, such as discrimination and harassment, (b) 25% identified stress in their primary relationships, including not being currently involved with someone or breaking up with a partner, (c) 11% identified their family of origin as the primary source of stress (e.g., lack of acceptance by family members or family members not taking their intimate relationships seriously), (d) 10% identified financial stressors; (e) 8% reported stress related to children and child care, such as custody issues; and (f) 24% reported miscellaneous stressors, including those related to identity development or lack of a social network. Although a few of the stressors were not directly related to a lesbian sexual orientation, most of the stressors reported by the women would not exist separately from the issue of sexual orientation.

Miranda and Storms' (1989) study of 50 lesbians and 50 gay men, and a sample of gay and lesbian college students, revealed that a positive gay or lesbian identity significantly correlated with lower rates of "neurotic anxiety" as measured by the Eysenck Personality Inventory. High scores on the neuroticism scale are indicative of anxiety and worry.

Similar to depression, hate crime victimization appears to increase lesbians' levels of anxiety. Herek et al. (1999) noted that lesbians and gay men who were the victims of hate or bias crimes within five years prior to the survey reported significantly more traumatic stress symptoms than did (a) non-victims, (b) victims of non-bias crimes, or (c) victims of hate crimes that occurred more than five years before the survey. Lesbians and gay men who had been hate crime victims in the previous five years reported significantly greater levels of general anxiety than did lesbians and gay men who had not been victims of any crime or of a hate or bias crime. There were no significant differences in levels of anxiety between recent victims of hate or bias crimes and those who were victimized more than five years before the study. Women who were victims of a hate crime prior to age 16 reported more psychological distress than did women who reported no victimization or adult victimization that occurred more than five years before the study. The researchers concluded that being the victim of a hate crime prior to reaching adulthood is associated with a greater level of psychological distress (Herek et al., 1999).

Two studies investigated the role of self-disclosure on levels of anxiety. Jordan and Deluty (1998) found that women who disclosed their sexual orientation were significantly less anxious than those who did not self-disclose. Driscoll, Kelley, and Fassinger (1996) expected to find that self-disclosure would affect workplace stress. Using a snow-ball method, they obtained a sample of 123 employed lesbians (85% were Caucasian, 8.1% African-American, and 6.4% Latina, Native American, or women who did not specify their ethnicity). The sample had low disclosure scores, although there was a great deal of variance in scores. Contrary to the original hypothesis of the researchers, disclosure was not linked to workplace stress. Of interest however, is the finding that length of time in a partnered relationship was negatively correlated with occupational stress. In other words, the longer a woman had been in a partnered relationship, the less workplace stress she reported.

COPING WITH STRESS, ANXIETY, AND DEPRESSION

Research reveals that lesbians use a variety of adaptive and mal-adaptive coping strategies to combat depression, stress and anxiety. Gillow and Davis's (1987) study of stress and coping among lesbians led them to conclude that there is a strong tendency for lesbians to use ineffective coping strategies such as suicidal behavior and alcoholism. Rates of attempted suicide among lesbians range from 18% (Bradford et al., 1994; Sorensen & Roberts, 1997) to 27% (Lehmann et al., 1998). When asked why they attempted suicide, lesbians in Bernhard and Applegate's (1999) study most frequently identified feeling depressed or sad. Lehmann et al. (1998) also found a significant relationship be-tween reports of being seriously depressed in the past and having made a suicide attempt. However, it is important to note that more than half of the suicide attempts reported in Sorensen and Roberts's (1997) study were made during adolescence.

Substance use, including alcohol, is another way that lesbians have coped with depression and anxiety. The percentage of lesbians report-ing substance abuse problems has varied. More than one-third of participants in Lehmann et al.'s (1998) sample reported drug and alcohol problems. Lehmann et al. found that lesbians who had experienced a seri-ous depression were also significantly more likely to report substance abuse problems. Fifteen percent of the respondents in the Boston Lesbian Health Project identified themselves as alcoholic, and 29% reported that they had attended Alcoholics Anonymous meetings (Sorensen & Rob-erts, 1997).

Self-disclosure of one's lesbian sexual orientation was linked to in-creased positive affectivity and decreased anxiety (Jordan & Deluty, 1998). Not only does self-disclosure emerge as a risk factor, it can also be viewed as an adaptive coping strategy. Jordan and Deluty suggested that self-disclosure may reduce anxiety by eliminating the need to hide an important aspect of one's identity, making it easier to locate support systems. They acknowledged that greater positive affectivity and reduced anxiety may increase the likelihood that a lesbian will disclose her identity to others.

Lesbians appear to use therapy as a means of addressing emotional problems such as depression and anxiety, with usage rates ranging from 30% (Bernhard & Applegate, 1999) to 80% (Sorensen & Roberts, 1997). Half of the participants in the Boston Health Project reported seeing a counselor more than once. The Bradford et al. (1994) extensive health care survey found that 75% of their sample of 1925 lesbians had received counseling and the most frequently cited reason for seeing a counselor was feeling sad or depressed (50%), followed by feeling anxious or scared (31%). Twenty-eight percent of the participants in the Boston Lesbian Health Project reported seeing a counselor because of depression (Sorensen & Roberts, 1997), while 50% of Tait's (1997) sample of lesbians saw a psychiatrist or psychologist to help deal with stress. There are mixed findings regarding the length of time spent in therapy. Bernhard and Applegate (1999) found no difference in the length of time spent in therapy. Griffith et al. (1997) found that twice as many lesbians as heterosexual women without sexual abuse histories reported long-term (3-10 years) therapy. Griffith et al. (1997) also found that a larger percentage of lesbians than heterosexual women participated in Adult Children of Alcoholics (20% lesbian, 3% heterosexual), Overeater's Anonymous (18% lesbian, 11% heterosexual), and Incest Survivors (10% lesbian, 0% heterosexual) self-help groups. It is possible that lesbian participation in individual and group therapy may result from being more psychologically-minded due to their higher educational levels (Griffith et al., 1997) or because of the introspection that goes with lesbian identity development and coming out (Morgan, 1992).

Other coping strategies have been identified in the literature. Gillow and Davis (1987) asked lesbians to identify coping strategies that they had used in the past six months or at the time of the survey. Ninety-four percent of participants said that they currently tried to see the humor in a situation, 92% said that they cried, 89% temporarily withdrew, 63% talked with parents, and 58% used relaxation techniques in order to cope with stress. These authors also found that lesbians who reported more social support networks were significantly more likely to use adaptive coping behaviors. Finally, Bernhard and Applegate (1999) found that lesbians were significantly more likely than heterosexual women to use meditation as a coping strategy.

DISCUSSION

The majority of participants in research examining depression and anxiety among lesbians were Caucasian, relatively young, and well-educated. Due to the homogeneity across samples, one must exercise caution when attempting to generalize findings to ethnic minority, older, and less educated lesbians. It is difficult to know whether the high percentages of educated lesbians in mental health research is due to (a) a greater willingness on the part of educated lesbians to participate in research, (b) the possibility that lesbians tend to be better educated than heterosexual women, or (c) an artifact of snowball sampling, which may lead to samples of lesbians who resemble each other in terms of ethnicity, age, and educational background. Although preliminary findings suggested that depression and anxiety among lesbians may decrease with age, the limited age range of most samples makes it inadvisable to draw definitive conclusions without additional research.

There is clearly a paucity of research focusing specifically on depression and anxiety among ethnic minority lesbians. This type of research seems especially important in light of one study's finding that the lifetime prevalence for depression is highest for African-American women between the ages of 35-44 (Blazer et al., 1994). One research study found that African-American lesbian and bisexual women were more depressed than African-American women in general (Cochran & Mays, 1994).

In summary, it is clear that few, if any, definitive conclusions can be drawn from the literature pertaining to depression, stress, and anxiety among lesbians. It seems safe to say that these mental health issues are problematic for lesbians, but one cannot say that they are more, or less, problematic than for women in general. Several possible risk factors and mediating variables for depression and anxiety emerge from this review, including social support, hate crime victimization, self-esteem, and satisfaction with relationship status. Internalized homophobia and self-disclosure of sexual orientation were not as directly linked to depression or anxiety as one might expect. However, these assertions are based only on one or two studies of each variable. More research is needed to enhance the credibility of these research findings. Although the body of research devoted to the mental health of lesbians is growing, the existing literature raises more questions than answers. Future researchers need to further examine the prevalence, risk factors, consequences, and coping strategies related to depression and anxiety among lesbian women.

REFERENCES

American Psychiatric Association. (1994). Diagnostic and statistical manual of mental disorders (4th ed.). Washington DC: Author.

Ayala, Jessica & Coleman, Heather. (2000). Predictors of depression among lesbian women. *Journal of Lesbian Studies, 4*, 71-86.

Barbee, James G. (1998). Mixed symptoms and syndromes of anxiety and depression: Diagnostic, prognostic, and etiological issues. *Annals of Clinical Psychiatry, 10*, 15-29.

Bernhard, Linda A. & Applegate, Julia M. (1999). Comparison of stress and stress management strategies between lesbian and heterosexual women. *Health Care for Women International, 20*, 335-347.

Blazer, Dan G., Kessler, Ronald C., McGonagle, Katherine A., & Swartz, Marvin, S. (1994). The prevalence and distribution of major depression in a national community sample: The National Comorbidity Survey. American Journal of Psychiatry, 151, 979-986.

Bradford, Judith, Ryan, Caitlin, & Rothblum, Esther D. (1994). National Lesbian Health Care Survey: Implications for mental health care. *Journal of Consulting and Clinical Psychology, 62*, 228-242.

Clark, Lee Anna, Watson, David, & Mineka, Susan (1994). Temperament, personality, and the mood and anxiety disorders. *Journal of Abnormal Psychology, 103*, 103-116.

Cochran, Susan D., Greer, J. Sullivan, & Mays, Vickie M. (2003). Prevalence of mental disorders, psychological distress, and mental health services use among lesbian, gay, and bisexual adults in the United States. *Journal of Counseling and Clinical Psychology, 71*, 53-61.

Cochran, Susan D. & Mays, Vickie M. (1994). Depressive distress among homosexually active African-American men and women. *American Journal of Psychiatry, 151*, 524-529.

Derogatis, Leonard. (1983). *SCL-90: Administration, scoring, and procedures manual-I for the revised version.* Towson, MD: Clinical Psychometric Research.

Driscoll, Jeanine M., Kelley, Frances A., & Fassinger, Ruth E. (1996). Lesbian identity and disclosure in the workplace: Relation to occupational stress and satisfaction. *Journal of Vocational Behavior, 48*, 229-242.

Eliason, Michele J. & Morgan, Kris, S. (1998). Lesbians define themselves: Diversity in lesbian identification. *Journal of Gay, Lesbian, and Bisexual Identity, 3*, 47-63.

Gillow, Kim E. & Davis, Linda L. (1987). Lesbian stress and coping methods. *Journal of Psychosocial Nursing, 25*, 28-32.

Griffith, Penny L., Myers, Rita W., Cusick, Gary M., & Tankersley, Melody J. (1997). MMPI-2 profiles of women differing in sexual abuse history and sexual orientation. *Journal of Clinical Psychology, 53*, 791-800.

160   LESBIAN AND BISEXUAL WOMEN'S MENTAL HEALTH

Grossman, Arnold H., D'Augelli, Anthony R., & Hershberger, Scott. (2000). Social support networks of lesbian, gay, and bisexual adults 60 years of age and older. *Journal of Gerontology, Psychological Sciences, 55B,* 171-179.

Grossman, Arnold H., & Kerner, Matthew S. (1998). Self-esteem and supportiveness as predictors of emotional distress in gay male and lesbian youth. *Journal of Homosexuality, 35,* 25-39.

Herek, Gregory M., Gillis, J. Roy, & Cogan, Jeanine C. (1999). Psychological sequelae of hate-crime victimization among lesbian, gay, and bisexual adults. *Journal of Consulting and Clinical Psychology, 67,* 945-951.

Herek, Gregory M., Gillis, J. Roy, Cogan, Jeanine C., & Glunt, Eric K. (1997). Hate crime victimization among lesbian, gay, and bisexual adults: Prevalence, psychological correlates, and methodological issues. *Journal of Interpersonal Violence, 12,* 195-215.

Joiner, Thomas E., & Blalock, Janice A. (1995). Gender differences in depression: The role of anxiety and generalized negative affect. Sex Roles, 33, 91-108.

Jordan, Karen M. & Deluty, Robert H. (1998). Coming out for lesbian women: Its relation to anxiety, positive affectivity, self-esteem, and social support. *Journal of Homosexuality, 35,* 41-63.

Jorm, A. F. (2000). Does old age reduce the risk of anxiety and depression? A review of epidemiological studies across the adult life span. *Psychological Medicine, 30,* 11-22.

Katon, Wayne & Roy-Byrne, Peter P. (1991). Mixed anxiety and depression. *Journal of Abnormal Psychology, 100,* 337-345.

Kendler, Kenneth S., Neale, Michael C., Kessler, Ronald C., Heath, Andrew C., Eaves, Lindon, J. (1992). Major depression and generalized anxiety disorder: Same genes, (partly) different environments? *Archives of General Psychiatry, 49,* 716-722.

Kurdek, Lawrence A. (1988). Perceived social support in gays and lesbians in cohabiting relationships. *Journal of Personality and Social Psychology, 54,* 504-509.

Kurdek, Lawrence A. & Schmitt, J. Patrick. (1987). Perceived emotional support from family and friends in members of homosexual, married, and heterosexual cohabiting couples. *Journal of Homosexuality, 14,* 57-68.

Kessler, Ronald C., McGonagle, Katherine A., Zhao, Shanyang, Nelson, Christopher B., Hughes, Michael, Eshleman, Suzann, Wittchen, Hans-Ulrich, & Kendler, Kenneth S. (1994). Lifetime and 12-month prevalence of DSM-III-R psychiatric disorders in the United States: Results from the National Comorbidity Study. *Archives of General Psychiatry, 51,* 8-19.

Lehmann, Joan B., Lehmann, Christoph U., & Kelly, Patricia J. (1998). Development and health care needs of lesbians. *Journal of Women's Health, 7,* 379-387.

Lewinsohn, Peer M., Gotlib, Ian H., Lewinsohn, Mark, Seeley, John R., & Allen, Nicholas B. (1998). Gender differences in anxiety disorders and anxiety symptoms in adolescents. *Journal of Abnormal Psychology, 107,* 109-117.

Luhtanen, Riia K. (2003). Identity, stigma management, and well-being: A comparison of lesbians/bisexual women and gay/bisexual men. *Journal of Lesbian Studies, 7,* 85-100.

McGrath, Ellen, Keita, Gwendolyn P., Strickland, Bonnie R., Russo, Nancy F. (1990). *Women and Depression: Risk Factors and Treatment Issues.* Washington, D.C.: American Psychological Association.

Mental health: A report of the Surgeon General. (2000). [On-line]. Available: http://www.mentalhealth.org/specials/surgeongeneralreport/home.html.

Miranda, Jeanne & Storms, Michael. (1989). Psychological adjustment of lesbians and gay men. *Journal of Counseling and Development, 68,* 41-45.

Morgan, K. S. (1992). Caucasian lesbians' use of therapy. *Psychology of Women Quarterly, 16,* 127-130.

Oetjen, Helen & Rothblum, E. D. (2000). When lesbians aren't gay: Factors affecting depression among lesbians. *Journal of Homosexuality, 39,* 49-73.

Otis, Melanie D. & Skinner, William F. (1996). The prevalence of victimization and its effects on mental well-being among lesbian and gay people. *The Journal of Homosexuality, 30,* 93-121.

Procidano, Mary E. & Heller, Kenneth. (1983). Measures of perceived social support from friends and from family. *American Journal of Community Psychology, 11,* 1-14.

Radloff, Lenore S. (1977). The CES-D Scale: A self-report depression scale for research in the general population. *Applied Psychological Measurement, 1,* 385-401.

Reinherz, Helen Z., Giaconia, Rose M., Hauf, Amy M. C., Wasserman, Michelle, S., & Silverman, Amy B. (1999). Major depression in the transition to adulthood: Risks and impairments. *Journal of Abnormal Psychology, 108,* 500-510.

Robinson, Nancy S. & Garber, Judy. (1995). Social support and psychopathology across the life span. Dante Ciccheti & Donald J. Cohen (Eds.). Developmental Psychopathology, Volume 2, pp. 162-209. New York: John Wiley & Sons.

Rogers, Tracey L., Emanuel, Kristen, & Bradford, Judith. (2003). Sexual minorities seeking services: A retrospective study of the mental health concerns of lesbian and bisexual women. *Journal of Lesbian Studies, 7,* 127-146.

Rothblum, Esther D. (1990). Depression among lesbians: An invisible and unresearched phenomenon. *Journal of Gay and Lesbian Psychotherapy, 1,* 67-87.

Sarason, I. G., Levine, H. M., Basham, R. B., & Sarason, B. R. (1983). Assessing social support: The Social Support Questionnaire. *Journal of Personality and Social Psychology, 44,* 127-139.

Solarz, Andrea L., Ed. (1999). Lesbian Health: Current Assessment and Directions for the Future. Washington, DC: National Academy Press.

Sorensen, Lena & Roberts, Susan J. (1997). Lesbian uses of and satisfaction with mental health services: Results from Boston Lesbian Health Project. *Journal of Homosexuality, 33,* 35-49.

Spielberger, C. D., Gorsuch, R. L., & Lushene, R. (1968). *State-Trait Anxiety Inventory.* Palo Alto, CA: Consulting Psychologists Press.

Sprock, June & Yoder, Carol Y. (1997). Women and depression: An update on the report of the APA task force. *Sex Roles, 36,* 269-303.

Tait, Diane. (1997). Stress and social support networks among lesbian and heterosexual women: A comparison study. *Smith College Studies in Social Work, 67,* 213-224.

Trippet, Susan E. (1994). Lesbians mental health concerns. *Health Care for Women International*, *15*, 317-323.

Tuel, Beverly D. & Russell, Richard K. (1998). Self-esteem and depression in battered women: A comparison of lesbian and heterosexual survivors. *Violence Against Women*, *4*, 344-362.

Zea, Maria Cecilia, Reisen, Carol A., and Poppen, Paul J. (1999). Psychological well-being among Latino lesbians and gay men. *Cultural Diversity & Ethnic Minority Psychology*, *5*, 371-379.

Zuckerman, Diana M. (1989). Stress, self-esteem, and mental health: How does gender make a difference? *Sex Roles*, *20*, 429-444.

The Effects of Sexual Orientation, Gender Identity, and Gender Role on the Mental Health of Women in Taiwan's *T-Po* Lesbian Community

Mei-Fun Kuang, MPhil
Robin M. Mathy, MSW, LGSW, MSc, MSt, MA
Helen M. Carol, MPhil
Kazuhiko Nojima, PhD

SUMMARY. We obtained via the Internet a convenience sample of Taiwanese heterosexual ($n = 287$) and sexual minority females ($n =$

Mei-Fun Kuang is affiliated with the Graduate School of Human-Environmental Studies, Kyushu University, Higashiku, Hakozaki 6-19-1. Robin M. Mathy is Director of Research and Assistant Professor of Arts & Sciences at Presentation College in Aberdeen, South Dakota, and is a Licensed Graduate Social Worker in Minnesota. Helen M. Carol is affiliated with the Departments of Pediatrics and Psychiatry, University of Minnesota Medical School. Nojima Kazuhiko is affiliated with the Faculty of Human-Environmental Studies, Kyushu University, Higashiku Hakozaki 6-19-1.

Address correspondence to Mei-Fun Kuang (E-mail: fukuron2000@yahoo.co.jp) or Robin M. Mathy (E-mail: math5577@umn.edu).

This work was supported, in part, by a grant from the American Foundation for Addiction Research, as well as a National Institute of Mental Health Supplemental Grant for an Individual with a Disability (5RO1MH063328) to Robin M. Mathy.

The authors would like to express special thanks for kind comments from Professor Kitayama of the Faculty of Human-Environment Studies in Kyushu University.

[Haworth co-indexing entry note]: "The Effects of Sexual Orientation, Gender Identity, and Gender Role on the Mental Health of Women in Taiwan's *T-Po* Lesbian Community." Kuang et al. Co-published simultaneously in *Journal of Psychology & Human Sexuality* (The Haworth Press, Inc.) Vol. 15, No. 4, 2003, pp. 163-184; and: *Lesbian and Bisexual Women's Mental Health* (ed: Robin M. Mathy, and Shelly K. Kerr) The Haworth Press, Inc., 2003, pp. 163-184. Single or multiple copies of this article are available for a fee from The Haworth Document Delivery Service [1-800-HAWORTH, 9:00 a.m. - 5:00 p.m. (EST). E-mail address: docdelivery@haworthpress.com].

260). A significantly greater percentage of sexual minorities (lesbian and bisexual females) than heterosexuals reported they had used tobacco or alcohol. Relative to heterosexuals, sexual minorities were significantly more likely to report a serious suicide attempt. Overall, gender identity (masculine, feminine, and androgynous) and gender role (butch, femme, and pure or undifferentiated) were poor discriminators of lesbian mental health. Differences between sexual minorities and heterosexuals were more robust than were the variations in gender identities and gender roles among lesbian and bisexual women. We discuss the implications of these findings for further clinical research. *[Article copies available for a fee from The Haworth Document Delivery Service: 1-800-HAWORTH. E-mail address: <docdelivery@haworthpress.com> Website: <http://www.HaworthPress.com> © 2003 by The Haworth Press, Inc. All rights reserved.]*

KEYWORDS. Gender, lesbian, mental health, suicide attempt, Taiwan

Homosexuality was removed in 1973 from the official list of mental disorders included in the *Diagnostic and Statistical Manual of Mental Disorders*, when the American Psychiatric Association (APA) adopted the official policy that homosexuality *per se* does not constitute a mental health impairment. The American Psychological Association urged mental health professionals to take the lead in removing the stigma of mental illness associated with lesbian and gay sexualities. Researchers in the United States and Western Europe have since then studied lesbian, gay, and bisexual (LGB) mental health issues from a non-pathological view. In part to further these goals, the APA approved in 1984 the establishment of Division 44, dedicated to the psychological study of LGB issues (Perez, DeBord, & Bieschke, 1999). The British Psychological Society (BPS) officially inaugurated the Lesbian and Gay Psychology Section at the organization's London Conference on 18th December 1998 (Coyle & Kitzinger, 2002). Thus, in recent decades homosexuality has been a topic of scientific inquiry rather than a subject of social deviance.

Concurrent with the change from pathological to non-pathological views of homosexuality, psychological explanations derived from psychodynamic and psychoanalytic perspectives aligned with Freudian psychotherapy have become less viable. The perspective that homosexuality is a normal variant of human sexual experience also was advanced by researchers such as Kinsey, Pomeroy, Martin, and Gebhard (1953), Armon (1960), Bell and Weinberg (1973), and Whitam and Mathy (1986). The non-clinical samples used in these studies focused on homosexuality as part of a common human sexual experience rather than psychological deficits seen in small groups of psychiatric patients (Ponse, 1978).

We have known for several decades that lesbians and heterosexual women have similar mental health profiles, with some notable exceptions. Hopkins (1969) compared lesbians to heterosexual women and found that they were more independent, resilient, reserved, dominant, bohemian, self-sufficient, and composed. Loney (1972) studied non-clinical lesbians and concluded that most sexual minority women were involved in stable, ongoing relationships. Consistent with the findings of Hopkins (1969), Freedman (1971), Saghir and Robins (1973), and Thompson, McCandless, and Strickland (1971), and Seigelman (1972) found that lesbians were better adjusted than a matched control group of heterosexual women (Ponse, 1978).

Far fewer studies have examined the possibility that gender identity (masculine, feminine, or androgynous) or gender role (butch, femme, or neither) moderates lesbian and bisexual women's mental health. Women are more likely than men to be judged as mentally ill or dysfunctional when they evidence gender-incongruent behavior (Broverman et al., 1970, 1972). Sexual minorities are more likely than heterosexuals to have gender atypical behaviors or appearances (Bailey, Kim, Hills, & Linsenmeier, 1997). Androgyny is associated with greater mental health and self-efficacy than masculine, feminine, or undifferentiated gender identities (Bem, 1975). Therefore, we might expect that relatively androgynous sexual minorities have better mental health outcomes than their gender-typed gay, lesbian, and bisexual peers. For example, Harry (1983) reevaluated data from Bell and Weinberg (1978) and found that gender atypical males (but not females) were more likely to attempt suicide than were their gender typical same-sex peers, regardless of sexual orientation. However, Harry's finding may suggest that gender-incongruous identities (androgynous, feminine, or masculine) or roles (butch or femme) pose mental health risks for males but not for females.

As psychologists have developed an empirically balanced view toward lesbian mental health, researchers have focused more on the relationship between social stress and sexual minority mental health. There is an underlying presumption in this research that sexual minorities have the same mental health issues as heterosexuals. However, social stress associated with oppression, discrimination, and stigma creates a greater burden for sexual minorities. Because homosexuality is not a psychopathology, we must assume that sexual minorities and hetero-sexuals have a similar threshold for succumbing to mental illness.

Sexual minorities have somewhat greater risks of succumbing to stress-related disorders because they carry a disproportionate burden of society's oppression, discrimination, and stigma, not because they are more intrinsically prone to psychological maladies or social dysfunctions. Studies have found that sexual minorities have somewhat higher rates of stress-related disorders than do heterosexuals, including increased risks of suicidal intent (Cochran & Mays, 2000). This research has found that lesbians are significantly more likely than heterosexual women to report that they have issues with identity and psychosocial development, social support, and social stress (Bradford, Ryan, & Rothblum, 1994). Sexual minority females also face biased treatment when they seek help from professional clinicians (Perez, DeBord, & Bieschke, 1999; see also Kerr, Walker, Warner, and McNeill, this volume).

Researchers have conducted a disproportionate amount of research regarding sexual orientation and mental health in the United States, Western Europe, and Australia. Mathy (2002) argued that research concerning the mental health of lesbians in Asia is needed. This paper attempts to address the need for research regarding mental health of sexual minorities on the Asian continent, with attention to the possibility that cultural factors may have significant effects on lesbians' mental health outcomes and receipt of mental health services.

THE MENTAL HEALTH OF LESBIANS IN TAIWAN

The goal of this study was to examine the relationship between mental health and social stress among lesbians in Taiwan. In traditional Taiwan and Chinese culture, lesbianism is a neglected and often misunderstood subject. Writers sometimes argue that lesbians as a group do not actually exist (Chan, 2000). Influenced by lesbian and gay activism occurring in the Western hemisphere since the 1969 Stonewall Inn uprising as well as the local homosexual rights movement in Taiwan, scholars in the last decade have published more research regarding lesbians. In Psychology, these studies have been in the areas of counseling and guidance, often focused on identity development. Case studies have been the principal research method of these studies (e.g., Jeng, 1997;

Jian, 1997). Kao (1994), Jia (1996), and Liu (2000) used school counselor cases to analyze attitudes toward sexual minority clients. These cases consisted primarily of individuals who needed psychological help or who sought and received counseling. However, it is difficult to generalize these case studies to lesbians in the general population. Data from non-clinical populations of Taiwan sexual minorities are extremely rare. Research about lesbians in the general population is needed to provide a non-clinical baseline regarding lesbian mental health. Thus, the primary goal of this study was to examine the relationship between mental health and sexual orientation in a non-clinical sample of Taiwan women.

Butch versus Femme Gender Role

Another important goal of this study was to test the hypothesis that mental health and social oppression experienced by lesbians varies by gender roles in the *T-Po* community, which generally centers on butch-femme distinctions (Chao, 2000). The *T-Po* community is predominant relative to the smaller feminist lesbian community. We use "butch" and "femme" to refer to masculine and feminine role-playing, respectively, consistent with the terms used in the Taiwan *T-Po* lesbian community. It is important to note that the Taiwan feminist lesbian community contends that butch-femme distinctions perpetuate rigid gender roles via domestic colonialism. A similarly rigid gender role system developed in the early stages of the emergence of lesbian culture in the United States (Faderman, 1991). Theoretically, rigid gender roles within lesbian subculture parallel the relatively staid gender roles between men and women in the dominant heterosexual culture of Taiwan (Hong, Veach, & Lawrenz, 2003). Cross-culturally, we might expect that gender-role playing within lesbian communities mirrors the rigidity and extent of sex role stereotyping in a mainstream, predominantly heterosexual culture. One could test this hypothesis with cross-cultural, longitudinal, or multi-panel research. We anticipate that cross-cultural collaboration can facilitate a comparison of lesbians in Taiwan and the United States.

Since lesbian activism and Queer theory have flourished in Taiwan, the gender roles of lesbians often have been a subject of debate due to the intrinsic nature of gender roles, social oppression, and political correctness. Studies have shown that although there are lesbians who follow gender roles from a specific subculture, there are lesbians without such role definitions who lead a different subcultural lifestyle (Jian, 1997). According to academic reports and real-time communication in

Internet chat rooms for lesbians, the gender roles of lesbians are an active and lively phenomenon in Taiwan lesbian culture. This study does not discuss the intrinsic issue of gender roles *per se*. Instead, it analyzes the mental health status of lesbians by their self-identified gender (feminine, masculine, androgynous) and their chosen gender role. Researchers have categorized several gender roles of lesbians. These normally include butch, femme, and pure (undifferentiated). A woman playing a masculine role is "butch," whereas the "femme" plays a stereotypically feminine (traditional) gender role. The "butch," "femme," and "pure" terms remain loosely defined in the research literature. Some women interpret these terms simply in terms of a role that one plays. Lesbians in Taiwan may consider gender roles when forming their gender identities. A sense of playfulness, fun, and experimentation has characterized the adaptation of gender roles by some lesbians (Ponse, 1978). Often lesbian sexual relationships differentiate between a partner who has a role as "top" (active) or "bottom" (passive). "The top is the person who conducts and orchestrates" the intimate interlude. "The bottom is the one who responds, acts out, makes visible or interprets the sexual initiatives and language of the top" (Walton 1984, p. 246). Preference for an active or passive sexual role in Taiwan lesbian subculture is associated with adult gender identity. "Butch" lesbians tend to prefer the active sexual role, whereas "femme" lesbians prefer the passive sexual role (Bailey et al., 1997; Singh, Zambarano, & Dabbs, 1999). In Taiwan lesbian subculture, "pure" types do not play either masculine or feminine gender roles. Consistent with its use in Taiwan, this study uses the term "pure" to refer to an undifferentiated gender role.

Although adherence to gender roles has been a polemic issue, prior studies have found that members of Taiwan's lesbian culture do not have difficulty categorizing themselves when asked. Most lesbians readily self-identified as "butch," "femme" or "no difference" (i.e., pure or undifferentiated), and participants readily identify with one of these labels more than another (Brown, Finn, Cooke, & Breedlove, 2002). In sum, in addition to studying differences between lesbians and heterosexual women, we examined the relationships between mental health and gender identity or gender role.

METHODS

Instrument

Due to social oppression and stigma, sexual minority populations are not very visible in three-dimensional space. In cyberspace (i.e., on the

Internet), this population is more apparent in certain Websites, homepages, or chat rooms. This study used the Internet as a research tool (Mathy, 2002) in order to establish contact with participants. It used the confidential and anonymous nature of the Internet to facilitate their responses to sensitive questions about their sexual orientation and mental health status. To compare the mental health of self-identified heterosexual and sexual minority females (lesbians and bisexuals), we used two questionnaires adapted from an English-language version that has been previously published elsewhere (Cooper, Morahan-Martin, Mathy, & Maheu, 2002).

The first author used two versions of the questionnaire because some items were specific to the within-group comparisons among lesbians rather than tests of differences between heterosexuals and sexual minority women. The sexual minority and heterosexual versions of the questionnaire contained 55 and 45 items, respectively. One of the challenges of studying sexual minorities often is the lack of a control group for comparison. "However, inherent to research on this population, there is truly no perfect control group" (Safren and Heimbreg, 1999, p. 865). Both questionnaire versions were adapted and revised from a prior study of sexual orientation and mental health by permission of its senior methodologist, the second author (Mathy, 2002; Cooper, Morahan-Martin, Mathy, & Maheu, 2002).

To be compatible with the study's goals and Taiwan culture, we revised and translated into Chinese the questionnaire used by Cooper et al. (2002) and Mathy (2002). We agreed by consensus that back-translation into English was of sufficient adequacy to ensure that the questionnaires addressed the same items addressed by Mathy's (2002) cross-cultural study of sexual orientation and mental health. Questions addressed demographics, mental health history, access to treatment, and satisfaction with being female. The first author administered the questionnaire confidentially, using interactive HTML Web design in a data center employed for this purpose. Participants were required to select an answer in order to move to a subsequent page and finally chose the 'send' button to submit the completed questionnaire. When submitted, the information was saved automatically in the Web data center.

All participants were self-selected and responded to research postings on lesbian forums, bulletin board systems, individual homepages (self-disclosed lesbian), personal Internet newspapers, heterosexual commercial portal Websites, recreational Websites, and other informal sources. Participants could link to the questionnaire Web page to start the response procedure. The questionnaire was posted in a commercial portal Website that is not limited to sexual minorities. Within seven days, 308 participants had answered the heterosexual questionnaire and 302 individuals had responded to the sexual minority version. Advertisements for this study mentioned the goal of the study and asked the prospective participants to answer the questionnaire and recommend the research page to lesbian friends. This snowball methodology is useful when studying less visible populations and minorities. It is an effective methodology previously used for referrals and as a way to build a sample. Other studies with similar minority populations have utilized this methodology successfully (Radonsky & Borders, 1995; Weiss, 1994). However, using the Internet as the research tool could decrease the possibility of concerns about coming out and privacy (Cooper et al., 2002; Mathy, 2002; Mathy, Schillace, Coleman, & Berquist, 2002). Conversely, the reliability and validity of the Internet is still in doubt, although recent research suggests that the Internet is just as valid and reliable as other media (Mathy & Cooper, 2003, Mathy, Schillace, Coleman, & Berquist, 2002; Mathy, Kerr, & Haydin, 2003).

Measures

Demographics. Participants were asked to select their age from a list with 5-year increments. Gender was assessed with responses to, "I am (check only one) [Female] [Transgender]." Education was determined by responses to, "My education level (check only one) [Junior high school or below][Senior high school or Vocational school][College or university][Graduate School]." Occupation was assessed with answers to, "My current occupation is (check only one)" and a list of 16 choices, including "Other" and "Unemployed." Income was evaluated with responses to, "My income status is (NT) (check only one)" and 10,000 in increments from "19999" through "70000+." Residence was evaluated with responses to, "I reside in (check only one)" and predominant counties and cities in Taiwan as well as "China," "Hong Kung and Macao," "Japan," and various continents, including Europe, North America, South and Central America, Asia and Pacific Ocean, and Africa. Participants' rural-urban gradient was determined by answers to, "The location I live in has a population of and can best be described as (check only one) [Urban (50,001 or more people)][Suburban (10,001 to 50,000 people)] [Rural (10,000 or fewer people)]. Sexual orientation was based on responses to, "I identify my sexual orientation as: (check only one) [Heterosexual/Straight][Gay/Lesbian][Bisexual][None of the above]." Lesbian participants were asked to indicate whether their gender identity is feminine, androgynous, masculine, not definite, or other. Also, lesbian participants were asked to indicate whether their gender role preference was butch, femme, pure, or none of the above.

Mental health. Frequency of smoking and drinking were based on participants' answers to, "I Smoke" or "I drink" and 5 response categories: [Every day][More than once per week][More than once per month][Less than once per month][Never]." The remaining items were scored dichotomously ("Yes" or "No"). Following the appropriate question stem, "In the past, I have been" or "In the past, I have had," participants were asked about "medications for a psychiatric condition," being "in psychotherapy," having "had depression," having "wondered if I had depression," and having "considered psychotherapy" or "considered counseling. "Participants then provided "yes" or "no" responses to whether they were "currently on medications for a psychiatric condition," "currently in psychotherapy," "wonder that I have depression now," "considering psychotherapy now," "considering counseling now," and, "I do not know how to seek psychotherapy and counseling."

Suicidal Intent. Participants were asked to provide a "yes" or "no" response to the statements, "I have had serious thoughts of suicide" and "I have made a serious suicide attempt or gesture," and "When I made a serious suicide attempt or gesture, I really wanted to die."

Self-Acceptance. Participants gave "yes" or "no" responses to the statements, "I feel happy for being female," and the lesbian and bisexual females who responded to the lesbian version of the questionnaire indicated whether they "feel happy for being lesbian."

The questionnaire concluded with mental health information available at the Taiwan Health Department.

Sample

Recruitment efforts resulted in 610 completed questionnaires. Of these, 63 questionnaires were excluded because they indicated a residence outside Taiwan (n = 38), the response to the sexual orientation question was "none of the above" (n = 14), or transgender was the gender reported (n = 11). On the sexual minority questionnaire, 77% of participants identified their sexual orientation as gay/lesbian, 21.4% as bisexual, and 1.6% as heterosexual/straight (n = 257). On the heterosexual questionnaire, 3.8% identified their sexual orientation as gay/lesbian, 5.5% as bisexual, and 90.7% as heterosexual/straight (n = 290).

After combining the two versions of the questionnaire ($N = 547$), there were 267 participants who reported their sexual orientation as heterosexual/straight, 209 who identified as lesbian, and 71 who indicated they are bisexual. The lesbian and bisexual response categories were collapsed (n = 280), and the final sample for analysis included almost equal percentages of heterosexual (48.8%) and lesbian and bisexual (51.2%) participants. Our references to "lesbian" herein are inclusive of bisexual females.

Statistical Analyses

We applied the chi-square test of independence to cross-tabulated data. To examine the hypothesized relationships between sexual orientation and mental health, we evaluated bivariate differences in mean percentages with a t-test, and we assessed analyses of variance with an omnibus F-test when comparing three groups. When the omnibus F-test was statistically significant, we conducted post-hoc analyses for pairwise differences. We used an alpha level of .05, such that $p < .05$ indicated statistically significant evidence of independence. Although the Chi-Square test statistic is sensitive to sample size, the sample sizes for the lesbian and heterosexual groups were not large enough to encounter an unacceptably high risk of a Type II error (i.e., erroneously refraining from rejecting the null hypothesis when it was in fact incorrect). With $n = 267$ and $n = 280$, and $p < .05$, the two-sample power was computed to be .86, which is conventionally acceptable.

RESULTS

Demographic Information

Seventy-five percent of lesbian participants were aged 25 or younger, with a modal age group of 16-20 years (39.3%). Heterosexual participants appeared to be somewhat older; 51% were aged 25 or younger, with a modal age group of 26-30 years (35.6%). College or university education was the modal category for both the lesbian and heterosexual groups (47.1% and 58.8%, respectively). The median income (New Taiwan dollars) fell between 0-19999 for lesbians (61.1% of sample) and 20000-29999 for heterosexuals (53.2% at or below this income). The difference in incomes between the two groups reflects the significantly greater number of lesbian vis-à-vis heterosexual participants who reported their occupation as student (51.8% and 24.3%, respectively). Relative to lesbians, a significantly greater proportion of heterosexual participants were drawn from the Taiwan capitol of Taipei City (23.2% and 37.1%, respectively), $X^2_{(1)} = 12.52$, $p < .01$. More than three-fourths of lesbian and heterosexual participants reported that they grew up in urban areas (78.9% and 83.9%, respectively). There was no statistically significant difference in proportions of lesbians and heterosexuals raised in suburban environments (11.8% and 13.1%, respectively). However, a disproportionately large number of lesbians were raised in rural Taiwan (9.3% and 3.0%, respectively), $X^2_{(1)} = 9.27$, $p < .01$.

Sexual Orientation and Relationship Intimacy

Significant differences in relationship status were found between heterosexual and lesbian participants, $X^2_{(5)} = 47.91$, $p < .01$. Sexual orientation and relationship status were not independent, partly because nearly twice as many lesbians as heterosexuals reported they were in a committed relationship (38% and 20%, respectively), although four times as many heterosexuals as lesbians reported they were married (20% and 5%, respectively). Relative to single heterosexual participants, single lesbians were more likely to be dating (13% and 21%, respectively).

Sexual Orientation and Mental Health

We asked participants about the frequency of tobacco and alcohol use. We found statistically significant differences between heterosexuals and lesbians for both smoking ($X^2_{(4)} = 64.1$, $p < .01$) and drinking ($X^2_{(4)} = 25.9$, $p < .01$). Compared to lesbians (50.7%), a much higher percentage of heterosexuals (79%) reported that they do not use tobacco at all, and a higher percentage of lesbians than heterosexuals reported daily, weekly, monthly, and less-occasional smoking. The percentages of participants who stated that they refrained from drinking any alcohol was higher in the heterosexual (44.9%) than in the sexual minority group (32.9%), although heterosexuals (6.4%) were more likely than lesbians to report daily drinking (2.5%).

A significantly higher percentage of lesbians (38.2%) than heterosexuals (27.3%) reported a prior suicide attempt, $t(544) = 2.72$, $p < .01$ (see Table 1). There were no statistically significant differences in percentages of sexual minority (51.4%) and heterosexual women (45.3%) who reported that they had seriously considered suicide, $t(545) = 1.43$, $p =$

TABLE 1. Mental Health and Service Utilization by Sexual Orientation (Percent)

	Heterosexual (N = 267)	Lesbian (N = 280)	|t| / df / p
Past psychiatric meds	8.2	10.0	0.71 / 545 / .48
Past psychotherapy	9.0	10.4	0.54 / 545 / .59
Past depression	11.2	14.6	1.19 / 543 / .59
Past wondered about depression	43.8	50.4	1.53 / 544 / .13
Past considered psychotherapy	28.1	29.6	0.40 / 545 / .69
Past considered counseling	35.6	39.6	0.98 / 545 / .33
Current psychiatric meds	6.4	5.7	0.32 /545 / .75
Current psychotherapy	7.1	5.4	0.85 / 545 / .40
Currently wonder about depression	22.5	22.1	0.09 / 545 / .93
Currently consider psychotherapy	15.7	13.6	0.71 / 545 / .48
Currently consider counseling	19.1	17.1	0.59 / 545 / .55
Serious thoughts of suicide	45.3	51.4	1.43 / 545 / .15
Serious suicide attempt	27.3	38.2	2.72 / 544 / .01**
Really wanted to die	33.3	37.9	1.10 / 545 / .27
Don't know how to seek therapy	40.4	31.8	2.11 / 540 / .04*
Happy being female	88.0	79.6	2.68 / 531 / .00***
Pressure being female, family	38.6	43.6	1.19 / 545 / .24
Pressure being female, work/school	41.9	30.4	2.83 / 537 /.01**

* p < .05, ** p < .01, *** p < .001

.153, or who "really wanted to die" as a result of a suicide attempt (33.3% and 37.9%, respectively).

A higher percentage of heterosexual (40.4%) than sexual minority participants (31.8%) indicated that they did not know how to seek psychotherapy and counseling, $t(540) = 2.11$, p < .05. T-tests revealed that there were no statistically significant differences between heterosexuals and sexual minorities for past or current mental health questions. Similar percentages of heterosexuals and sexual minorities reported a history of medications for a psychiatric condition, history of psychotherapy, self-doubt regarding depression, and consideration of psychotherapy and counseling. Heterosexuals and sexual minorities also reported similar current psychiatric conditions, including denial of depression and consideration of participating in psychotherapy and counseling. This finding is similar to the results of past studies of depression and sexual orientation among females (e.g., Bradford et al., 1994). Bradford et al. reported that the high rate of depression among lesbians was similar to heterosexual women in the United States.

Self-Acceptance. As a group, lesbians were more likely to report that they were happy to be lesbian (87%) than they were to be female (81%), paired $t(252) = 22.45, p < .05$. Although there were no differences by gender identity in happiness with being lesbian, the three gender identity groups differed significantly with regard to happiness with being female. A positive response to the question was reported by 97.8% of feminine-identified participants, 77.8% of androgynous-identified peers, and only 57.9% of masculine-identified lesbians, $F_{(2,247)} = 10.42, p < .01$).

Lesbians' Mental Health

Gender identity. Feminine, androgynous, and masculine-identified lesbians differed in two aspects of mental health; specifically, currently considering psychotherapy, $F_{(2,247)} = 3.61, p < .05$, and serious thoughts of suicide, $F_{(2,247)} = 3.39, p < .05$ (see Table 2). Post-hoc comparisons revealed that feminine and androgynous-identified lesbians differed significantly (24.4% and 9.6%, respectively). In addition, a lower percentage of androgynous-identified lesbians (47.9%) than their masculine-identified peers (71.1%) reported serious thoughts of suicide. Fifty-three percent of feminine-identified lesbians reported serious thoughts of suicide, which did not distinguish them from either of the other two gender identities.

Gender role. The percentages of lesbians ($n = 247$) who indicated that their gender role was butch, femme, or pure (undifferentiated) were 49.8%, 23.9%, and 26.3%, respectively (see Table 3). The definition of lesbian "role play" is inconsistent and varies among writers (Jian, 1997). In this study, gender role was not associated with suicide ideation, attempt, or lethality of intent. There were no lesbian gender role differences in receipt of mental health services, including past or current psychiatric medications, therapy, or counseling. Compared to lesbians who had adopted a femme role, a lower percentage of butch participants reported happiness with being female (94.9% and 70.7%, respectively), $F_{(2,244)} = 8.32, p < .01$. A higher percentage of butch (61.0%) than either femme (6.8%) or pure (20.0%) lesbians reported that they had tried to conceal their breasts, $F_{(2,247)} = 40.30, p < .01$.

TABLE 2. Mental Health and Service Utilization by Lesbians' Gender Identity (Percent)

	Feminine (N = 45)	Androgynous (N = 167)	Masculine (N = 38)	F	p	ph[a]
Past psychiatric meds	15.6	10.2	5.3	1.18	.31	
Past psychotherapy	17.8	9.6	10.5	1.21	.30	
Past depression	20.0	16.2	7.9	1.21	.30	
Past wondered about depression	46.7	52.1	47.4	.29	.75	
Past considered psychotherapy	37.8	28.7	23.7	1.07	.35	
Past considered counseling	44.4	40.1	23.7	2.20	.11	
Current psychiatric meds	11.1	4.8	5.3	1.28	.28	
Current psychotherapy	11.1	3.6	10.5	2.61	.08	
Currently wonder about depression	26.7	19.2	21.1	.60	.55	
Currently consider psychotherapy	24.4	9.6	15.8	3.61	.03*	fa
Currently consider counseling	22.2	14.4	18.4	.86	.43	
Serious thoughts of suicide	53.3	47.9	71.1	3.39	.04*	am
Serious suicide attempt	40.0	34.7	50.0	1.58	.21	
Really wanted to die	37.8	34.1	55.3	2.97	.053	
Don't know how to seek therapy	40.0	26.9	39.5	2.13	.12	
Happy being female	97.8	77.8	57.9	10.42	.00***	all
Happy being lesbian	89.7	87.4	82.4	.46	.63	
Have tried to hide breasts	10.3	37.1	73.5	17.77	.00***	all

p < .05, ** p < .01, *** p < .001
Note: ph[a] = post hoc differences: feminine (f), androgynous (a), masculine (m), with letters representing statistically significant pairwise difference in means; "all" indicates all pairwise comparisons were significant. N = 250 for this table. Of the original 280 women who indicated a minority sexual orientation, 29 answered "Not definite" and 1 answered "other" on the gender identity item. Ns for these items are: feminine n = 39, androgynous n = 151, masculine n = 34. These questions were not administered to sexual minority participants who answered the heterosexual questionnaire.

DISCUSSION

This study advances our understanding of the relationship between sexual orientation and mental health in cross-cultural contexts, particularly in non-Western areas of the world. Taiwan is more similar to the West than many other parts of Asia. Nonetheless, we found that there

TABLE 3. Mental Health and Service Utilization by Lesbians' Gender Role (Percent).

	Femme (N = 59)	Pure (N = 65)	Butch (N = 123)	F	P	Ph[a]
Past psychiatric meds	8.5	16.9	7.3	2.29	.10	
Past psychotherapy	10.2	13.8	8.1	.76	.47	
Past depression	13.6	20.0	13.0	.87	.42	
Past wondered about depression	52.5	53.8	45.5	.74	.48	
Past considered psychotherapy	33.9	33.8	22.8	1.88	.16	
Past considered counseling	37.3	49.2	32.5	2.55	.08	
Current psychiatric meds	3.4	6.2	5.7	.28	.76	
Current psychotherapy	1.7	6.2	4.9	.77	.46	
Current wonder about depression	2.2	23.1	17.1	.60	.55	
Current consider psychotherapy	16.9	15.4	9.8	1.14	.32	
Current consider counseling	16.9	23.1	13.8	1.29	.28	
Serious thoughts of suicide	57.6	50.8	43.9	1.56	.21	
Serious suicide attempt	44.1	38.5	31.7	1.39	.25	
Really wanted to die	39.0	46.2	30.9	2.22	.11	
Don't know how to seek therapy	32.2	33.8	31.7	.04	.96	
Happy being female	94.9	84.6	70.7	8.32	.00***	fb
Happy being lesbian	91.5	87.7	85.4	.69	.50	
Have tried to hide breasts	6.8	20.0	61.0	40.30	.000***	fb, pb

* p < .05, ** p < .01, *** p < .001, ph[a] = post hoc differences:
Note: feminine (f), androgynous (a), masculine (m), with letters representing statistically significant pairwise difference in means. N = 247 for this table. Of the original 280 women indicating a minority sexual orientation, 27 answered the heterosexual questionnaire which did not include the sexual role item. An additional 6 sexual minority women selected the "None of the above" response to the sexual role item.

were significant differences between heterosexual and lesbian females. Moreover, there were more differences between heterosexual and lesbian females than there were among lesbians of varying gender roles (butch, femme, or pure) or gender identities (masculine, feminine, or androgynous).

There is considerable gender-role playing in Taiwan lesbian culture. These roles appear to reflect the relatively rigid gender differences in the mainstream Taiwan culture. The island nation (22.6 million people; 35,980 sq km, separated from mainland China by the 100-mile wide Taiwan Strait) did not hold a gay rights march until November 1, 2003 (Talberg, 2003). Although it did so with the full support of Taiwan Mayor Ma Ying-jeou, sexual minorities in Taiwan nonetheless continue to experience fierce discrimination and oppression. Taiwan does not yet permit same-sex marriage or civil unions. Therefore, it is not particularly surprising that heterosexuals were four times as likely as lesbians to report they were married (20% and 5%, respectively). Several days prior to its first gay rights March, however, the Taiwan government announced that it was proposing legislation to permit same-sex marriage (Hogg, 2003). This makes it somewhat more interesting and noteworthy that nearly equal percentages of lesbians and heterosexuals were in either married or committed relationships (43% and 40%, respectively). It seems possible that equal access to marriage for sexual minorities would mediate the relationship between sexual orientation and relationship status. As noted by Mathy and Lehmann (2004) as well as Mathy, Kerr, and Lehmann in this volume, marriage is a protective factor against suicidal intent and some forms of psychopathology. Thus, depriving sexual minorities of the benefits of marriage may have avoidable public health risks. The amelioration of these associated public health risks consumes scarce resources in the U.S. and elsewhere.

In addition to depriving sexual minorities of the protective benefits of marriage, societies also subject them to greater oppression and discrimination. Therefore, it is understandable (yet unacceptable) that a significantly greater proportion of sexual minorities than heterosexuals develop stress-related disorders (Cochran & Mays, 2000). The findings of our study may help generalize these findings to Taiwan. However, population-based studies are needed to corroborate these findings.

We found that a significantly greater percentage of lesbians than heterosexuals reported that they do not refrain from smoking (79.0% and 50.7%, respectively) or drinking (44.9% and 32.9%). This is important because smoking and drinking have notable public health risks, and both can become maladaptive ways of coping with stress. The higher proportion of alcohol consumers and tobacco users among sexual minorities than heterosexuals may relate to the cultural aspects of lesbian bars. These are some of the most important meeting and activity places for lesbians in Taiwan, and tobacco and alcohol use is more prevalent in these environments. Bars were a widely available social resource for lesbians in the current study. This finding was consistent with those obtained by Bradford et al. (1994) in the U.S.

Perhaps of far greater concern was our finding that lesbians were significantly more likely than heterosexuals to report they had made a serious suicide attempt (38.2% and 27.3%, respectively), despite the lower percentage of lesbians than heterosexuals who indicated that they did not know how to seek therapy (31.8% and 40.4%, respectively). It is also possible that a serious suicide attempt led to intervention. This intervention may have resulted in a higher percentage of lesbians than heterosexuals who obtained therapy and hence were more familiar with the mental health service system. Despite a significant difference regarding suicide attempts, we did not find differences in suicidal ideation or the lethal intent of attempts. Our findings are similar to the those of Safren and Heimberg (1999), who reported that "persons who reported a past attempt (42% sexual minority, 66% heterosexual) indicated that they attempted to kill themselves but did not really hope to die" (p. 861).

Mathy's (2002) cross-cultural research found a relationship between sexual orientation and suicide attempts for females only in North America. Our results were inconsistent with this cross-cultural work. The difference may be attributable to the fact that the first author wrote the questionnaire in Chinese, whereas Mathy's cross-cultural study was limited to participants able to comprehend English. Our findings also were inconsistent with other U.S. studies which reported that lesbians were not at higher risk of suicide attempts than were their heterosexual same-sex peers (Remafedi, French, Story, Resnick, & Blum, 1998).

The incessant oppression and discrimination experienced by lesbians in this study may account for the significantly lower percentage of lesbians than heterosexuals who indicated that they were happy being female (79.6% and 88.0%, respectively). Nonetheless, it should be noted that nearly four-fifths of lesbians were, indeed, happy being female. Because we removed transgender-identified participants from the sample, we can be certain that about one-fifth of female-identified lesbians were unhappy being female even though they did not identify as transgender. This may suggest that the identity salience of sexual orientation supersedes that of gender among masculine-identified sexual minorities in contemporary Taiwan society. The relation between self-acceptance of minority sexual orientation and gender identity salience may warrant further research. This finding also may have been due to the perceived gender nonconformity among lesbians, with more oppression of masculine-identified lesbians and hence increased dissatisfaction with being female.

Our analyses of mental health and gender identity among lesbians yielded few noteworthy results. Overall, gender identity did not differentiate lesbians on indices of mental health, past or present. There was a notable exception. A significantly greater percentage of masculine than androgynous-identified lesbians reported that they had experienced serious suicidal ideations (71.1% and 47.9%, respectively). In addition, a significantly greater percentage of feminine than androgynous lesbians indicated that they were considering psychotherapy at the time they answered the questionnaire (24.4% and 9.6%, respectively). It is also noteworthy that there was a gender identity-related linear trend toward happiness with being female. A significantly greater percentage of feminine than androgynous or masculine-identified lesbians reported they were happy being female (97.8%, 77.8%, and 57.9%).

Gender roles also failed to distinguish differences in the mental health or treatment histories of lesbians. As expected, we found that happiness with being female was significantly greater among lesbians who adopted a femme vis-á-vis butch role. It is not surprising that a disproportionately large percentage of butch lesbians had tried to conceal their breasts. Doing so would be consistent with a butch role.

The dearth of differences in psychopathology by gender identity and gender role suggest that gender identity and gender role *per se* are insufficient explanations for the differences in mental health found between lesbians and heterosexual females. Gender may be too complex a construct to permit a simple explanation of the variance between sexual orientation and mental health. In the future, researchers should consider the ego dystonic effects that occur when others perceive one to have a gender identity or gender role discordant with one's identity. As evidenced by the experience of transsexuals, this is psychically quite painful and potentially debilitating. Thus, we would predict that dissatisfaction with one's gender identity, gender role, or sexual orientation would pose a greater challenge to mental health than gender-incongruent orientations, identities, or roles per se. Our alternative explanation about gender role, gender identity, and sexual orientation in relation to mental health also would predict a relatively high incidence of depression and stress-related disorders among effeminate heterosexual males and extremely masculine heterosexual females.

The *relatively* high prevalence of psychopathology among sexual minorities relative to heterosexuals presents a challenge for researchers. Sexual orientation is not a psychopathology. In part because there is an association between gender nonconformity and homosexuality, it may appear reasonable to ask whether gender atypical gay men, lesbian women, and bisexuals are more likely to develop a mental illness than are their gender-congruent peers. At least for lesbian and bisexual females in Taiwan, our research suggests not. In part because most sexual minorities do not succumb to psychopathology and there is a clear relation between sexual orientation and gender nonconformity (Bell & Weinberg, 1983; Whitam & Mathy, 1986), we believe the explanation lies elsewhere. Specifically, again, we would argue that gender-incongruous identities or roles are not a factor in psychopathology. Rather, we would suggest that discordance between one's self-perception as masculine, feminine, or androgynous and social expectations about one's sexual orientation, gender identity, or gender role can significantly contribute to the burden of oppression that contributes to stress-related disorders. Gender-role playing may provide an unusually creative and adaptive outlet for sexual minority individuals living in areas in which gender stereotypes are rigid and culturally entrenched.

Thus, the sexual minority groups at greatest risk of succumbing to psychopathology are not masculine women and feminine men. Instead, they are sexual minorities to whom others deny the right to be, unable to have their sense of self phenomenologically endorsed by others. This is simultaneously a function of self-efficacy and social oppression, weighed heavily by the ongoing reification of sex, gender, and sexual orientation as a binary system aligned with genitalia rather than self-concept.

This study is an important start for understanding lesbian mental health in Taiwan. Our results revealed a need for further research in this area. Further examination of identity, mental health, and Chinese culture may help us learn more about the variations of human sexuality in complex social ecologies. There is a long history of lesbians in Chinese and other Asian cultures. It is time to increase our knowledge and understanding of these long forgotten cultures and the peoples who inhabit places that Westerners think of as foreign and exotic. On the journey toward understanding psychology and human sexuality, we are all foreigners in exotic lands.

LIMITATIONS

Self-report and retrospective recall may have affected the results of this study. Use of the Internet as a research tool may have increased the integrity of self-disclosure. The Internet fosters a sense of anonymity and confidentiality. However, the study relied upon convenience sampling. Therefore, the reliability to generalizing our results to Taiwan is unknown. There is no population-based demographic information with which to compare our sample with lesbian and bisexual females in Taiwan. Further research with more robust sampling designs will need to corroborate our findings.

Despite these limitations, the study included a heterosexual control group obtained with a similar survey instrument via the Internet. It provides information about lesbian and bisexual women, who remain underrepresented in the empirical research literature. Moreover, it provides information about lesbian and bisexual women in an Asian culture. Further cross-cultural research, as well as studies with more rigorous sampling designs, could facilitate our understanding of women and sexual minorities in non-clinical contexts.

REFERENCES

Armon, V. S. (1960). Some personality variables in overt female homosexuality. *Journal of Projective Techniques, 24,* 292-309.

Bailey, J. M., Kim, P. Y., Hills, A., & Linsenmeier, J. A. W. (1997). Butch, femme, or straight acting? Partner preferences of gay men and lesbians. *Journal of Personality & Social Psychology, 73*(5), 960-973.

Bell, A. P., & Weinberg. M. S. (1978). *Homosexualities: A study of diversity among men and women.* New York: Simon & Schuster.

Bem, S. (1975). Sex role atypicality: One consequence of psychological androgyny. *Journal of Personality and Social Psychology, 31,* 634-643.

Bradford, J., Ryan, C. & Rothblum, E.D. (1994) National Lesbian Health Care Survey: Implications for mental health care. *Journal of Consulting and Clinical Psychology, 62*(2), 228-242.

Broverman, I. K., Broverman, D. M., Clarkson, F. E., Rosenkrantz, P. S., & Vogel, S. R. Sex-role stereotypes and clinical judgments of health. *Journal of Consulting & Clinical Psychology, 34*(1), 1-7.

Brown, W. N, Finn, C. J., Cooke, B.M., and Breedlove, S. M. (2002). Differences in finger length ratios between self-identified "butch" and "femme" lesbians. *Archives of Sexual Behavior, 31*(1), 123-127.

Chan, C.(1989). Issues of identity development among Asian American lesbians and gay men. *Journal of counseling and Development, 68,* 16-20.

Chan, C. (1992). Cultural considerations in counseling Asian American lesbians and gay men. In S. Dworkin & F. Gutierrez (Eds.), *Counseling gay men and lesbians.* (pp.115-124). Alexandria, VA: American Association for Counseling and Development.

Chan, L.R. (2000). Their stories: Seven lesbians' identity process. Master Dissertation.

Chao, A. (2000). Global metaphors and local strategies in the construction of Taiwan's lesbian identities. *Culture, Health, & Sexuality, 2*(4), 377-390.

Cochran, S. D., and Mays, S. M. (2000). Relation between psychiatric syndromes and behaviorally defined sexual orientation in a sample of the US population. *American Journal of Epidemiology, 151,* 516-523.

Cooper, A., Morahan-Martin, J., Mathy, R. M., & Maheu, M. (2002). Toward an increased understanding of user demographics in online sexual activities. *Journal of Sex & Marital Therapy, 28,* 105-129.

Coyle, A. & Kitzinger, C. (2002). *Lesbian and gay psychology.* Oxford: Blackwell.

D'Augelli, A. R. & Hershberger, S.L. (1993). Lesbian, gay, and bisexual youth in community settings: Personal challenges and mental health problems. *American Journal of Community Psychology, 21,* 421-448

Freedman, M. (1971). *Homosexuality and psychological functioning.* Belmont, CA: Brooks/Cole.

Harry, J. (1983). Parasuicide, gender, and gender deviance. *Journal of Health & Social Behavior, 24*(4), 350-361.

Hogg, C. (2003). Taiwan moves to allow gay unions. *BBC News UK Edition.* Retrieved February 14, 2004, from http://news.bbc.co.uk/1/hi/world/asia-pacific/3219721.stm

Hong, Z., Veach, P. M., & Lawrenz, F. (2003). An investigation of the gender stereotyped thinking of Taiwanese secondary school boys and girls. *Sex Roles, 48*(11/12), 495-504.

Hopkins, J. H. (1969). The lesbian personality. *British Journal of Psychiatry, 115,* 1433-1436.

Jeng, M.L. (1997) Daughter's Circle, the identity of Taiwanese lesbian, family and circle life. Taipei: Female Culture.

Jia, H. Y. (1996) The knowledge of adolescent homosexuality's inclination and guidance. *Counseling and Guidance, 126,* 12-16.

Jian, J. S. (1997). 90s' lesbian gender struggle culture, the deconstruction of T and P, reconstruct and overcome. *Think and Word, 35,* 145-209.

Kao, L. A. (1994). The counseling of homosexuality. *Guidance Quarter, 30*(2), 50-57.

Kinsey, A. C., Pomeroy, W. B., Martin, C. E., & Gebhard, P. H. (1953). *Sexual behavior in the human female.* Philadelphia: W. B. Saunders Co.

Liu, A. J. (2000) The rethink of homosexuality guidance. *Counseling and Guidance, 171,* 23-27.

Loney, J. (1972). Background factors, sexual experiences, and attitudes toward treatment in two 'normal' homosexual samples. *Journal of Consulting & Clinical Psychology, 38,* 57-65.

Mathy, R. M. (2002). Suicidality and Sexual Orientation in Five Continents: Asia, Australia, Europe, North America, and South America. *International Journal of Sexuality and Gender Studies, 7*(2/3), 215-225.

Mathy, R. M., & Cooper, A. (2003). The duration and frequency of Internet use in a nonclinical sample: Suicidality, behavioral problems, and treatment histories. *Psychotherapy: Theory, Research, Practice, Training, 40*(1/2), 125-135.

Mathy, R. M., Kerr. D. L., & Haydin, B. M. (2003). Methodological rigor and ethical considerations in Internet-mediated research. *Psychotherapy: Theory, Research, Practice, Training, 40*(1/2), 77-85.

Mathy, R. M., Schillace, M., Coleman, S. M., & Berquist, B. E. (2002). Methodological rigor with Internet samples: New ways to reach underrepresented populations. *CyberPsychology & Behavior, 5*(3), 253-266.

Perez, R. M., DeBord, K. A. & Bieschke, K. J. (1999). *Handbook of counseling and psychotherapy with lesbian, gay, and bisexual clients.* American Psychological Association.

Ponse, B. (1978). *Identities in the lesbian world: The social construction of self.* Westport, CT: Greenwood.

Radonsky, S. E., & Borders, L. D. (1995). Factors influencing lesbians' direct disclosure of their sexual orientation. *Journal of Gay & Lesbian Psychotherapy, 2,* 17-37.

Safern, S.A. & Heimberg, R. G. (1999). Depression, hopelessness, suicidality, and related factors in sexual minority and heterosexual adolescents. *Journal of Consulting and Clinical Psychology, 67*(6), 859-866.

Saghir, M., & Robins, E. (1973). *Male and female homosexuality: A comprehensive investigation.* Baltimore, MD: Williams & Wilkins.

Seigelman, M. (1972). Adjustment of homosexual and heterosexual women. *British journal of psychiatry, 120,* 477-481.

Singh, D., Vidaurri, M., Zambarano, R. J., and Dabbs, J. M. Jr. (1999). Lesbian erotic role identification: Behavioral, morphological, and hormonal correlates. *Journal of Personality and Social Psychology, 76,* 1035-1049.

Talberg, C. (2003, November 1). Taiwan holds it first gay parade. *BBC News World Edition.* Retrieved February 14, 2004, from http://news.bbc.co.uk/1/hi/world/asia-pacific/3233905.stm

Thompson, N., McDandless, B., & Strickland, B. (1971). Personal adjustment of male and female homosexuals and heterosexuals. *Journal of Abnormal Psychology, 78,* 237-240.

Tremble, B., Schneider, M., & Appathurai, C. (1989). Growing up gay or lesbian in a multicultural context. *Journal of Homosexuality, 17,* 253-267.

Weiss, R. S. (1994). Learning from strangers: The art and method of qualitative interview studies. New York: Free Press.

Whitam, F. L., & Mathy, R. M. (1986). Male homosexuality in four societies: Brazil, Guatemala, the Philippines, and the United States. Westport, CT: Praeger.

Ye, Z. T. (2001) Case Study: The counseling of homosexuality. *Counseling and guidance, 189,* 9-14.

Lesbian and Bisexual Women's Sexual Fantasies, Psychological Adjustment, and Close Relationship Functioning

Jessica Dawn Robinson, PhD
Carlton W. Parks, PhD

SUMMARY. This study focused on the impact of relationship functioning, relationship satisfaction, psychological adjustment, and the thematic content of sexual fantasies endorsed by lesbian and bisexual
couples during masturbation and sexual relations. The sample consisted
of 129 women (85 lesbian, 44 bisexual) who were part of a same-sex
couple (average relationship duration of 5-10 years). Participants (94%

Jessica Dawn Robinson is affiliated with Individual, Family, and Child Psychology,
California School of Professional Psychology of Alliant International University at
Los Angeles. Carlton W. Parks is affiliated with Multicultural Community-Clinical
Psychology, California School of Professional Psychology and Graduate Programs in
School and Educational Psychology, Graduate School of Education of Alliant Interna-
tional University at Los Angeles.

Address correspondence to Carlton W. Parks, Alliant International University, 1000
South Fremont Avenue, Unit 5, Bldg. 7, Alhambra, CA 91803 (E-mail: cparks@alliant.
edu).

The authors would like to acknowledge Wendy E. Stock, PhD, of Alliant International University, San Francisco Bay Campus, who provided assistance during the preliminary phases of this research endeavor. Portions of this data set have been presented
at the Society for the Scientific Study of Sexuality Western Region Meeting as well as
the American Psychological Association Convention.

[Haworth co-indexing entry note]: "Lesbian and Bisexual Women's Sexual Fantasies, Psychological Adjustment, and Close Relationship Functioning." Robinson, Jessica Dawn, and Carlton W. Parks. Co-published simultaneously in *Journal of Psychology & Human Sexuality* (The Haworth Press, Inc.) Vol. 15, No. 4,
2003, pp. 185-203; and: *Lesbian and Bisexual Women's Mental Health* (ed: Robin M. Mathy, and Shelly K.
Kerr) The Haworth Press, Inc., 2003, pp. 185-203. Single or multiple copies of this article are available for a
fee from The Haworth Document Delivery Service [1-800-HAWORTH, 9:00 a.m. - 5:00 p.m. (EST). E-mail
address: docdelivery@haworthpress.com].

Digital Object Identifier: 10.1300/J056v15n04_03

Euro-Americans) were recruited through advertisements placed in national gay and lesbian periodicals. Relationship functioning significantly predicted the thematic content of sexual fantasies. However, psychological adjustment did not significantly predict the thematic content of non-traditional sexual fantasies. The authors discuss the implications of these findings for clinicians who practice with lesbian and bisexual women who are in same-sex relationships. *[Article copies available for a fee from The Haworth Document Delivery Service: 1-800-HAWORTH. E-mail address: <docdelivery@haworthpress.com> Website: <http://www.HaworthPress.com> © 2003 by The Haworth Press, Inc. All rights reserved.]*

KEYWORDS. Bisexual and lesbian couples, relationship functioning, psychological adjustment, sexual fantasies

A paucity of research has focused on the sexual fantasies of lesbians, gay men, or bisexual men or women (Leitenberg & Henning, 1995). The limited data that do exist have generated rather mixed findings (e.g., Masters, & Johnson, 1979; Price, Allenworth, & Hillman, 1985; Lehne, 1978). Adults currently involved in same-sex couple relationships may be more likely to express the full spectrum of sexual fantasies (McKinney, & Sprecher, 1991). Therefore, researchers may need to include both same-sex partners in their close-relationship research designs. However, such a task can be challenging given the "invisibility" of gay male, lesbian, and bisexual couples.

Another reason that research with lesbian, gay, and bisexual (LGB) populations has generated mixed findings may be the reluctance of sexology researchers to directly assess the sexual orientation identity status of participants. Sexology researchers often presume participants are heterosexual or neglect to consider the impact of race, ethnicity, gender, SES, geographic region, cohort influences, and sexual orientation identity status on the expression of sexual behavior. A growing body of literature has focused on the production of sexual fantasies by women "presumed to be heterosexual" (Herek, Kimmel, Amaro, & Melton, 1991). For instance, Stock (1982) found that women who fantasized frequently during masturbation had a greater genital response during sexual fantasy and tape-elicited arousal than women who reported lower levels of masturbatory fantasy. Women who fantasize about sex more frequently were more orgasmic with their partner during masturbation. Moreover, they reported being more satisfied with their sexuality than women who rarely fantasized. Finally, when they reported a broader spectrum of sexual fantasies, they were more likely to have elevated rates of masturbation as well as partner-induced orgasms (Arndt, Foehl, & Good, 1985).

Lentz and Zeiss (1984) indicated that mixed fantasies (a combination of both erotic and romantic ideas) were the best predictor of coital orgasms. Women fantasized primarily about romantic (non-erotic fantasies) and had fewer orgasms during intercourse. Erotic sexual fantasies during masturbation were the best predictor of coital orgasms when compared to women who fantasized about romance without the thought of engaging in sexual behavior. Research by Purifoy, Grodsky, and Giambra revealed that sexual fantasies "occur as daydreams or as deliberate, consciously manipulated thoughts" (1992, p. 369). Sexual fantasies, according to the authors, were always fantastic or unreal. In their sample of women ranging from their middle 20s to late 70s, increases in age were associated with reduced levels of sexual interest and activity, reduced levels of sexual desire, and more negative attitudes about sexuality. Women with negative attitudes about sex were less likely to report sexual daydreams. When women had sexual partners available, the effect of age was eliminated.

Hariton and Singer (1974) tested three theoretical models, including (a) drive-reduction, (b) adaptive, and (c) personality-cognitive models. Their sample consisted of 141 housewives from suburban Long Island, New York who responded to questionnaires involving general daydreaming tendencies, fantasies and other ideations during coitus, sexual patterns, marital adjustment, and measures of intelligence, personality, and personality adjustment. Factor analyses revealed statistical support for the "personality-cognitive" and "adaptive" models as compared to the "drive-reduction" model.

Finally, another major methodological limitation within the sexual fantasy literature has been the failure of researchers to directly assess for child sexual abuse history. A growing literature has focused on the long-term effects of child sexual abuse on adult female sexual functioning, particularly within the context of close (intimate) relationships (Gil, 1983; Bass & Davis, 1988; Brown, 1995; Hunter, 1995; Schwartz, Galperin, & Masters, 1995; Button & Dietz, 1995; Kerewsky & Miller, 1996; Wyatt, Newcomb, & Riederle, 1993). It can be challenging for partners since the sexual domain is often the final area where changes occur for adult female survivors of child sexual abuse who are undergoing treatment (Button, & Dietz, 1995). When researchers are focusing on partners' functioning within the context of close relationships, they need to directly assess participants for history of child sexual abuse. They should not presume the sexual orientation identity status of their participants when studying sexuality within the context of close relationships (e.g., McKinney & Sprecher, 1991).

Altogether, the preceding findings provided the framework and rationale for this study. The questions generated from this empirical literature include: (a) What impact would child sexual abuse history have on the production of sexual fantasies within the context of a lesbian or bisexual couple's relationship? (b) What would be the level of psychological adjustment of a national sample of lesbian and bisexual women with a history of child sexual abuse? (c) What impact would such a history have on their close relationship functioning? (d) Would we be able to replicate Hariton and Singer's (1974) findings concerning the adaptive function of sexual fantasies in a "presumed-to-be heterosexual" female convenience sample when replicated with a national sample of lesbian and bisexual female couples with a history of childhood sexual abuse? Specifically, what would be the relationship between the thematic content categories of lesbian and bisexual women's sexual fantasies and other standardized relationship functioning variables? Based on Kurdek's (1988) findings with a sample of lesbian and bisexual female couples, we hypothesized that our national sample would appear more similar in all dimensions to Kurdek's sample than to a traditional clinical sample, with an identical sampling strategy used for both studies. Moreover, because there are limited data focusing on the sexual fantasies of lesbians and bisexual women in the literature, we expected that the thematic content categories of our participants' sexual fantasies (and their relationship to other psychological constructs) would generally mirror Hariton and Singer's (1974) findings.

METHOD

Participants

The participants consisted of 129 women (85 lesbian and 44 bisexual) who had been in cohabiting relationships with their lesbian or bisexual female partner for at least six months. The participants were recruited through an announcement placed in national gay and lesbian periodicals. The announcement placed in these publications recruited couples interested in participating in a relationship satisfaction survey.

The participants were 94% Euro-Americans, with a median age of 29. The median duration of participants' relationships was 4 years, with a positively skewed distribution as indicated by a mean duration of 5-10 years. The typical participant had some college education and was employed as machine operator or semiskilled worker. About 15 percent of the participants reported having children, of whom 84.6% were biological and 15.4% were adopted. About 91% of the participants reported they were in a sexually monogamous relationship. Finally, 75% of the participants reported having a history of childhood sexual abuse.

Materials

Demographic Questionnaire

Participants responded to questions documenting demographic characteristics for themselves and their partners. The questions focused on (a) gender, (b) chronological age, (c) relationship status, (d) race, (e) occupation, (f) education, (g) income, and (h) duration of current relationship. Participants also were asked to disclose whether they had children and, if so, the child's age, sex, and relationship to the participant (e.g., adopted or biological). No reliability or validity data were available for the demographic questionnaire.

Sexual History Questionnaire

Participants were asked a series of questions concerning their sexual abuse (e.g., "Before you were 18, were you ever upset by anyone exposing their genitals to you?"; "Did anyone ever try or succeed in getting you to touch their breasts or genitals against your wishes before you were eighteen?"; "Did anyone ever try or succeed in touching your breasts or genitals against your wishes before you turned eighteen?"; "Before you turned eighteen, did anyone ever feel you, grab you, or kiss you in a way you felt was sexually threatening?"; "Did anyone ever try to succeed in having any kind of sexual relations (intercourse) with you against your wishes before you turned eighteen?"). Participants were asked the identity of the perpetrators and multiple responses were made available to the respondent. Child sexual abuse history was coded as a separate linear variable: no history = 0; rape as an adult without childhood abuse = 1; extrafamilial history only = 2; extrafamilial abuse and rape as an adult = 3; incest = 4; incest and rape as an adult = 5; both extrafamilial abuse and incest histories = 6, and extrafamilial abuse and incest as a child as well as rape after the age of 18 = 7. We used this coding scheme to assess child sexual abuse history because Russell (1986), Courtois (1988), and Briere (1988) asserted that trauma builds with the circumstances of the abuse. Thus, rape as an adult would be considered less traumatic than extrafamilial abuse as a child. Incest would be considered more traumatic than either, and the combination of rape and childhood sexual abuse would be more traumatic than either alone.

Sexual orientation identity was assessed using the Kinsey Sexual Orientation Continuum (Kinsey, Pomeroy, & Martin, 1948; Kinsey, Pomeroy, Martin, & Gebhard, 1953), as well as questions concerning the sexual monogamy of the couple. We did not assess the reliability or validity of the sexual history questionnaire used for this study.

Hobart Scale (Hobart, 1958)

The Hobart Scale measured the level of romanticism of each respondent. The scale consisted of 12 statements about close relationships, such as, "To be truly in love is to be in love forever," or "Most of us could sincerely love any one of several people equally," and the respondent either agreed or disagreed with each statement. There were no published reliability or validity data based on this instrument. The Cronbach alpha coefficient for the Hobart Scale for this sample was .82.

Trust Scale (Rempel, Holmes, & Zanna, 1985)

The Trust Scale measured the degree of trust that participants felt toward their partners. It used the following three subscales: (a) predictability, (b) dependability, and (c) faith. Each item was scored on a 7-point Likert scale ranging from 1 = strongly disagree, 4 = agree, and 7 = strongly agree. Higher scores reflected greater participant endorsement of the three constructs: (a) predictability, (b) dependability, and (c) faith in their intimate relationship. The overall Cronbach alpha was .81, with subscale reliabilities of .70, .72, and .80, respectively (Rempel, Holmes, & Zanna, 1985). Cronbach's alpha for the summed composite score for the Trust Scale score was .87 based on the Kurdek data set (Kurdek, 1988), and the subscale reliabilities for this sample were .22, .59, and .91, respectively.

Motivation Scale (Rempel, Holmes, & Zanna, 1985)

The Motivation Scale measured the extent to which an individual participant was in a coupled relationship due to intrinsic, instrumental, or extrinsic motivation. The scale consisted on 20 items assessing the respondent and their partners on how important each item was in motivating them with respect to their close relationship. The overall reliability of the Motivation Scale was .83 for attributions about partners' motives and .80 for inferences about personal motives. The subscale reliabilities (Cronbach's alphas) were .82, .77, and .76 for the partners' motives, and .69, .76, and .79 for the personal motives (Rempel, Holmes, & Zanna, 1985). The subscale reliabilities (Cronbach's alphas) for personal motives for this sample were .72, .70 and .85, respectively, and the subscale reliabilities (Cronbach's alphas) for the partners' motives were .70, .67, and .85, respectively.

Relationship Beliefs Inventory (RBI) (Eidelson, & Epstein, 1982)

The RBI assessed four dysfunctional (irrational) relationship beliefs: (a) disagreement is destructive, (b) mindreading is expected, (c) partners cannot change, and (d) sexual perfectionism. Bradbury and Fincham (1993) asserted that the Disagreement is Destructive subscale was positively correlated with the RBI total score, and it was used as the measure of dysfunctional relationship beliefs for the current study. Psychometric information is available in the Appendix of Baucom and Epstein (1990). Additional psychometric data are presented in Bradbury and Fincham (1993). The Cronbach alpha coefficient for the RBI's Disagreement is Destructive scale was .79 for this sample.

Dyadic Adjustment Scale (DAS) (Spanier, 1976)

The DAS consisted of four scales: (a) consensus, (b) satisfaction, (c) cohesion, and (d) affectional expression. The participants rated 32 statements concerning their close (intimate) relationship and the extent to which they agreed or disagreed with each statement. Cronbach's alphas for the summed composite scores were .83, .63, .81, and .72 based on the Kurdek (1986) data set. The Cronbach's alpha for the summed composite score based on the Kurdek (1988) data set was .89. Additional psychometric data are presented in Spanier (1976). The subscale reliabilities (Cronbach's alphas) for this sample were .85, .86, .62, and .66 respectively, and the DAS total score for this sample was .92.

SCL 90-R (Derogatis, 1977)

The SCL90-R consisted of 90 items that assessed psychological distress over the past seven days through self-report symptoms: The 90 items form the following 9 scales: (a) Somatization, (b) Obsessive-Compulsive, (c) Interpersonal Sensitivity, (d) Depression, (e) Anxiety, (f) Hostility, (g) Phobic Anxiety, (h) Paranoid Ideation, and (i) Psychoticism. It yielded a global severity index, with each item rated along a 5-point scale. A score of 0 represented no symptoms and a score of 4 indicated that a symptom was extremely problematic. Some examples of questions for the SCL90-R include, "Worrying too much about things," or "Having thoughts that are not your own." The Cronbach's alpha for the summed composite score (global severity index) ranged from .95 to .97 based on the Kurdek (1993) data set. Similarly, the Cronbach's alpha for the Depression score was .89 across partners and the Cronbach's alpha for each score exceeded .86 (Kurdek, 1987; 1993). The subscale reliabilities (Cronbach's alpha) for the SCL-90-R for this sample were (Somatization) .86, (Obsessive-Compulsive) .86, (Interpersonal Sensitivity) .86, (Depression) .90, (Anxiety) .91, (Hostility) .79, (Phobic Anxiety) .74, (Paranoid Ideation) .72, and (Psychoticism) .84.

Sexual Fantasy Questionnaire

The Sexual Fantasy Questionnaire was constructed from parts 2 and 3 of the Hariton and Singer's (1974) Daydreaming Inventory for married women. Part 2 of the Sexual Fantasy Questionnaire consisted of fantasies involving the participation of the partner. It was referred to as "stimulus dependent positive thoughts" (Hariton & Singer, 1974). Part 3 of the Sexual Fantasy Questionnaire consisted of 15 erotic fantasy items that were "stimulus independent." The stimulus independent items were fantasies about events or people outside of the sexual situation. For example, "I imagine that I am being overpowered or forced to surrender" (Hariton & Singer, 1974). These items were combined to assess fantasies that the respondent had experienced during masturbation. The respondents were asked to circle all the letters corresponding to themes that have occurred in their fantasies during masturbation. The second section of the Sexual Fantasies Questionnaire was designed to assess personal descriptions of respondents' sexual fantasies during masturbation. The respondents were instructed to "describe briefly (in sentence or phrase) the typical content of each of your masturbation fantasies (e.g. 'I'm seduced by a stranger,' 'My lover and I are making love,' or 'I'm an Arabian harem girl.').'"

Both sections of the Sexual Fantasies Questionnaire were coded and placed into one of six factors: (a) genital, (b) romantic, (c) power-dominance, (d) non-traditional, (e) sexual-aggression, and (f) non-sexual fantasies. The non-traditional category was labeled as such based on sexual fantasies that would be in violation of community standards (e.g., sex in public settings) if they were to be evaluated according to traditional heterosexual community standards. The constructs were based on previous factorial research conducted by Meuwissen and Over (1991). A random selection of the fantasies were scored by an independent observer and yielded an inter-rater agreement of 90.2%.

Design and Procedure

The design of this study was a descriptive exploratory study designed to empirically document the sexual fantasies of lesbian and bisexual females currently living within the context of a coupled relationship between two women. Couples ($N = 232$ women) expressed interest in participating in the relationship satisfaction survey by providing their names and addresses to the principal investigator. Each couple was mailed a pair of identical questionnaire packets with separate, addressed, stamped return envelopes. Participants were asked not to discuss their responses with their partner. A total of 157 questionnaire packets were returned to the principal investigator, yielding a return rate of 67.67 percent, including 54 lesbian and bisexual female couples and 22 lesbian and bisexual female individuals who were living in couple relationships.

The mean value of each missing value was inserted into this data set in order to address the issue of missing data. Normality was assessed statistically using the nonparametric test, one-sample K-S test. Variables that yielded $p < .05$ were transformed using the Windsorize method, with the outlier value replaced by the nearest non-outlier subject plus one. The following variables were Windsorized after yielding one-sample K-S test results with $p < .05$: (a) Hobart scale, (b) Trust Faith scale, (c) Trust Dependability scale, (d) Trust Predictability scale, (e) Motivation Intrinsic scale, (f) Motivation Extrinsic scale, (g) Motivation Instrumental scale, and (h) SCL 90-R Global Severity Index Score.

Because 75% of the sample reported a history of child sexual abuse, 25% of these respondents were selected and compared to the 25% of the non-abused respondents. The alpha level was raised to .01. There was only one significant difference between respondents with and without a history of childhood sexual abuse. Respondents with a history of child sexual abuse were more likely than their non-abused counterparts to report more problem-solving in their daydreams ($F(1,72) = 4.254$, $p < .01$). This variable was omitted from all subsequent simultaneous multiple linear regression analyses. Post-hoc statistical analyses were generated to determine if there were any significant differences between bisexual female and lesbian respondents with respect to the dependent variables associated with this study. The analysis of variance generated no significant differences, and the sexual orientation identity variable was consequently omitted from all subsequent simultaneous multiple linear regression analyses.

RESULTS

We hypothesized that one of the three factors (i.e., sexual relations *vis-à-vis* power and dominance or non-traditional) generated by the research from the six thematic content factors would yield the most elevated frequency of reported sexual fantasies. We hypothesized that the frequency of these sexual fantasies would be followed by the non-traditional factor and the power and dominance factor. This hypothesis was confirmed, and 98.4% of the respondents reported having sexual fantasies that fit under the sexual relations factor, followed by 79.1% of the respondents who endorsed fantasies that fit under the non-traditional factor and 62.8% who endorsed sexual fantasies that fit under the power and dominance factor. Although respondents were able to endorse more than one factor when reporting all of their sexual fantasies, only one factor per sexual fantasy based on the action described in the sexual fantasy description was permitted.

Relationship Functioning and the Thematic Content Factors (Sexual Relations, Non-Traditional, and Power-Dominance)

We hypothesized that the relationship functioning variables (e.g., Hobart Scale, Relationship Beliefs Inventory, Trust Scale, Motivation Scale, and the Dyadic Adjustment Scale) were significant predictors of the thematic content factors. More specifically, we hypothesized that the (a) Relationship Beliefs Inventory Disagreement is Destructive scale would significantly predict a positive association with the non-traditional factor; (b) Hobart Scale would significantly predict a positive association with the sexual relations factor; (c) Trust subscales would separately predict a negative association with the power and dominance factor, (d) the Motivation subscales would significantly predict a positive association with the sexual relations factor, and (e) the Dyadic Adjustment Scale total score and the 4 subscales would separately predict a positive association with the sexual relations factor.

The Relationship Beliefs Inventory's Disagreement is Destructive scale significantly predicted the non-traditional factor, $F(1,127) = 6.58$, $p < .01$, $R = .22$, R-square = .05, Adjusted R-square = .04, and standard error = .40. Women who endorsed the dysfunctional relationship irrational belief, disagreement is destructive (RBI), reported an elevated frequency of non-traditional fantasies during masturbation and sexual relations.

Psychological Adjustment and the Sexual Relations Thematic Content Factor

We hypothesized that the SCL 90-R's nine scales and the global severity index would significantly predict the criterion variable, the non-traditional thematic content factor. This hypothesis was not empirically supported.

Motivation Subscales and the Power/Dominance Thematic Content Factor

The results of post-hoc analyses revealed that when the 3 Motivation subscales were entered separately into a simultaneous multiple linear regression analysis, they significantly predicted the power and dominance factor, $F(6,122) = 2.19$, $p < .049$, $R = .31$, R-square = .10, Adjusted R-square = .05, standard error = .47. Participants who endorsed the three subscales had a lower frequency score on the power and dominance thematic content factor.

DISCUSSION

These findings revealed that relationship functioning measures (Motivation subscales and the RBI's Disagreement is Destructive subscale) significantly predicted subsets of the thematic content factors. However, psychological adjustment, as assessed by the SCL-90 R, did not significantly predict the thematic content factors. The sexual relations sexual fantasy thematic content factor was the most prevalent factor, followed by the non-traditional sexual fantasy thematic content factor and the power and dominance sexual fantasy thematic content factor. These findings corroborate Kurdek's study (1991). Our results did not reveal a unique pattern of sexual fantasies in this sample, and sexual fantasies appeared to serve an adaptive function for our participants. These findings appear similar to Hariton and Singer's (1974) in these respects.

Sexual orientation identity status and child sexual abuse history did not serve as potent predictors for the sexual fantasy thematic content factors. Morris, Waldo, and Rothblum (2001) found that sexual orientation identity status (lesbian versus bisexual) was a predictor of emotional distress for bisexual women. However, more systematic empirical attention needs to be paid in documenting the phenomenological experiences of lesbian and bisexual women.

Contributions to the Existing Literature

These findings make a contribution to the growing literature that focuses on sexuality in the form of sexual fantasies within the context of close relationships (e.g., Kurdek, 1991; McKinney & Sprecher, 1991; Hariton & Singer 1974). However, the generalizability of our findings was limited. Due to the small sample size, we were unable to analyze these data with couples as the unit of analysis. Nonetheless, we were able to replicate Hariton and Singer (1974) and Kurdek (1991).

Issues of Internal and External Validity

Given the reality that conducting sexology research with lesbians and gay men involves working with an "invisible" population, it is impossible to address whether or not the researcher has been able to tap a "representative" sample. Therefore, these sexual fantasy findings generalize only to lesbians and bisexual women who read national gay and lesbian periodicals, self-label as a "lesbian" or "bisexual female," and are willing to respond to sensitive questions about their sexual victimization histories. Only through the direct assessment of sexual orientation identity status, sexual fantasies, and sexual victimization histories can we uncover the relationships between these variables and dramatically improve the lives of lesbians and bisexual women within the general population. Recently, survey items about sexual behavior and sexual orientation identity have been successfully administered to probability samples (Miller, Turner, & Moses, 1990).

According to Haugaard and Emery (1989), when there is a low response rate, the number of respondents wanting to tell their story of sexual abuse will outnumber the ones who cannot tell it and the few non-survivors. This will make it appear as though there are more survivors of sexual abuse within the general population than there is in reality. Likewise, when there is a medium response, there are enough non-survivors to balance out the survivors who want to talk about their sexual abuse history, and the ones who do not want to talk result in a representative sample of the general population. Finally, when there is a high response rate the frequency of non-survivors outweighs the survivors who want to talk coupled with the absence of the ones who cannot talk and chose not to respond. This reality gives one the impression that there are less survivors of sexual abuse than is actually the case. Because the response rate for this study was 68%, this sample was somewhat skewed and may appear to have more non-survivors than there actually are in the general population. This issue cannot be fully resolved until more investigators directly assess participants for child sexual abuse history and we can compare the sample and population percentages of participants who report having a history of childhood sexual abuse.

A major limitation of our research effort is its over-reliance on self-report data based on long-term recall memory, as compared to prospective assessments grounded in the present. The limitations inherent in long-term recall data have been well documented and discussed extensively within the empirical literature and will not be discussed further here. Respondent bias was a limitation of this research effort since both partners' data were utilized in all data analyses. One option would have been to analyze the data of only one of the partners or determine statistically if there were any significant differences between couples' data versus couples where only one participant submitted their data. The rationale behind including both partners in data analyses was a serious concern about having too small a sample size, which was another limitation of this research effort. Finally, the collection of data at one specific time of measurement (i.e., cross-sectional data) does not permit the measurement of age-related changes (e.g., longitudinal data), which was yet another limitation of this research effort.

Future Research Directions

Future research endeavors need to take a more systemic approach to these issues and sample culturally and racially diverse samples of lesbian and bisexual female couples (e.g., Pearlman, 1996; Greene & Boyd-Franklin, 1996; Hays, 1996). Moreover, the direct assessment of sexual orientation identity status and sexual victimization history should utilize a multi-method assessment strategy. An emphasis should be placed on the collection of empirical data based on national samples in order to control for possible regional influences. Instruments selected for inclusion in this program of research should be systemic in orientation and have a history of being used previously with lesbian and bisexual female samples. There is a pressing need for a systematic examination of the impact of lesbians' views concerning their body image, weight, and physical appearance on their expression of lesbian sexuality (including their sexual fantasies; e.g., Atkins, 1998; Cogan & Erickson, 1991; Rapi & Chowdhry, 1998; Rose, 1994; Rothblum, 1994). This program of research is still in its embryonic stages, but it is quite likely that it will play a critical role in broadening our understanding of the expression of lesbian sexuality within the context of close relationships (Rose, 1994; Rothblum, 1994). As a case in point, Loulan (1987) reported that less than 10% of her lesbian sample had ever acted out a sexual fantasy with their partner. Mediating variables (e.g., internalized sexism, internalized homophobia, and internalized racism) need to be systematically assessed and incorporated into any design that hopes to be sufficiently comprehensive and inclusive to address the intrapsychic dynamics that serve as the foundation for the expression of lesbian sexuality (e.g., Loulan, 1987; Rose, 1994; Rothblum, 1994).

Clinical Implications

Practitioners need to ensure that their assumptions concerning human behavior are based upon the "realities" that exist outside of the clinic setting. They need to systematically assess clients at intake to ensure that they have accurate information concerning the histories and realities of lesbian and bisexual female couples (e.g., Swartz, 1989; Roth, 1985). The practitioner's genuine validation of the lesbian couple relationship within the treatment context is the most critical ingredient of culturally-informed sex therapy with lesbian couples (Brown, 1995). For instance, being comfortable with the terminology associated with lesbian and bisexual female couples' relationships is a first step in this process (Zimbardi, 1997).

Therapists who feel uncomfortable or seriously question the viability of lesbian couples as a committed relationship (e.g., Green & Clunis, 1989; Rothblum & Brehony, 1993) need to refer these couples to other qualified practitioners for couple therapy. Likewise, the therapist needs to be completely comfortable in addressing issues related to the expression of lesbian sexuality. Lesbian couples rely heavily on their therapist to assist them in openly expressing their desires and fantasies within the arena of lesbian sexuality. Therapists who are uncomfortable assisting in this process only serve to sabotage the treatment of lesbian and bisexual female couples.

These data suggest (e.g., Rose, 1994) that there is considerable shame associated with the expression of lesbian sexuality and the therapist needs to be prepared to address this reality with relative ease (e.g., Rothblum & Brehony, 1993; Queen, 1996). Kurdek (1991) asserted that it is important to keep in mind that lesbian couples (a) deal daily with the lack of institutional supports for their relationship, (b) deal with the lack of adequate role models of lesbian couples in committed relationships, (c) deal with sexuality that does not always serve a procreative function, which is at the foundation of our nation's Puritan religious origins, (d) deal with the restricted "eligible" and "suitable" partner availability within the lesbian community, and (e) deal with the pressures of living in a racist, sexist, and homophobic society, with the resultant minority stressors (i.e., DiPlacido, 1998) that negatively impact lesbians' mental health, psychological adjustment, sexual fantasies, and behavior. Given these realities, it is incumbent upon practitioners to empower their clients to directly address these realities in their daily lives (Brown, 1995).

Clinicians must be prepared to treat effectively partners who have a history that includes multiple levels of victimization (e.g., race, gender, and sexual orientation). These histories may be expected to exacerbate a couple's relationship functioning. Alternatively, there may be occasions when couples may not evidence the symptoms associated with a history of childhood sexual abuse. Clinicians need to be prepared for this reality, without discounting such information despite the absence of objective manifestations of the phenomena.

Finally, practitioners need to address their own cultural biases concerning lesbian couples and their expression of lesbian sexuality. After being socialized within a homophobic and heterosexist culture, it is not particularly surprising that we carry with us vestiges of those socialization experiences. These need to be directly addressed lest they negatively impact our verbal as well as nonverbal communications and result in "mixed messages" within the context of lesbian and bisexual female couple therapy.

The goal of this study was to initiate a dialogue concerning the expression of sexual fantasies within the context of lesbian and bisexual female close relationships that involve a history of childhood sexual abuse. It was intended, in part, to empower this often stigmatized, marginalized, and oppressed group. There is considerable work ahead if we are to enlighten, educate, and inform our society about the varieties and complexities of human sexualities. In particular, further empirical work is needed to study the impact of culture on the expression of sexual fantasies among lesbian and bisexual women in committed, close, same-sex relationships.

REFERENCES

Arndt, Jr., W.B., Foehl, J.C., & Good, F.E. (1985). Specific sexual fantasy themes: A multidimensional study. *Journal of Personality and Social Psychology, 48(2),* 472-480.

Atkins, D. (Ed.). (1998). *Looking queer: Body image and identity in lesbian, bisexual, gay, and transgender communities.* Binghamton, NY: Harrington Park Press.

Bass, E., & Davis, L. (1988). *The courage to heal: A guide for women survivors of child sexual abuse.* New York, N.Y.: Harper & Row, Publishers, Inc.

Baucom, D.H., & Epstein, N. (1990). *Cognitive–behavioral marital therapy.* New York, N.Y.: Brunner/Mazel Publishers.

Bradbury, T.N., & Fincham, F.D. (1993). *American couples: Money, work, and sex.* New York, N.Y.: William Morrow and Company, Inc..

Briere, J. (1988). The long-term clinical correlates of childhood sexual victimization. In R.A. Prenky, & V.L. Quinsey (Eds.), *Human sexual aggression: Current perspectives, Annals of the New York Academy of Sciences, Vol. 528* (pp. 327-334). New York, N.Y: New York Academy of Sciences.

Brown, L.S. (1995). Therapy with same-sex couples: An introduction. In N.S. Jacobsen, & A.S. Gurman (Eds.), *Clinical handbook of couple therapy* (pp. 274-291). New York, N.Y.: Guilford Press.

Button, B., & Dietz, A. (1995). Strengthening the heartline: Working with adult survivors of childhood sexual abuse and their partners. In M. Hunter (Ed.), *Adult survivors of sexual abuse: Treatment innovations* (pp. 136-153). Thousand Oaks, CA: Sage Publications.

Cogan, J., & Erickson, J. (Eds.). (1999). *Lesbians, levis, and lipstick: The meaning of beauty in our lives.* Binghamton, New York: Harrington Park Press.

Courtois, C.A. (1988). *Healing the incest wound: Adult survivors in therapy.* New York, NY: W.W. Norton, & Company, Inc.

Derogatis, L.R. (1977). *SCL 90-R*. Baltimore, Maryland: Baltimore Clinical Psychometric Research.

DiPlacido, J. (1998). Minority stress among lesbians, gay men, and bisexuals: A consequence of heterosexism, homophobia, and stigmatization. In G. M. Herek (Ed.), *Psychological perspectives on lesbians and gay issues, Volume 4, Stigma and sexual orientation: Understanding prejudice against lesbians, gay men, and bisexuals* (pp. 138-159). Thousand Oaks, CA: Sage Publications.

Eidelson, R.J., & Epstein, N. (1982). Cognitions and relationship maladjustment: Development of a measure of dysfunctional relationship beliefs. *Journal of Consulting and Clinical Psychology, 50*, 715-720.

Gil, E. (1983). *Outgoing the pain: A book for and about adults abused as children*. New York, N. Y.: Bantam Doubleday Dell Publishers.

Green, G.D., & Clunis, D.M. (1989). Married lesbians. *Women & Therapy, 8(1/2)*, 41-49.

Greene, B., & Boyd-Franklin, N. (1996). African-American lesbians: Issues in couples therapy. In J. Laird & R. Jay-Green (Eds.), *Lesbians and gays in couples and families: A handbook for therapists* (pp. 251-271). San Francisco, California: Jossey-Bass Publishers, Inc.

Hariton, E.B., & Singer, J.L. (1974). Women's fantasies during sexual intercourse: Normative and theoretical implications. *Journal of Consulting and Clinical Psychology, 42*, 313-322.

Haugaard, J., & Emery, R. (1989). Methodological issues in child sexual abuse research. *Child Abuse and Neglect, 13*, 89-100.

Hays, P.A. (1996). Cultural considerations in couples therapy. *Women & Therapy, 19(3)*, 13-23.

Herek, G.M., Kimmel, D.C., Amaro, H., & Melton, G.B. (1991). Avoiding heterosexist bias in psychological research. *American Psychologist, 46(9)*, 957-963.

Hobart, C.W. (1958). The incidence of romanticism during courtship. *Social Forces, 36*, 362-367.

Hunter, M. (1995). Uncovering the relationship between a client's adult compulsive sexual behavior and childhood sexual abuse. In M. Hunter (Ed.), *Adult survivors of sexual abuse: Treatment innovations* (pp. 56-79). Thousand Oaks, CA: Sage Publications.

Kerewsky, S.D., & Miller, D. (1996). Lesbian couples and childhood trauma: Guidelines for therapists. In J.Laird & R. Jay-Green (Eds.), *Lesbians and gays in couples and families: A handbook for therapists* (pp. 298-315). San Francisco, CA: Jossey-Bass Publishers, Inc.

Kinsey, A.C., Pomeroy, W.B., & Martin, C.E. (1948). *Sexual behavior in the human male*. Philadelphia, PA: W.B. Saunders

Kinsey, A.C., Pomeroy, W.B., Martin, C.E., & Gebhard, P.H. (1953). *Sexual behavior in the human female*. Philadelphia, PA: W.B. Saunders.

Kurdek, L.A. (1993). The allocation of household labor in gay, lesbian, and heterosexual couples. *Journal of Social Issues, 49(3)*, 127-139.

Kurdek, L.A (1992). Assumptions versus standards: The validity of two relationship cognitions in heterosexual and homosexual couples. *Journal of Family Psychology, 6(2)*, 164-170.

Kurdek, L.A. (1991). Sexuality in homosexual and heterosexual couples. In K. McKinney & S. Sprecher (Eds.), *Sexuality in close relationships* (pp. 177-191). Hillsdale, N.J.: Lawrence Erlbaum Publishers, Inc.

Kurdek, L.A. (1988). Perceived social support in gays and lesbians in cohabiting relationships, *Journal of Personality and Social Psychology, 54(3)*, 504-509.

Kurdek, L.A. (1987). Sex-role self schema and psychological adjustment in coupled homosexual and heterosexual men and women. *Sex Roles, 17 (9/10)*, 549-562.

Kurdek, L.A., & Schmitt, J.P. (1986a). Early development of relationship quality in heterosexual married, heterosexual cohabiting gay, and lesbian couples. *Developmental Psychology, 22*, 305-309.

Kurdek, L.A., & Schmitt, J.P. (1986b). Relationship quality of gay men in closed or open relationships. *Journal of Homosexuality, 12*, 85-99.

Kurdek, L.A., & Schmitt, J.P. (1986c). Relationship quality of partners in heterosexual married, heterosexual cohabiting, and gay and lesbian relationships. *Journal of Personality and Social Psychology, 51*, 711-720.

Lehne, G.K. (1978). Gay male fantasies and realities. *Journal of Social Issues, 34*, 28-37.

Leitenberg, H., & Henning, K. (1995). Sexual fantasy. *Psychological Bulletin, 117*, 469-496.

Lentz, S.L., & Zeiss, A.M. (1984). Fantasy and sexual arousal in college women: An empirical investigation. *Imagination, Cognition, and Personality, 3*, 185-202.

Loulan, J. (1987). *Lesbian passion*. San Francisco, CA: Spinsters Ink.

Marsella, A.J., Friedman, M.J., Gerrity, E.T., & Scurfield, R.M. (Eds.). (1996). *Ethnocultural aspects of posttraumatic stress disorder: Issues, research, and clinical applications*. Washington, D.C.: American Psychological Association.

Masters, W.H., & Johnson, V.E. (1979). *Homosexuality in perspective*. Boston, MA: Little Brown, & Company, Inc.

McKinney, K., & Sprecher, S. (Eds.). (1991). *Sexuality in close relationships*. Hillsdale, N.J.: Lawrence Erlbaum Publishers, Inc.

Meuwissen, I., & Over, R. (1991). Multidimensionality of the content of female sexual fantasy. *Behavior, Research, and Therapy, 29*, 179-189.

Miller, H.G., Turner, C.F., & Moses, L.E. (Eds.). (1999). *AIDS: The second decade*. Washington, D.C.: National Academy Press.

Morris, J.F., Waldo, C.R., & Rothblum, E.D. (2001). A model of predictors and outcomes of outness among lesbians and bisexual women. *American Journal of Orthopsychiatry 71*, 61-71.

Pearlman, S.F. (1996). Loving across race and class divides: Relational challenges and the interracial lesbian couple. *Women & Therapy, 19(3)*, 25-35.

Price, J.H., Allensworth, D.D., & Hillman, K.S. (1985). Comparison of sexual fantasies of homosexuals and heterosexuals. *Psychological Reports, 57*, 871-877.

Puriofy, F.E., Grodsky, A. & Giambra, L.M. (1992). The relationship of sexual daydreaming to sexual activity, sexual drive, and sexual attitudes for women across the life-span. *Archives of Sexual Behavior, 21*, 369-385.

Queen, C. (1996). Women, S/M, and therapy. *Women & Therapy, 19(4)*,65-73.

Rapi, N., & Chowdhry, M. (Eds.). (1998). *Acts of passion: Sexuality, gender, and performance*. Binghamton, New York: Harrington Park Press.

Rempel, J.K., Holmes, J.G., & Zanna, M.P. (1985). Trust in close relationships. *Journal of Personality and Social Psychology, 49*, 95-112.

Rose, S. (1994). Sexual pride and shame in lesbians. In B. Greene, & G.M. Herek (Eds.), *Psychological perspectives in lesbian and gay issues: Volume 1, Lesbian and gay psychology: Theory, research, and clinical applications* (pp. 71-83). Thousand Oaks, CA: Sage Publications, Inc.

Roth, S. (1985). Psychotherapy with lesbian couples: Individual issues, female socialization, and the social context. *Journal of Marital and Family Therapy, 11(3)*, 273-286.

Rothblum, E.D. (1994). Lesbians and physical appearance: Which model applies? In B. Greene, & G.M. Herek (Eds.), *Psychological perspectives on lesbian and gay issues: Volume 1, Lesbian and gay psychology: Theory, research, and clinical applications* (pp. 84-97). Thousand Oaks, CA: Sage Publications.

Rothblum, E.D., & Brehony, K.A. (1993). *Boston marriages: Romantic but asexual relationships among contemporary lesbians.* Amherst, MA: University of Massachusetts Press.

Russell, D.E. H. (1986). *The secret trauma: Incest in the lives of girls and women.* New York, N.Y.: Basic Books Publishers, Inc.

Schwartz, M.F., Galperin, L.D., & Masters, W.H. (1995). Dissociation and treatment of compulsive reenactment of trauma: Sexual compulsivity. In M. Hunter (Ed.), *Adult survivors of sexual abuse: Treatment innovations* (pp. 42-55). Thousand Oaks, CA: Sage Publications.

Spanier, G.B. (1976). Measuring dyadic adjustment: New scales for assessing the quality of marriages and similar dyads. *Journal of Marriage and the Family, 38*, 15-38.

Stock, W.E., & Geer, J.H. (1982). A study of fantasy-based sexual arousal in women. *Archives of Sexual Behavior, 11*, 33-47.

Swartz, V.J. (1989). Relational therapy with lesbian couples. In G.R. Weeks (Ed.), *The intersystem model of the Marriage Council of Philadelphia* (pp. 236-257). New York, N.Y.: Brunner/Mazel Publishers, Inc.

Wyatt, G.E. (1990). Sexual abuse of ethnic minority children: Identifying dimensions of victimization. *Professional Psychology: Research and Practice, 21*, 338-343.

Wyatt, G.E., Newcomb, M.D., & Riederle, M. H. (1993). *Sexual abuse and consensual sex: Women's developmental patterns and outcomes.* Newbury Park, CA: Sage Publications, Inc.

Zimbardi, A. (1997, March). Defining a gay relationship: Finding a label which works for both of you. *4Front*, 28.

Lesbian Body Image
and Eating Issues

Paula Wagenbach, PhD

SUMMARY. Research on body-image dissatisfaction and eating issues has emphasized the impact of culture's obsession on women's appearance. This paper reviews a study that examined body image issues, eating behavior, and identification with sexual identity in a sexually diverse sample that included lesbians ($n = 47$), heterosexual women ($n = 47$), and gay men ($n = 51$). The degree to which women identified as lesbian did not influence their body satisfaction or eating issues. However, lesbians were less invested in their appearance and less involved in maintaining it than heterosexual women or gay men. Further, lesbians were less concerned with dieting and thinness than the two other groups. The lesbian community may be less concerned with dieting and thinness than heterosexual women. Implications of findings are discussed. *[Article copies available for a fee from The Haworth Document Delivery Service: 1-800-HAWORTH. E-mail address: <docdelivery@ haworthpress.com> Website: <http://www.HaworthPress.com> © 2003 by The Haworth Press, Inc. All rights reserved.]*

KEYWORDS. Lesbian, mental health, body image, eating issues

Paula Wagenbach is affiliated with the Epidemiology Genetics Program, Department of Psychiatry, Johns Hopkins University School of Medicine, Baltimore, MD.

[Haworth co-indexing entry note]: "Lesbian Body Image and Eating Issues." Wagenbach, Paula. Co-published simultaneously in *Journal of Psychology & Human Sexuality* (The Haworth Press, Inc.) Vol. 15, No. 4, 2003, pp. 205-227; and: *Lesbian and Bisexual Women's Mental Health* (ed: Robin M. Mathy, and Shelly K. Kerr) The Haworth Press, Inc., 2003, pp. 205-227. Single or multiple copies of this article are available for a fee from The Haworth Document Delivery Service [1-800-HAWORTH, 9:00 a.m. - 5:00 p.m. (EST). E-mail address: docdelivery@haworthpress.com].

205

BODY IMAGE AND EATING ISSUES

American culture's obsessive focus on the appearance of women has been linked to a variety of ills: eating disorders, body dissatisfaction, and a billion-dollar diet industry (Silverstein, Perdue, Peterson, & Kelly, 1986). Most research on body-image dissatisfaction and eating issues has examined the impact of these problems on heterosexual women. Although lesbians are immersed in mainstream culture, they also have a unique culture, albeit neither homogeneous nor all-inclusive. A variety of researchers have examined the prevalence of body dissatisfaction and eating issues in lesbians. However, the results have been far from consistent. Previous studies have not assessed the impact on body image based on the degree to which individuals identify with their sexual orientation.

The literature suggests that body-image dissatisfaction and eating disorders are significantly related to gender and, to some degree, sexual orientation. The research on body-image dissatisfaction and eating disorders in lesbians, however, is equivocal. Some studies have found that lesbians have greater satisfaction with body image and lower incidence of eating disorders than heterosexual women (Gettleman & Thompson, 1993; Herzog, Newman, Yeh, & Warshaw, 1992; Siever, 1994). Other studies have found no differences (Heffernan, 1996; Striegel-Moore, Tucker, & Hsu, 1990). Although researchers have examined the epidemiology of these issues, little research has attempted to explain these discrepancies. Siever (1994) found that both heterosexual women and gay men were more vulnerable to body dissatisfaction and eating pathology. He suggested that stage of sexual identity formation may be a significant factor in body-image satisfaction. Identity formation may influence an individual's acceptance of mainstream cultural values.

Media exposure in our daily lives illustrates how greatly our culture values appearance. The ideal body displayed on television and in magazines is slimmer for women than for men, and the standards of attractiveness are thinner now than they were a few decades ago (Silverstein et al., 1986). There has been an increasing emphasis on a thinner figure for women since the 1950s despite the fact that women under 30 have become heavier (Garner, Garfinkel, Schwartz, & Thompson, 1980). This dichotomy between the socio-cultural pressure to be thin and the reality of a heavier body weight may have contributed to the growth of anorexia nervosa among young women during the past few decades (Andersen & DiDomenico, 1992; Boskind-Lodahl, 1976). Silverstein and colleagues (1986) noted that in the 1920s, when thinness standards for attractiveness were most similar to current ones, there was a significant rise in eating disorders. By the close of the twentieth century, the extent to which the majority of women in U.S. culture experienced dissatisfaction with appearance and constant striving to be thinner had become a "normative discontent" (Rodin, Silberstein, & Striegel-Moore, 1985).

Exposure to mass culture appears to affect different groups in diverse ways. Racial groups, such as African Americans, may be less affected because of identification with their own culture and less emphasis on the values of mainstream culture (Cash & Henry, 1995; Rucker & Cash, 1992). Other groups, especially feminists, actively reject the images and themes of popular culture by exploring its harms for women and society in general (Freedman, 1986; Lakoff & Scherr, 1984; Wolf, 1991). Conversely, teenagers often embrace mainstream culture in their attempts to form an identity and fit in with their peers.

Mainstream culture's emphasis on thinness, especially for women, is important because a significant relationship exists between body-image disturbance and eating pathology. Early research on eating disorders described body-image distortion as a primary component of anorexia nervosa (Bruch, 1962). The DSM-IV-TR includes body-image disturbance as diagnostic criteria for anorexia nervosa and bulimia nervosa (American Psychiatric Association, 2000). Poor body image and the propensity to diet, when body dissatisfaction is linked with weight, are believed to predispose the person to an eating disorder (Striegel-Moore et al., 1990; Striegel-Moore, Silberstein, & Rodin, 1986). Society's cultural imperative equating thinness with beauty and attractiveness with self-worth appears to have an impact on the formation of a woman's body image. However, the impact of popular culture must be interpreted with caution. The popular media depict women as dissatisfied with their bodies, but stereotypes and misperceptions may lead us to believe that women experience more distress than they actually do (Cash & Brown, 1989).

Body-image disturbance and dissatisfaction, especially among heterosexual women, has been widely researched in recent years. Current research suggests that body image is not improving for women, and distress actually may be more acute than in the past. In their landmark survey on the body image of 62,000 Americans, Berscheid, Walster, and Bohrnstedt (1973) found that 45% of women were satisfied with their overall body image, 16% reported being slightly dissatisfied and 7% were "quite or extremely dissatisfied." Nearly half of women reported being dissatisfied with their weight. In general, women were less satisfied with their bodies than were men, and this trend continued throughout the lifecycle. In a nationwide survey conducted a decade later, Cash, Winstead, and Janda (1986) found that respondents reported more dissatisfaction with their bodies than did those surveyed by Berscheid et al. (1973). Relative to men, women were more critical of their bodies and less satisfied with their overall appearance.

Cash and Henry's (1995) study of 803 women found that 48% of women expressed preoccupation with their weight and 47% endorsed an overall negative evaluation of their appearance. Dissatisfaction was centered on weight, lower torso, and middle torso in over 45% of respondents. Relative to Cash, Winstead, and Janda's (1985) survey, women reported significantly more negative evaluation of their overall appearance, although they endorsed less preoccupation with weight. Garner (1997) studied respondents from a *Psychology Today* survey and found that body dissatisfaction has increased for women in recent years.

At least 90% of patients with anorexia nervosa and bulimia nervosa are female (APA, 2000). There is likely to be a strong socio-cultural component in the development of eating disorders for women due to powerful messages equating thinness with desirability and attractiveness (e.g., Boskind-Lodahl, 1976; Striegel-Moore et al., 1986). Striegel-Moore et. al (1986) hypothesized that the women at greatest risk for bulimia are those who accept and internalize most deeply the socio-cultural mores about thinness and attractiveness. Some theorists have suggested that lesbian subculture actively resists the dominant culture's emphasis on appearance and thinness (Blumstein & Schwarz, 1983; Brown, 1987). Brown (1987) noted that anecdotal reports suggested a relationship between body satisfaction and acceptance of lesbian identity. Lesbians who were more "closeted" or who expressed internalized homophobia were less accepting of their bodies and weight. Other theorists disagree that lesbian subculture is protective. Dworkin (1988) asserted that lesbians are like all women in that they "have been oppressed by the standardization of one body image for women" (p. 33).

Research examining body image in lesbians has yielded conflicting results. Some studies have found that lesbians have more positive body image than heterosexual women, whereas others have failed to find significant differences. Striegel-Moore et. al's (1990) study of undergraduate women found no significant differences between heterosexual women and lesbians in body image and disordered eating. The authors suggested that despite increased contact with the lesbian community, lesbians remain embedded in a greater cultural context that places inordinate emphasis on thinness and beauty. Brand, Rothblum, and Solomon (1992) surveyed both gay and heterosexual women and men on measures of weight, dieting, preoccupation with weight, and exercise. Heterosexual women and gay men were more similar in their desire for a low ideal weight and their preoccupation with weight. Lesbians expressed less preoccupation with weight than both groups. Women in general scored higher on eating disorder measures than men. The results of this study indicated that both lesbians and heterosexual women are affected by the cultural imperative to be thin, but heterosexual women are affected more than lesbians.

Beren, Hayden, Wilfley, and Grilo (1996) found that gay men, lesbians, and heterosexual women reported similar levels of body dissatisfaction. They also concluded that gay men were at increased risk for body-image problems and vulnerability to eating disorders, whereas lesbian women reported significant body dissatisfaction, which was not buffered by lesbian culture. Other studies have found significant differences between lesbians and heterosexual women. Herzog, Newman, Yeh, and Warshaw (1992) found that lesbians were less concerned about their appearance and weight, had less desire to lose weight, and chose a higher ideal body weight than heterosexual women. These researchers suggested that lesbians may be more satisfied with their bodies and less accepting of the societal ideal for female thinness. Finch (1991) found that lesbians were significantly more satisfied with their body image, less concerned about being or becoming overweight, and expressed less dissatisfaction with their bodies than heterosexual women. Lesbians also were concerned less with the physical appearance of their partners than were heterosexual women. In comparison with heterosexual women and gay men, lesbians were the least concerned that their own appearance was a significant factor in attracting a partner. Gettelman and Thompson (1993) found that heterosexual women had the greatest body image concerns and the highest ratings of disturbed eating compared to lesbians, gay and heterosexual men. Lesbians were less concerned with weight, dieting, and appearance than were gay men and heterosexual women and also were less appearance-oriented than were gay men.

Heffernan (1996) explored eating disorders and weight concern among lesbians from a community sample. One percent of the women met the clinical criteria for bulimia and 49% met the clinical criteria for anorexia. Heffernan found that binge eating disorder was more strongly related to negative affect regulation than to body dissatisfaction or dieting. Heffernan also assessed non-clinical eating concerns. Nearly half of the women were "dieters" (restricting food intake on at least half of the days in the previous three months) and one-quarter were "bingers" (at least one episode of binge eating in the previous three months). The author also found that a higher level of involvement in lesbian activities was related to less concern with weight.

HYPOTHESES

Research clearly supports the hypothesis that gender has an effect on body-image dissatisfaction and eating behaviors and concerns. Women experience more distress than men. However, sexual orientation appears to alter the effects of gender, especially for gay men. The effect of lesbian identification is more ambiguous. Some studies have found a lower emphasis on body image in lesbians and fewer eating issues, whereas other studies have found that lesbians' body image and eating issues are similar to those of heterosexual women.

The author hypothesized that gender and sexual orientation would interact on body satisfaction, importance of body image, satisfaction with fitness, importance of fitness, and eating behavior and concerns. Specifically, the hypothesis specified that lesbians would report less dissatisfaction with their bodies, place less emphasis on appearance, and report less disordered eating than heterosexual women. The author expected that lesbians would be more satisfied with their fitness and place less importance on fitness than heterosexual women. Hypothetically, one would expect the stage of sexual identification to be a critical factor in body satisfaction and eating behavior and concerns for lesbians. One would expect gender and stage of sexual identity to predict body satisfaction, importance of body image, satisfaction with fitness, importance of fitness, and disturbances in eating. Specifically, one would expect that women who identified more with being lesbian would report more body satisfaction, less importance of appearance, more satisfaction with their fitness, less importance on fitness, and less disordered eating than women who identified less with being lesbian.

METHODS

Participants

The sample consisted of 47 lesbian women, 47 heterosexual women, 51 gay men, and 37 heterosexual men. Lesbians and gay men were recruited from gay and lesbian student groups at colleges in Washington DC, Maryland, and Virginia, community organizations, flyers placed in bookstores, and from other researchers contacted through the GLBT Network at the University of Alabama, Auburn. Heterosexual participants were recruited from the human subjects pool at The College of William and Mary, student organizations, and flyers placed in bookstores. All participants were at least 18 years of age. Approximately 50% of the gay and lesbian participants came from campus gay and lesbian organizations; the remainder were recruited through bookstores and community organizations.

Eighty-three percent of the participants were Caucasian, 6% African American, 7% Asian, 2% Hispanic, and 2% "other" ethnic groups (Native Americans, biracial). Forty-six percent of the participants designated themselves as exclusively or primarily heterosexual, whereas 53% described themselves as "equally heterosexual and gay or lesbian" to "exclusively gay or lesbian." Bisexual participants ($N = 8$) were retained in this study in order to reflect the continuum of sexuality. Two participants chose not to answer the Kinsey scale (item 7) and were excluded from all analyses.

Participants self-selected to answer the Gay Identity Questionnaire (GIQ) based on whether they believed that the material was relevant to them. The stage designations for female respondents were as follows: 5.7% Stage 1, 9.4% Stage 2, 5.7% Stage 3, 13.2% Stage 4, 17.0% Stage 5, and 49.0% Stage 6. The stage designations for male respondents were as follows: 2.0% Stage 1, 0% Stage 2, 2.0% Stage 3, 13.7% Stage 4, 31.4% Stage 5, and 51.0% Stage 6. Forty-four percent of the participants did not respond to the GIQ.

Measures

Body Image. The Multidimensional Body-Self Relations Questionnaire (MBSRQ) is a 69-item self-report inventory designed to assess cognitive, behavioral, and affective facets of body-image and weight-related variables (four items, comprising the Overweight Preoccupation scale were not included in the current survey). Originally derived from the 140-item Body-Self Relations Questionnaire (BSRQ) (Winstead & Cash, 1984), the MBSRQ was subsequently validated and normed on a large national body-image survey (Cash et al., 1986).

The MBSRQ contains six factor scales to assess the participants' attitudes toward the somatic domains of appearance, fitness, and health. Each scale assesses two separate areas: evaluation and orientation. Appearance Evaluation (APPEV) assesses how attractive a person feels or how satisfied the person is with his or her appearance. Appearance Orientation (APPOR) assesses the importance of appearance and how much the person engages in behaviors to enhance appearance. Fitness Evaluation (FITEV) assesses the person's evaluation of his or her physical fitness. Fitness Orientation (FITOR) assesses the degree to which fitness is valued and the degree to which the person actively pursues or maintains his or her fitness. Two health scales were not used in this study (Health Orientation and Health Evaluation). These six scales have been confirmed and replicated by a principal components factor analysis (Brown, Cash, & Mikulka, 1990). Subscale reliability for the four scales used in this study, as measured by Cronbach's alphas, range from .76 to .91 (Brown et al., 1990).

The Body-Areas Satisfaction Scale (BASS) assesses satisfaction with discrete aspects of appearance and focuses on nine body areas: face, hair, lower torso, mid torso, upper torso, muscle tone, weight, height, and overall appearance. Cash (1994) reported Cronbach's alphas of .73 for women and .77 for men.

Eating Behavior and Concerns. The Eating Disorders Inventory (EDI) (Garner, Olmsted, & Polivy, 1983) is a self-report measure of eating behaviors and concerns associated with anorexia nervosa and bulimia nervosa. A newer form, the EDI-2, was published in 1992 and contains the original eight scales plus three new scales. For use with a non-clinical sample, the authors note that the EDI can be used as a screening instrument for individuals who are likely to be very preoccupied with their weight.

Two of the EDI scales were analyzed in this research: Drive for Thinness and Bulimia. The Drive for Thinness subscale contains items such as, "I eat sweets and carbohydrates without feeling nervous" (negatively keyed), and "I exaggerate or magnify the importance of weight." The Bulimia subscale contains items such as, "I eat when I am upset" and "I eat moderately in front of others and stuff myself when they're gone." In the original scoring method, the most pathological response receives a score of 3, the second most extreme a 2, the next response a 1, and all other responses a score of 0. For the analyses in this study, all responses were considered meaningful and were scored from 1 to 6, with higher scores indicating more pathology. This scoring method is suggested by Siever (1994) for use in epidemiological studies because the traditional scoring collapses the three responses most likely to be endorsed by a non-clinical population and creates a skewed distribution. Internal consistency reliability coefficients for the Drive for Thinness subscale were .86 and .87 with an anorexia patient sample and female control sample, respectively. For the Bulimia subscale, Cronbach's alphas were .88 and .83 for the same samples (Garner & Olmsted, 1984).

Sexual Identity Formation. The Gay Identity Questionnaire (GIQ) (Brady & Busse, 1994) was developed as a brief measure for identifying gay males' homosexual identity formation (HIF), based on Cass's theory (Cass, 1979, 1984). The items represent the six stages of HIF. Inter-item consistency, established using the Kuder-Richardson formula, was $r = .76$ for Stage 3, $r = .71$ of Stage 4, $r = .44$ for Stage 5, and $r = .78$ for Stage 6. Inter-item consistency could not be determined for stages one and two because of small sample sizes (Stage 1, $N = 1$; Stage 2, $N = 4$). In the original study to validate the measure, 42 items were used to determine Stage of HIF and three items were used as validity checks. Stage of HIF was not correlated with any demographic variables (age, education, income, religiosity, or political values); the authors asserted that the absence of confounds with these variables provides some support for the validity of the model to predict a stage of coming out. Brady and Busse (1994) noted that further studies are needed to establish external validity for the measure.

Brady and Busse (1994) developed the stage designations using inter-item and inter-rater measures of consistency and subsequently refining the measure through two pilot tests. They found that two factors emerged: Stages 1-3 grouped together (Stage I) and Stages 4-6 grouped together (Stage II). In this study, the author analyzed the data based on the participants' actual stage designation. If a participant had equal scores in two high stages, the participant was given the higher identification rating; conversely, if the participant had equal scores in two lower stages, he or she was given the higher of the low-identification rating.

This measure was included in all packets provided to participants. At the top of the measure, a statement instructed participants as to whether or not they should choose to answer this questionnaire. It read as follows: "This questionnaire contains items that may not be relevant to all people. Please complete this questionnaire if you believe its content pertains to you."

Self-Esteem. The Rosenberg Self-Esteem Scale (Rosenberg, 1965) consists of 10 questions that participants answer on a four-point scale ranging from "strongly agree" to "strongly disagree." Answers were scored continuously. A score of 10 indicated low self-esteem; a score of 40 indicated high self-esteem. Rosenberg (1965) reported a test-re-test correlation coefficient of .85 and the measure correlates with other measures of self-esteem, ranging from .56 to .83.

Social Desirability. The Social Desirability Scale (SDS) (Reynolds, 1982) is an abbreviated version of the original 33-item Marlowe-Crowne Social Desirability Scale (Crowne & Marlowe, 1960). Because social desirability may confound self-report measures, the use of such a scale is relevant to self-report research. The SDS consists of 13 true/false items that describe culturally approved behaviors with a low probability of occurrence. Zook and Sipps (1985) validated the SDS on males and females; they reported an overall Kuder-Richardson reliability coefficient of .74 and a test-retest correlation coefficient of .74. Previous research demonstrated that the SDS correlated .93 with the standard form (Reynolds, 1982). A higher score indicates a greater tendency to respond in a socially desirable manner.

Demographic Questionnaire. A demographic questionnaire, designed by this author, assessed participants' age, sex, race, socioeconomic status, relationship status, current weight and height (in order to determine Body Mass Index) (BMI = kg weight/m^2 height), and ideal weight. Socioeconomic status was defined using income, level of education, and occupation, as suggested by Hollingshead and Redlich (1958).

Sexual Orientation. Sexual orientation was measured using the seven-item rating scale developed by Kinsey and colleagues (Kinsey, Pomeroy, & Martin, 1948). The scale assesses sexual orientation, based on both psychological and overt experience along a continuum from "0: Exclusively heterosexual" to "6: Exclusively gay or lesbian." A seventh question was added to protect the participants' risk of responding to sensitive material: #7: "I choose not to answer this question." Because their sexual orientation could not be determined, participants who responded "7" were not included in the analyses.

RESULTS

For the correlation and reliability analyses, participants were placed into groups based on gender and sexual orientation: lesbian (3-6 on the Kinsey scale), heterosexual female or male (0-2 on the Kinsey scale), or gay male (3-6 on the Kinsey scale).

Group differences on demographic variables and BMI were analyzed using 2 (gender) x 2 (sexual orientation) analyses of variance (ANOVAs). Because there was a significant main effect for sexual orientation on age ($p < .001$), income ($p < .05$), years of education ($p < .001$), and body mass index ($p < .001$), these variables were statistically controlled in subsequent analyses. Gay and lesbian participants were significantly older than their heterosexual peers and they had more years of education. Most heterosexual participants were students and younger, whereas the gay and lesbian participants were older. The mean income of heterosexual participants was higher than the mean income of gay and lesbian participants. However, it is important to note that the majority of heterosexual participants were reporting family of origin income and the gay and lesbian participants were more likely to report their own income. There was also a significant interaction effect for sexual orientation and gender ($p < .05$) on education and body mass index. Simple effects analyses (contrasts) revealed that lesbians reported more years of education than gay men [$t (3, 173) = 2.78, p < .05$]. Lesbians also had a significantly higher BMI than heterosexual women [$t (3, 173) = -5.05, p < .001$].

To assess the reliability of the measures, the author calculated Cronbach's alphas for each group on the measures of body image, eating behavior and concerns, self-esteem, and social desirability. For the MBSRQ, each subscale had adequate reliability for all groups, with Crohnbach's alphas ranging from .85 to .89 on the APPEV, .80 to .90 on the APPOR, .70 to .84 on the BASS, .71 to .86 on the FITEV, and .90 to .91 on the FITOR. For the EDI scales, Cronbach's alphas were acceptable for all groups, with ranges from .94 to .83 on the Drive for Thinness scale (DFT) and .91 to .79 on the Bulimia scale. The Cronbach's alphas on the Rosenberg Self-Esteem Scale were acceptable, ranging from .84 to .93. On the Social Desirability Scale, reliability ranged from marginal (.69) for heterosexual men and women and gay men to an acceptable range for lesbians (.77). These reliability estimates are comparable to those obtained by Zook and Sipps (1985).

Due to low numbers of participants in some stages, the author calculated the reliability for the Gay Identity Questionnaire (GIQ) stages by combining the gay and lesbian participants. Kuder-Richardson reliability coefficients for Stages 1-6 were respectively: .73, .65, .72, .83, .61, and .73. These results are congruent with previously reported estimates of reliability. Stage of identity was highly correlated with the Kinsey scale ($r = .64, p < .0001$). This correlation was expected because people who identify with being gay or lesbian are more likely to be in the later stages of gay identity than those who identify with being heterosexual.

To compare this sample with the population norms for the EDI, the data were rescored using the clinical scoring. Nine percent of heterosexual women and 2% of lesbians expressed elevated concerns with dieting and preoccupation with weight. One percent of heterosexual women and 0% of lesbians expressed elevated concerns with overeating. In keeping with the other analyses of group differences, 2 (gender) x 2 (sexual orientation) analyses of covariance (with age and BMI as covariates) were used to compare the mean scores. On the DFT scale, the interaction was significant ($F(5, 174) = 13.20, p < .001$), with lesbians being less concerned with dieting and thinness than were heterosexual women. On the Bulimia scale, the interaction was significant ($F(5, 174) = 5.70, p < .05$), with lesbians being less concerned with overeating and controlling food intake than were heterosexual women.

Because the groups differed significantly in body mass index (BMI) and age, correlations were examined to assess for confounds with these variables in further analyses. For heterosexual women, there was a significant correlation between scores on the BMI and the APPEV, BASS, and Drive for Thinness scale. Heterosexual women who were heavier in proportion to their height were less satisfied with their overall attractiveness (including specific aspects of their appearance) and were more concerned about dieting and thinness. For lesbians, BMI was significantly correlated with APPEV, BASS, FITOR, Drive for Thinness, and Bulimia. Lesbians who were heavier in proportion to their height had less satisfaction with their overall attractiveness and certain aspects of their appearance. They also were invested less in their physical fitness and were more concerned with weight, dieting, and overeating.

There was a significant correlation between age and APPEV for heterosexual women, suggesting that the older heterosexual women in this study were more satisfied with their appearance. Age also correlated with FITEV and FITOR for lesbians. Older lesbians were invested more in physical fitness or athletic ability and had a more positive evaluation of their fitness. The author used age as a covariate in subsequent analyses because the groups differed significantly on this item.

No significant correlations were found between the Social Desirability Scale (SDS) (Reynolds, 1982) and any of the measures for any group. Groups were compared using a 2 (gender) x 2 (sexual orientation) ANOVA. The main effects and the interaction effect were not significant. The groups appeared to be equivalent on social desirability.

Summary of the Analyses

The author performed two sets of analyses after assessing potential confounds and calculating reliability for the measures. The first set of analyses investigated group differences in body image (appearance orientation and evaluation), fitness orientation and evaluation, and eating behavior and concerns. In comparisons of the dependent variables, the author statistically controlled Age and BMI. Differences between the means on the measures were analyzed using 2 (gender) x 2 (sexual orientation) analyses of covariance (ANCOVA) with age and BMI as covariates. Table 1 shows the results of these analyses.

The author performed a second set of analyses on the data from lesbian and gay participants. Dependent variables were included in multiple regression analyses, with gender, age, BMI, and stage of identity as the independent variables. The author tested the overall model with backward elimination to determine which variables made statistically

TABLE 1. Group Differences on Measures with Age and BMI as Covariates

	Gay Men	Heterosexual Women	Lesbians	*F*
APPEV	3.30	3.53	3.30	<1
M	.81	.76	.82	<1
SD				1.67
APPOR	3.64	3.54	3.25	1.44
M	.64	.55	.55	<1
SD				12.15**
BASS	3.19	3.50	3.35	<1
M	.73	.58	.67	1.69
SD				5.79*
FITEV	3.12	3.61	3.65	2.19
M	.92	.75	.98	4.09*
SD				7.46**
FITOR	3.15	3.63	3.26	2.22
M	.89	.75	.81	8.00**
SD				<1
DFT	2.56	3.14	2.80	10.47**
M	1.25	1.37	.97	1.40
SD				12.71**
Bulimia	1.86	2.08	1.91	2.61
M	.96	.74	.64	1.31
SD				7.66**

*$p < .05$. **$p < .01$.
Note. *F* values are for gender, sexual orientation, and the interaction between gender and sexual orientation, respectively.

significant contributions to explaining the variance between the independent variables and outcome measures.

Appearance Evaluation (APPEV) and Orientation (APPOR). Analysis of covariance on APPEV did not yield a significant main effect for gender [F (5, 175) < 1], sexual orientation [F (5, 175) < 1], or an interaction effect [F (5, 175) = 1.67, p > .05]. All groups had similar evaluations of their attractiveness. Analysis of covariance on APPOR did not yield a significant main effect for gender [F (5, 175) = 1.44] or sexual orientation [F (5, 175) < 1]. The interaction between gender and sexual orientation was significant, [F (5, 175) = 12.15, p < .001]. Heterosexual women scored significantly higher than did lesbians, suggesting that heterosexual women placed more importance on their appearance and were more involved in maintaining it.

Body Areas Satisfaction Scale Measure (BASS). Analysis of covariance did not yield a significant main effect on the BASS for gender [F (5, 175) < 1] or sexual orientation [F (5, 175) = 1.69]. The interaction between gender and sexual orientation was significant [F (5, 175) = 5.79, p < .05]. Subsequent t tests found no difference between lesbians and heterosexual women [t (1, 90) < 1].

Fitness Evaluation (FITEV) and Orientation (FITOR). Analysis of covariance did not yield a significant main effect on FITEV for gender [F (5, 175) = 2.91]. There was a significant main effect for sexual orientation [F (5, 175) = 4.09, p < .05], and the interaction between gender and sexual orientation was significant [F (5, 175) = 7.46, p > .01]. However, there were no differences between lesbians and heterosexual women [t (1, 90) < 1]. Analysis of covariance did not yield a significant main effect on FITOR for gender [F (5, 175) = 2.22]. There was a significant main effect for sexual orientation [F (5, 175) = 8.00, p < .01], but the interaction between gender and sexual orientation was not significant [F (5, 175) < 1].

Eating Behavior and Concerns. On the Drive for Thinness scale, there was a significant main effect for gender [F (5, 174) = 10.47, p < .001]. Sexual orientation was not significant [F (5, 174) = 1.40]. Heterosexual women and lesbians scored significantly higher than did gay and heterosexual men, suggesting that women in general were more concerned with dieting and thinness. The interaction between gender and sexual orientation was significant [F (5, 174) = 12.72, p < .001]. Lesbians scored lower than did heterosexual women [t (1, 92) = 1.99, p < .05], suggesting that lesbians were less concerned with dieting and thinness. On the Bulimia scale, neither gender [F (5, 174) = 2.61] nor sexual orientation [F (5, 174) = 1.31] were significant. The interaction between gender and sexual orientation was significant [F (5, 174) = 7.67, $p <$ .01]. However, subsequent t tests failed to find significant differences among lesbians and heterosexual women [t (1, 92) < 1]. This suggests that the groups had similar concerns with overeating or controlling food intake.

Analyses for Lesbians and Gay Men

Prior to the multiple regression analyses, the author conducted separate analyses on gay men and lesbians to determine the correlation of stage of identity with the research measures. Table 2 presents the results of these analyses. Multiple regression analyses examined the predictors of APPEV, APPOR, BASS, FITEV, FITOR, DFT, and Bulimia for lesbians and gay men. For each criterion variable, the author entered gender, stage of identity, age, and BMI stepwise by backward elimination.

Appearance Evaluation (APPEV) and Orientation (APPOR). For APPEV, the overall model was significant [F (4, 95) = 5.92, $p < .001$]. BMI emerged as the significant predictor of appearance evaluation, accounting for 17% of the variance in appearance evaluation. For lesbians, greater satisfaction with attractiveness was associated with weighing less in proportion to height. For APPOR, the overall model was significant [F (4, 95) = −2.77, $p < .05$]. Gender emerged as the significant predictor, accounting for 7% of the variance in appearance ori-

TABLE 2. Correlations of Measures with Stage of Identity

Variable	Gay Men	Lesbians
APPEV	−.01	−.12
APPOR	−.09	.06
BASS	.17	−.18
FITEV	−.06	−.06
FITOR	.11	.08
DFT	−.08	−.27
Bulimia	−.07	−.04
Self-Esteem	.21	.31*

*$p < .05$, two-tailed.

entation. Lesbians were invested less in their appearance than were gay men.

Body Areas Satisfaction Scale Measure (BASS). For BASS, the overall model was significant [F (4, 95) = 4.30, $p < .01$]. Gender and BMI emerged as significant predictors of BASS, accounting for 12% of the variance in satisfaction with discrete aspects of appearance. Lesbians were more likely to be satisfied with discrete aspects of their appearance. There was also a relation between satisfaction with particular body areas and a lower weight to height ratio.

Fitness Evaluation and Orientation Measures. For FITEV and FITOR, the overall model was not significant [F (4, 95) = 2.33]. There was no relation between the predictor variables and the importance of fitness. Nor was there a relation between the predictor variables and the degree to which lesbians pursued fitness.

Eating Behavior and Concerns Measures. For DFT, the overall model was significant [F (4, 95) = 6.14, $p < .001$]. Stage of identity, gender, and BMI emerged as significant predictors, accounting for 17% of the variance. Lesbians in the earlier stages of identity formation were more concerned with thinness and dieting. Lesbians were less concerned with dieting and thinness than were gay men. There was an association between increased concern with diet and thinness relative to a higher weight to height ratio. The overall model was significant [F (4, 94 = 4.66, $p < .01$] for Bulimia. BMI was the significant predictor, accounting for 13% of the variance. There was a significant relation between more concern with overeating and controlling food intake relative to a higher weight to height ratio.

DISCUSSION

The research on eating disorders in lesbians is limited. As previously noted, some studies found no differences between lesbians and heterosexual women in pursuit of thinness or behaviors related to bulimia nervosa (Striegel-Moore et al., 1990), whereas others studies found that lesbians have fewer concerns or behaviors related to eating disorders (Brand et al., 1992; Herzog et al., 1992; Siever, 1994).

In this study, heterosexual women and lesbians had similar overall evaluations of their attractiveness and satisfaction with certain aspects of their appearance. These results were similar to those of many other researchers (Beren et al., 1996; Gettleman et al., 1993; Siever, 1994; Striegel-Moore et al., 1990). Finch (1991) also found that heterosexual women and lesbians were similar in their satisfaction with overall appearance, but lesbians were more satisfied with particular aspects of their bodies (e.g., muscle tone, upper torso, chest, breasts, arms, and weight). Given these consistent findings, it seems well established that lesbians and heterosexual women do not differ in the degree to which they are dissatisfied with their appearance.

Relative to heterosexual women, lesbians rated their appearance significantly lower in importance, and they were less involved in maintaining their appearance. This provides further support for studies examining the importance of appearance for lesbians (Finch, 1991; Gettleman & Thompson, 1993; Herzog et al., 1990; Siever, 1994). In fact, Siever reported that lesbians were less concerned with physical appearance than any other group.

There was a negative relation between evaluation of appearance and body mass index for both heterosexual women and lesbians, suggesting that both heterosexual women and lesbians feel less attractive when they are overweight. It is important to note that the heterosexual women, on average, weighed significantly less than did their lesbian peers. It is likely that the heterosexual women made their evaluation of being less attractive regarding a much thinner body, and lesbian women can evaluate themselves positively despite weighing more. However, when the author assessed participants' evaluation of attractiveness controlled for BMI, there were no differences in evaluation of appearance among lesbians and heterosexual women. This is in contrast to Siever's study (1994), in which lesbians with higher BMI were more dissatisfied with their weight, although there was a consistent trend for lesbians to be less dissatisfied with their bodies overall. Herzog and colleagues (1992) found that lesbians of average weight were more satisfied with their bodies than were heterosexual women of average weight. Heffernan (1996) reported a strong negative relationship between BMI and overall body esteem among lesbians, as well as a strong positive relationship between BMI and weight dissatisfaction. Altogether, these studies suggest that lesbians are not immune to the societal ideals of thinness.

Lesbians scored lower than did heterosexual women on EDI measures of dieting behaviors, but there were no differences between the two groups on the Bulimia scale. Using the same measures, Finch (1991) found that lesbians were less worried about being or becoming overweight. For both lesbians and heterosexual women, concern with thinness significantly correlated with higher BMI. This suggests that, regardless of sexual orientation, overweight women are more concerned with dieting and thinness. The finding that lesbians were similar to heterosexual women on the Bulimia scale is consistent with Heffernan's (1996) findings that 5.4% of lesbians reported clinical levels of binge eating disorder and 1% scored in the clinical range for bulimia. Heffernan also reported that nearly half of the lesbians reported dieting and one quarter reported episodes of binge eating.

Previous studies have suggested that sexual minority women involved in lesbian activities were less concerned with their weight than other lesbians (Heffernan, 1996) and that coming out as lesbian resulted in more positive body esteem (Heffernan, 1996; Siever 1994). Siever (1994) noted that many lesbians in his study made comments in the margins that they experienced greater body dissatisfaction and more dysfunctional eating before they "came out." In this study, stage of sexual identity formation contributed significantly only to the prediction of desire for thinness. Greater identification with being lesbian contributed to decreased concern with dieting and thinness. Although the moderating effect of lesbian identification supports previous research findings that greater levels of involvement and higher stages of development may influence concerns about dieting and thinness, the results of this study do not support the hypothesis that there is a relation between stage of identity and body satisfaction.

In summary, these results suggest that lesbians may be less concerned with dieting and thinness than are heterosexual women, but lesbians still are more similar to heterosexual women than to men regarding issues with food. Although lesbians in the earlier stages of identity formation appear to be more concerned with dieting and thinness than are those in later stages, research does not provide consistent evidence that lesbian identification is a protective factor against eating concerns for these women. The high rate of binge eating reported by Heffernan (1996), large percentage of lesbians who dieted, and the similarity of lesbians with heterosexual women on the Bulimia scale, indicate that eating issues are salient concerns for lesbians.

These findings have important clinical implications. Clinicians working with women should be sensitive to their clients' sexual orientation, aware of stereotypes about lesbians, and not erroneously assume that all lesbian women are less prone to eating concerns than are heterosexual women. Some evidence (Heffernan, 1996) suggests that the mechanisms for eating disorders may be different for lesbians (i.e., negative affect modulation) and clinicians should be sensitive to the influence of these factors, in addition to the socio-cultural emphasis on thinness for women. Clinicians should not assume that weight and appearance are unimportant to lesbians. Homophobia may motivate lesbians to want to fit in and thus may motivate them to maintain a more mainstream appearance, including the culturally promoted thin figure for women. There is great stigma for being overweight in U.S. culture, and lesbians who are heavy relative to cultural ideals may feel doubly subjected to discrimination.

Limitations of This Study and Suggestions for Future Research

Readers should use caution when evaluating conclusions regarding stage of identity formation and body satisfaction, in part because there was a limited range in the participants' stages of identity formation. The majority of the participants (74%) scored in Stages 5 and 6 of identity formation and very few scored in the earliest stages (10%). The groups from whom this sample was drawn were more likely to contain people more identified with being lesbian or gay. Stage of identity may have a greater impact on body satisfaction and eating issues and concerns, but the impact was not evident in this sample because of its relative homogeneity. Future studies that explore the relationship between stage of identity formation and body satisfaction should strive to obtain a diverse sample by contacting younger gay men and lesbians, accessing closeted gay men and lesbians through referrals from "out" friends, and advertising in gay and lesbian community papers.

Failure to find a relationship between most of the measures and stages of identity formation may also be associated with the reliability and validity of the GIQ. Due to low numbers of participants in the earliest stages of identity formation, the author could not conduct a separate assessment of the reliability for lesbians and gay men. It is unknown if the stages had adequate reliability for the separate groups.

Readers also should note that this study relied on self-report measures. There was no association between social desirability and any of the measures, but response bias still may have affected the results. For example, lesbians may have underreported the importance of their appearance or underreported eating issues because of attitudes in lesbian culture regarding evaluating women based on their appearance or stigma against dieting.

Small sample sizes and homogeneity of the lesbian and gay samples relative to heterosexuals also may have affected this study's results. The sample may not be representative of heterosexuals, gays, and lesbians in the general population. However, this study's sample size is consistent with most others in the literature.

Unlike most of the other studies regarding sexual orientation, body image, and eating issues, this study included bisexuals in order to reflect the full continuum of sexual orientation. The 8 bisexual female participants were grouped with lesbians in the analyses, so they may have affected the results and conclusions regarding sexual orientation and women.

In order to understand better the relationship between body image and eating concerns, sexual orientation, and sexual identity formation, researchers should attempt to survey groups who represent the continuum of sexual identity formation. It would be particularly interesting (and difficult) to perform a longitudinal study of lesbians throughout the stages of sexual identity formation. This would provide the best evidence for any effects on body satisfaction and eating issues that may occur during assimilation into lesbian culture and the development of a lesbian identity.

CONCLUSIONS

This study found a significant relation between lesbian identity formation and concerns with dieting and thinness for lesbians. However, body image and concern with overeating seemed to be unrelated to stage of sexual identity formation. This suggests that the impact of affiliation with lesbian culture may be less important than other researchers have suggested. However, body mass (particularly being overweight) played an important role in satisfaction with appearance, concern with dieting, thinness, and overeating. It is noteworthy that age was not a significant predictor for any of the variables.

Although lesbians may be less vulnerable to concerns with dieting and thinness, they are still concerned with overeating and controlling food intake. As other researchers have suggested, lesbians may be particularly at risk for binge eating disorder and may use food to help moderate negative emotions. Thus, their issues with food may be related less to the dominant culture's imperative of thinness for women than are those of heterosexual women, but it would be premature to conclude that this is not important to lesbians. There is evidence that identification with being lesbian provides some moderation for concern with dieting and thinness. Lesbian culture may moderate the pressure to be thin. Conversely, lesbian culture may not be protective against fat discrimination. Researchers have demonstrated a relation between being overweight and self-esteem among lesbians, and it is possible that lesbian culture is less tolerant of diverse body sizes (Blumstein & Schwarz, 1983; Brown, 1987).

Clearly, the relationships between sexual orientation, sexual identity formation, gender, body image, and eating concerns are complex. Future studies may need more reliable instruments and large and varied samples of participants to elucidate the relationships between these factors.

REFERENCES

American Psychiatric Association (2000). *Diagnostic and statistical manual of mental disorders (4th ed-TR.)*. Washington, DC: Author.

American Psychological Association (1994). *Publication Manual of the American Psychological Association (4th ed.)*. Washington, DC: Author.

Andersen, A. E., & DiDomenico, L. (1992). Diet vs. shape content of popular male and female magazines: A dose-response relationship to the incidence of eating disorders? *International Journal of Eating Disorders, 11*, 283-287.

Beren, S. E., Hayden, H. A., Wilfey, D. E., & Grilo, C. M. (1996). The influence of sexual orientation on body dissatisfaction in adult men and women. *International Journal of Eating Disorders, 20*, 135-141.

Berscheid, E., Walster, E., & Bohrnstedt, G. (1973, November). Body image: A survey report. *Psychology Today, 7*, 119-131.

Blumstein, P., & Schwarz, P. (1983). *American couples: Money, work, and sex*. New York: William Morrow.

Boskind-Lodahl, M. (1976). Cinderella's stepsisters: A feminist perspective on anorexia nervosa and bulimia. *Signs: Journal of Women in Culture and Society, 2*, 342-356.

Brady, S., & Busse, W. J. (1994). The Gay Identity Questionnaire: A brief measure of homosexual identity formation. *Journal of Homosexuality, 26*, 1-22.

Brand, P. A., Rothblum, E. D., & Solomon, L. J. (1992). A comparison of lesbians, gay men, and heterosexuals on weight and restrained eating. *International Journal of Eating Disorders, 11*, 253-259.

Brown, L. (1987). Lesbians, weight, and eating: New analyses and perspectives. In Boston Lesbian Psychologies Collective (Eds.), *Lesbian Psychologies* (pp. 294-309). Urbana, IL: University of Illinois Press.

Brown, T. A., Cash, T. F., & Mikulka, P. J. (1990). Attitudinal body-image assessment: Factor analysis of the Body-Self Relations Questionnaire. *Journal of Personality Assessment, 55*, 135-144.

Bruch, H. (1962). Perceptual and conceptual disturbances in anorexia nervosa. *Psychosomatic Medicine, 24*, 187-194.

Cash, T. F. (1994). *MBSRQ Users' Manual*.

Cash, T. F., & Brown, T. A. (1989). Gender and body images: Stereotypes and realities. *Sex Roles, 21*, 361-373.

Cash, T. F., & Henry, P. E. (1995). Women's body images: The results of a national survey in the USA. *Sex Roles, 33*, 19-28.

Cash, T. F., Winstead, B. A., & Janda, L. H. (1986). The great American shape-up. *Psychology Today, 20*, 30-37.

Cass, V. C. (1979). Homosexual identity formation: A theoretical model. *Journal of Homosexuality, 4*, 219-235.

Cass, V. C. (1984). Homosexual identity: A concept in need of definition. *Journal of Homosexuality, 9*, 105-124.

Crowne, D. P., & Marlowe, D. (1960). A new scale of social desirability independent of psychopathology. *Journal of Consulting Psychology, 24*, 349-354.

Dworkin, S. H. (1988). Not in man's image: Lesbian and the cultural oppression of body image. *Women and Therapy, 8*, 27-39.

Finch, C. B. (1991). *Sexual orientation, body image, and sexual functioning.* Unpublished master's thesis, Old Dominion University, Norfolk, Virginia.

Freedman, R. (1986). *Beauty bound.* Lexington, MA: Lexington Books.

Garner, D. M. (1997). Exclusive body image survey. *Psychology Today, 30*, 30-78.

Garner, D. M., Garfinkel, P. E., Schwartz, D., & Thompson, M. (1980). Cultural expectations of thinness in women. *Psychological Reports, 47*, 483-491.

Garner, D. M., Olmsted, M. P., & Polivy, J. P. (1983). Development and validation of a multidimensional Eating Disorder Inventory for anorexia nervosa and bulimia. *International Journal of Eating Disorders, 2*, 15-34.

Garner, D. M., & Olmsted, M. P. (1984). *Manual for eating disorders inventory (EDI).* Odessa, FL: Psychological Assessment Resources, Inc.

Gettleman, T. E., & Thompson, J. K. (1993). Actual differences and stereotypical perceptions in body image and eating disturbance: A comparison of male and female heterosexual and homosexual samples. *Sex Roles, 29*, 545-561.

Heffernan, K. (1994). Sexual orientation as a factor in risk for binge eating and bulimia nervosa: A review. *International Journal of Eating Disorders, 16*, 335-347.

Heffernan, K. (1996). Eating disorders and weight concern among lesbians. *International Journal of Eating Disorders, 19*, 127-138.

Herzog, D. B., Newman, K. L., Yeh, C. J., & Warshaw, M. (1992). Body image satisfaction in homosexual and heterosexual women. *International Journal of Eating Disorders, 11*, 391-396.

Hollingshead, A. B., & Redlich, F. C. (1964). *Social class and mental illness.*

Kinsey, A. C., Pomeroy, W. B., & Martin, C. E. (1948). *Sexual behavior in the human male.* Philadelphia and London: W. B. Saunders Company.

Lakoff, R. T., & Scherr, R. L. (1984). *Face value: The politics of beauty.* Boston: Routledge & Keegan Paul.

Reynolds, W. M. (1982). Development of reliable and valid short forms of the Marlowe-Crowne Social Desirability Scale. *Journal of Clinical Psychology, 38*, 119-125.

Rodin, J., Silberstein, L. M., & Striegel-Moore, R. H. (1985). Women and weight: A normative discontent. In T. B. Sonderegger (Ed.), *Nebraska symposium on motivation: Vol 32. Psychology and gender* (pp. 267-307). Lincoln, NE: University of Nebraska Press.

Rosenberg, M. (1965). *Society and the adolescent self-image.* Princeton, NJ: Princeton University Press.

Rucker, C. E., & Cash, T. F. (1992). Body images, body-size perceptions, and eating behaviors among African-American and white college women. *International Journal of Eating Disorders, 12*, 291-299.

Siever, M. D. (1994). Sexual orientation and gender as factors in socioculturally acquired vulnerability to body dissatisfaction and eating disorders. *Journal of Consulting and Clinical Psychology, 62*, 252-260.

Silberstein, L. R., Mishkind, M. E., Striegel-Moore, R. H., Timko, C., & Rodin, J. (1989). Men and their bodies: A comparison of homosexual and heterosexual men. *Psychosomatic Medicine, 51*, 337-346.

Silverstein, B., Perdue, L., Peterson, B., & Kelly, E. (1986). The role of mass media in promoting a thin standard of bodily attractiveness for women. *Sex Roles, 14*, 519-532.

Striegel-Moore, R. H., Silberstein, L. R., & Rodin, J. (1986). Toward an understanding of risk factors for bulimia. *American Psychologist, 41*, 246-263.

Striegel-Moore, R. H., Tucker, N., & Hsu, J. (1990). Body image dissatisfaction and disordered eating in lesbian college students. *International Journal of Eating Disorders, 9*, 493-500.

Winstead, B. A., & Cash, T. F. (1984, March). *Reliability and validity of the Body Self-Relations Questionnaire: A new measure of body image*. Paper presented at the Southeastern Psychological Association Convention. New Orleans, LA.

Wolf, N. (1991). *The beauty myth: How images of beauty are used against women*. New York: William Morrow.

Zook, A., & Sipps, G. J. (1985). Cross-validation of a short form of the Marlowe-Crowne Social Desirability Scale. *Journal of Clinical Psychology, 41*, 236-238.

Index

BOOK ORDER FORM!

Order a copy of this book with this form or online at:
http://www.haworthpress.com/store/product.asp?sku=5395

Lesbian and Bisexual Women's Mental Health

___ in softbound at $19.95 (ISBN: 0-7890-2682-1)
___ in hardbound at $34.95 (ISBN: 0-7890-2681-3)

COST OF BOOKS _____

POSTAGE & HANDLING _____
US: $4.00 for first book & $1.50
for each additional book
Outside US: $5.00 for first book
& $2.00 for each additional book.

SUBTOTAL _____
In Canada: add 7% GST. _____

STATE TAX _____
CA, IL, IN, MN, NJ, NY, OH & SD residents
please add appropriate local sales tax.

FINAL TOTAL _____
If paying in Canadian funds, convert
using the current exchange rate,
UNESCO coupons welcome.

❏BILL ME LATER:
Bill-me option is good on US/Canada/
Mexico orders only; not good to jobbers,
wholesalers, or subscription agencies.

❏ Signature _____

❏ Payment Enclosed: $ _____

❏ PLEASE CHARGE TO MY CREDIT CARD:
❏ Visa ❏ MasterCard ❏ AmEx ❏ Discover
❏ Diner's Club ❏ Eurocard ❏ JCB

Account # _____

Exp Date _____

Signature _____
(Prices in US dollars and subject to change without notice.)

PLEASE PRINT ALL INFORMATION OR ATTACH YOUR BUSINESS CARD

Name

Address

City   State/Province   Zip/Postal Code

Country

Tel   Fax

E-Mail

May we use your e-mail address for confirmations and other types of information? ❏Yes ❏No We appreciate receiving
your e-mail address. Haworth would like to e-mail special discount offers to you, as a preferred customer.
We will never share, rent, or exchange your e-mail address. We regard such actions as an invasion of your privacy.

Order From Your **Local Bookstore** or Directly From
The Haworth Press, Inc. 10 Alice Street, Binghamton, New York 13904-1580 • USA
Call Our toll-free number (1-800-429-6784) / Outside US/Canada: (607) 722-5857
Fax: 1-800-895-0582 / Outside US/Canada: (607) 771-0012
E-mail your order to us: orders@haworthpress.com

For orders outside US and Canada, you may wish to order through your local
sales representative, distributor, or bookseller.
For information, see http://haworthpress.com/distributors

(Discounts are available for individual orders in US and Canada only, not booksellers/distributors.)

Please photocopy this form for your personal use.
www.HaworthPress.com

BOF04

Printed in the United States
by Baker & Taylor Publisher Services